The Mystery of the Eucharist

Voices from the Saints and Mystics

The Mystery of the Eucharist

Voices from the Saints and Mystics

Dennis J. Billy, C.Ss.R.

New City Press
Hyde Park, New York

For my nieces,
Elizabeth and Michelle,
And my nephew,
Andrew,
May the Mystery of the Eucharist
Fill your minds with light,
Your souls with grace,
Your hearts with gratitude.

Published in the United States by New City Press
202 Comforter Blvd., Hyde Park, NY 12538
www.newcitypress.com
© 2014 Dennis J. Billy

Cover design by Leandro De Leon

Bible citations unless otherwise noted are from the Holy Bible: New Revised Standard Version with Apocrypha (New York/Oxford: Oxford University Press, 1989)

Library of Congress Cataloging-in-Publication Data

Billy, Dennis Joseph.
  The mystery of the eucharist : voices from the saints and mystics / by Dennis J. Billy, C.Ss.R.
       pages cm
  Includes bibliographical references and index.
  ISBN 978-1-56548-530-3 (alk. paper)
  1. Lord's Supper--Catholic Church--Meditations. 2. Christian saints. 3. Mystics. I. Title.
  BX2169.B55 2014
  234'.163--dc23
                              2014013734

Printed in the United States of America

Ever since Pentecost, when the Church, the People of the New Covenant, began her pilgrim journey towards her heavenly homeland, the Divine Sacrament has continued to mark the passing of her days, filling them with confident hope.

Pope John Paul II

Contents

Abbreviations 9

Introduction 13

Voice One: Pseudo-Dionysius
   Sacrament of Sacraments 19

Voice Two: John Damascene
   Living Rule of Faith 31

Voice Three: Anselm of Canterbury
   Faith Seeking Understanding 43

Voice Four: Bernard of Clairvaux
   Food for the Heart 57

Voice Five: Hildegard of Bingen
   Saving Souls 69

Voice Six: Aelred of Rievaulx
   Sabbath of Sabbaths 81

Voice Seven: Albert the Great
   Infinite Delight 93

Voice Eight: Bonaventure
   Rapturous Love 105

Voice Nine: Thomas Aquinas
   Transubstantial Change 117

Voice Ten: Meister Eckhart
   Returning to the Divine Ground 129

Voice Eleven: Catherine of Siena
   A Radiating Sun 141

Voice Twelve: Julian of Norwich
   God's Maternal Love 151

Voice Thirteen: Thomas à Kempis
   Intimacy with Christ 163

Voice Fourteen: Ignatius of Loyola
   Informing Daily Life 173
Voice Fifteen: Teresa of Avila
   Daily Bread 183
Voice Sixteen: John of the Cross
   Living Fountain 195
Voice Seventeen: Francis de Sales
   Health of the Soul 207
Voice Eighteen: Alphonsus de Liguori
   Friendship with God 219
Voice Nineteen: St. John Vianney
   Loving Presence 233
Voice Twenty: John Henry Newman
   Devotion to the Real Presence 245
Voice Twenty-One: Thérèse of Lisieux
   Kiss of Love 257
Voice Twenty-Two: Charles de Foucauld
   Nearness to Jesus 269
Voice Twenty-Three: Thomas Merton
   Living Bread 281
Voice Twenty-Four: Teresa of Calcutta
   Face of the Poor 293
Voice Twenty-Five: Chiara Lubich
   Forging Unity 305
Voice Twenty-Six: Pope John Paul II
   School for Peace 319

Conclusion 331

Acknowledgments 335

Abbreviations

AMHT B.O. Gaybba, *Aspects of the Medieval History of Theology: 12th to 14th Centuries* (Pretoria: University of South Africa, 1988).

CCC *Catechism of the Catholic Church* (Rome: Libreria Editrice Vaticana, 1994) [Internet access: http://www.vatican.va/archive/ENG0015/_INDEX.HTM].

CE *The Catholic Encyclopedia*, 15 vols. (New York: Robert Appleton Co., 1909) [Internet access: http://www.newadvent.org/cathen/]

CH Karl Bihlmeyer, *Church History*, revised by Hermann Tüchle, 13th ed., trans. Victor E. Mills, 3 vols. (Westminster: The Newman Press, 1968).

CLEW Chiara Lubich, *Essential Writings: Spirituality, Dialogue, Culture* (Hyde Park, NY: New City Press, 2007).

CS Louis Boyer et al., *Christian Spirituality*, 3 vols. (New York: Crossroad, 1985–89).

CSp *Compendium of Spirituality*, trans. and ed. Jordan Aumann, 2 vols. (New York: Alba House, 1996).

CT Jaroslav Pelikan, *The Christian Tradition: A History of the Development of Doctrine*, 5 vols. (Chicago/London: The University of Chicago Press, 1971–89).

CWS *The Classics of Western Spirituality*, multi-volume series (New York/Mahwah, NJ: Paulist Press, 1978–).

DES *Dizionario enciclopedico di spiritualità*, vol. 2 (Rome: Città Nuova, 1990).

DM *Dizionario de mistica* (Vatican City: Libreria Editrice Vaticana, 1998).

EE	*Pope John Paul II, Ecclesia de Eucharistia* [Internet Access: http://www.vatican.va/holy_father/john_paul_ii/encyclicals/documents/hf_jp-ii_enc_20030417_eccl-de-euch_en.html].
EN	Vicent F. Blehl, ed., *The Essential Newman* (New York: The New American Library, 1963).
FEF	William A. Jurgens, *The Faith of the Early Fathers*, 3 vols. (Collegeville, Minn.: The Liturgical Press, 1979).
HCS	*A History of Christian Spirituality*, 3 vols. (New York: The Seabury Press, 1982).
HCT	*Handbook of Catholic Theology*, eds. Wolfgang Beinert and Francis Schüssler Fiorenza (New York: Crossroad, 1995).
HD	J. Tixeront, *History of Dogmas*, trans. H.L.B. (Westminster, MD: Christian Classics, 1984).
HP	Frederick Copleston, *A History of Philosophy*, 9 vols. (Garden City, NY: Image Books ed, 1985).
HPMA	Etienne Gilson, *History of Christian Philosophy in the Middle Ages* (London: Sheed and Ward, 1955).
IPMT	Walter H. Principe, *Introduction to Patristic and Medieval Theology*, 2d ed. (Toronto: Pontifical Institute of Medieval Studies, 1982).
LG	Second Vatican Council, *Lumen Gentium*, no. 11 [Internet access: http://www.vatican.va/ archive/hist_councils/ii_vatican_council/ documents/vat-ii_const_19641121_lumen-gentium_en.html].
LLDG	Jean Leclercq, *The Love of Learning and the Desire for God: A Study of Monastic Culture*, trans. Catharine Misrahi (New York: Fordham University Press, 1982).
MND	*Pope John Paul II, Mane Nobiscum Domine* [Internet Access: http://www.vatican.va/holy father/john_paul_ii/apost_letters/ documents/hf_jp-ii_apl_20041008_mane-nobiscum-domine_en.html].

Abbreviations 11

MTCF	José Pereira and Robert Fastiggi, *The Mystical Theology of the Catholic Reformation: An Overview of Baroque Spirituality* (Lanham, MD: University of America Press, 2006).
NCDS	*The New Catholic Dictionary of Spirituality* (Collegeville, MN: The Liturgical Press, 1993).
NCE	*The New Catholic Encyclopedia*, 19 vols. (New York: McGraw-Hill, 1967–1996).
NCE2	*The New Catholic Encyclopedia*, 2d ed., 15 vols. (Detroit: Thomson-Gale, 2001–2011).
NDT	*The New Dictionary of Theology*, eds. Joseph A. Komonchak, Mary Collins, Dermot A. Lane (Wilmington, DE: Michael Glazier, 1987).
NMI	Pope John Paul II, *Novo Millennio Ineunte*, nos. 16–26 [Internet access: http://www.vatican.va/holy father/john_paul_ii/apost_letters/documents/hf_jp-ii_apl_20010106_novo-millennio-ineunte_en.html].
P	Berthold Altaner, *Patrology*, trans. Hilda C. Graef (New York: Herder and Herder, 1960).
Pat.	Johannes Quasten, *Patrology*, 3 vols. (Westminster, Md: Christian Classics, Inc., 1950; reprint ed. 1983).
PG	Bernard McGinn, *The Presence of God: A History of Western Christian Mysticism*, 6 vols. (New York: Crossroad, 1994-).
PO	Second Vatican Council, *Presbyterorum Ordinis*, (*Decree on the Life and Ministry of Priests*) [Internet access: http://www.vatican.va/archive/hist_councils/ii_vatican_council/documents/vat-ii_decree_19651207_presbyterorum-ordinis_en.html].
RPA	Michael L. Gaudoin-Parker, *The Real Presence through the Ages* (New York: Alba House, 1993).
SC	*Sources chrétienne*, multivolume series (Paris: Editions de Cerf, 1941-).

SNP	Pope John XXIII, *Sacerdoti Nostri Primordia*, Encyclical Letter on St. John Vianney, August 1, 1959 [Internet access: http://www.vatican.va/holy_father/john xxiii/encyclicals/documents/hf_j-xxiii_enc_19590801_sacerdotii_en.html].
SS	*The Study of Spirituality*, eds. Cheslyn Jones, Geoffrey Wainwright, Edward Yarnold (London: SPCK, 1986; second impression, 1992).
ST	Thomas Aquinas, *Summa thelogiae*, trans. Fathers of the English Dominican Province, 5 vols. (New York: Benziger Brothers, 1948; reprinted, Allen, TX: Christian Classics, 1981).
WDCS	*The Westminster Dictionary of Christian Spirituality* (Philadelphia: The Westminster Press, 1983).
WSCMA	R. W. Southern, *Western Society and the Church in the Middle Ages* (New York: Penguin Books, 1970; 7th reprint ed., 1979.

Introduction

A few years ago I wrote *The Beauty of the Eucharist: Voices from the Church Fathers*. My purpose was to highlight the teachings on the Eucharist of the fathers of the Church and to show how, despite their historical distance in time and space, as well as differences in language, culture, and educational background, their coherent body of insights resonated with each other to form a harmonious whole. Even today, this "living faith of the dead" forms a part of the Church's heritage and constitutes the marrow of its vibrant, living tradition.[1] The present Volume, which picks up where the first left off, is called, *The Mystery of the Eucharist: Voices from the Saints and Mystics*. Such a title raises a number of important questions. What is sanctity? What is mysticism? How are the two related? Who are the saints and mystics of our past and present? How are they recognized? What do they have to say about the Eucharist? How are their teachings continuous with the age of the fathers? How do they impact our everyday lives? This book approaches these and other questions by examining the lives and teachings of twenty-six figures from our Christian past, people who firmly and publicly professed their faith in Christ and whose teachings on the Eucharist had a great impact on Catholic spirituality.

The lives of the saints and mystics presented in this volume span more than fifteen centuries, from the end of the patristic era (Pseudo-Dionysius and John Damascene) to the age of Western monasticism (Anselm of Canterbury and Bernard of Clairvaux) to the period of high scholasticism (Bonaventure and Thomas Aquinas), to the late medieval

---

1. See Jaroslav Pelikan, *The Vindication of Tradition* (New Haven/London: Yale University Press, 1984), 65.

ages (Catherine of Siena and Thomas à Kempis), to early modern Catholicism (Ignatius of Loyola and Teresa of Avila), to the modern era (John Vianney and John Henry Newman), to twentieth-century Catholicism (Charles de Foucauld and Thomas Merton), up to the dawn of the new millennium (Chiara Lubich and Pope John Paul II). They are but a sampling of the voices from our past gathered in this volume dedicated to the Holy Eucharist. Others include such saintly figures as Aelred of Riveaulx, Hildegard of Bingen, Albert the Great, Meister Eckhart, Julian of Norwich, John of the Cross, Francis de Sales, Alphonsus de Liguori, Thérèse of Lisieux, and Teresa of Calcutta—to name but a few.

Taken together, these figures represent a cross-section of the centuries-old tradition of Eucharistic devotion. For the most part, they are voices of the Christian West steeped in the theological and liturgical tradition of Roman Catholic spirituality. They do not represent Orthodox and Protestant Christianity, which deserve special attention and will be examined elsewhere. The only exceptions are the first entries from Pseudo-Dionysius and John Damascene, two representatives from the Eastern patristic tradition included because of the wide diffusion of their writings in the Latin West, their impact on the development of Western spirituality, and their respect in each tradition. Their inclusion in this volume represents a point of continuity with my earlier book on the Eucharistic spirituality of eastern and western fathers, and I invite you to turn to it for further background on the theological, liturgical, and spiritual sources from which Roman Catholicism sprang and eventually flourished. Although this volume stands on its own merits, it complements *Voices from the Church Fathers* by showing how a common Catholic heritage surrounding the Eucharist resonates in polyphonic beauty from the patristic era down to the present. I have gathered this select and varied group of voices into a single volume to highlight the centrality of the Eucharistic mystery for the life and devotion of the Catholic faithful and to allow readers to see the beauty of this tradition as it resonates in lives dedicated to its transforming vision of faith.

This brings me to the question about sanctity. Who are the saints? What does it mean to be holy? Do the criteria for holiness change over time or vary from one cultural milieu to the next? Answers to such questions depend on the cultural background, philosophical and theological presuppositions, and religious persuasion of the one who replies. For my purposes, I identify the saints as people who embrace the Gospel of Jesus Christ and dedicate themselves entirely to fulfilling God's will. They are "holy" because they enjoy an intimate relationship with God and seek to share that intimacy with others. They realize their smallness in God's eyes, yet allow the Spirit of the Redeeming Christ to live within their hearts and transform every human characteristic: the physical, emotional, intellectual, spiritual, and social.

Saints are sinners who have opened their hearts and allowed God's transforming love to penetrate their lives. They are filled with the Spirit of God and manifest God's gifts and fruits in their dealings with others. They embody the words of St. Paul: "I have been crucified with Christ; and it is no longer I who live, but it is Christ who lives in me" (Gal 2:19–20). God wants everyone to be saved and extends the invitation to holiness freely. Sanctity is not a way of life but a way of being; it is a divinizing gift from God sustained by the Eucharist. The Church has canonized only a fraction of the multitude who have found their way to God and wear the crown of salvation. All who experience such union with God, both the living and the dead, compose what the Church calls the communion of saints.

And who are the mystics? What do ordinary believers have in common with them? How do they differ? What do mystics from various faiths have in common? What distinguishes Christian mysticism? Once again, answers to such questions vary depending on the cultural, philosophical, and religious outlook of the one who replies. In Catholic spirituality, mystics are people who live the gospel with deep awareness. They display in the present life the same intimacy with God that others hope for only in the next. They often experience ecstasy, experiences that transcend human expression. The finite cannot contain the infinite ; words and symbols cannot capture such transcendent experiences. The mystic's gift of intimacy with God reveals what is ultimately offered to everyone. They are aware of this intimacy to different degrees, however, just as attempts to express it also vary. The many schools of Christian mysticism that have arisen over time demonstrate the variety of experiences of God within the Catholic faith.

Just as everyone is called to holiness, everyone is called to mysticism, to encounter God face-to-face. Mystics and ordinary believers, however, do differ. Most who experience deep intimacy with God in the beatific vision do so only after death, in most cases only after a long process of purgation. Mystics, however, are blessed with an intense (albeit fleeting) foretaste of it in the here and now. Their experience is a gift to the Church that reveals the fullness of life in the hereafter. They have been set aside and specially blessed to manifest to God's people the great gifts that await them in the world to come. Everyone is called to holiness, and to mysticism. When and how we experience union with God may be different, but the end is the same. In this respect, every disciple of Christ is a pilgrim on a lifelong (and everlasting) journey into the mystery of the divine.

Although not all of the saints and mystics presented in this volume have been canonized, all have affected Catholic spirituality profoundly. They have lived in epochs that range from the late patristic and Medieval periods to early, late, and post-modernity; they share a common faith in the sacrificial death and redeeming love of Jesus Christ, a saving mystery uniquely present in the Eucharist. What is more, they have written about this "sacrament of sacraments," emphasizing its fundamental importance for the Catholic faith. Their ever deeper insights into the unfathomable mystery and beauty of the sacrament have shaped Catholic attitudes toward the Eucharist in the past and continue to do so today. Although they convey only a portion of the vibrancy and richness of our tradition, each demonstrates without exception his or her reverence for the Holy Eucharist and invites us to examine our own views toward this central mystery of the Catholic faith.

Heard from a distance and examined with historical perspective, the rhythms and melodies of the voices presented in this volume together provide a symphony of great beauty about the mystery of the Eucharist. Each of the twenty-six chapters (or "voices") begins with a biographical sketch of a saint or mystic, followed by a summary of his or her spirituality and teaching on the Eucharist with accompanying observations, a conclusion, and reflection questions. This structure unifies the whole, while allowing each chapter to be read alone. The reflection questions are meant to explore the issues raised by these saints and mystics and to encourage readers to apply them to their own lives. I hope that such reflection will deepen readers' reverence for and devotion to the Eucharist and focus their attention on its centrality in their lives.

These saints and mystics sing to God a joyful, thankful, and melodious song centered on their love for the Eucharist and its necessity for their spiritual life. Conducted by the Spirit moving in their lives, their music breaks transcends time and space, even to the threshold of the divine. This symphony's beauty can penetrate the silence of every believer's heart and awake the desire to glorify the Lord. Then at Eucharist, with the saints and mystics whose voices fill this volume, they can join in Christ's great hymn of praise and thanksgiving to the Father.

Voice One

Pseudo-Dionysius: Sacrament of Sacraments

> This is indeed the sacrament of sacraments, and, by making use of the sacred lore of scripture and of hierarchical understanding, I must discuss the divinely inspired accounts of it and, guided by the inspiration of the spirit of the Deity, I must be uplifted to the sacred contemplation of it.
>
> *Pseudo-Dionysius*

We begin our discussion of the beauty of the Eucharist in the thought of the great saints and mystics of the Church, by looking to the past and to the future. Looking back, we see the age of the fathers and the centrality of the sacrament in their spiritual and theological vision. Looking forward we see the rise of Christendom and its pivotal role in the development of Western civilization.

Our first voice stands at the intersection of these two historical currents. A voice from the age of the fathers, he would influence both eastern and western Christian thought, especially as it applies to the rise of Christian mysticism. This influence, in turn, would affect the development of other dimensions of Christian society: music, literature, art, theology, Church structures, architecture—to name but a few. He had great influence in part because it was thought that his voice, which predates the age of the fathers, comes from the earliest days of Christianity, the age of Paul and the apostles. Although this notion is mistaken, his voice has undisputed importance for Western culture. Of particular interest is the close connection he makes between the Eucharist and the mystical life.

A Disciple of Paul?

Pseudo-Dionysius (also known as Pseudo-Areopagite) probably wrote from Syria just before the turn of the sixth century A.D. The prefix "Pseudo-" has been attached to his name because he claimed to be Dionysius the Areopagite of Athens, whom the Apostle Paul converted in Acts 17:34. In the ancient world, it was not uncommon for an unknown author to assume the name of a well-known historical figure in order to add attention and prestige to his work.

In his case, the ploy worked extremely well. Although some Catholic authorities rejected the treatises and letters as apocryphal when they first surfaced early in the sixth century, they gradually gained prominence in both orthodox and heterodox circles and were eventually defended by such stalwarts of the faith as Maximus the Confessor (d. 662) and Gregory the Great (c. 540–604). In the ninth century, Hilduin of St. Denis (d. 840) and John Scotus Eriugena (d. after 877) translated the writings into Latin, giving them unquestioned sub-apostolic authority. In the Latin West especially the works had a profound influence on scholastic thought and the development of the Western Christian mystical tradition.

Not until the Italian humanist Lorenzo Valla (d. 1457) questioned the authenticity of these writings did the doubts about the author's identity arise. Prominent scholars and Christian spokesmen like Erasmus (1469–1536) and Martin Luther (1483–1546) also doubted the authenticity of these writings. Nevertheless, only at the end of the nineteenth century was it demonstrated that the writings were the work of a Christian disciple of Proclus (d. 485 A.D.), a fifth-century pagan Neoplatonic philosopher.[1] According to Walter Principe, "Many suggestions have been made about the identity of the author but none are convincing. Internal evidence suggests that he may have been a native of Syria and possibly a monk or a bishop."[2]

Pseudo-Dionysius' Spirituality

Pseudo-Dionysius' body of work includes four treatises and ten letters, all written in an uneven and often enigmatic literary style. The author was seeking to develop a Christian version of philosophy rooted in the writings of Plato (c. 427–347 B.C.) and developed in the early centuries of the Christian era by the pagan philosophers Plotinus (205–270 A.D.), Porphry (d. 306), and Proclus (412–485).

Neoplatonism envisions reality as emanating from a First Principle known as the One, which is independent of all things and beyond the reach of all thought. The first great emanation from the One is the divine mind, or Nous, in which exist the Ideas that all of reality is patterned upon. In the Neoplatonic perspective, in this first great emanation or "pouring forth," multiplicity enters the world. The second great emanation is the immaterial and indivisible World Soul, which acts as the intermediary between the intellectual and sensible worlds. It has two functions: (1) a principle of order without direct contact with the visible universe, and (2) Nature, the immanent principle of life for the visible world. The rest of invisible and visible reality flows from the Soul in a series of emanations that culminate in the visible, sensible world around us.[3]

---

1. See *P*, 604–9; Karl Bihlmeyer, *CH*, 1:414–16; *NCE2*, s.v. "Pseudo-Dionysius," by F.X. Murphy.
2. *IPMT*, 161.
3. For a general treatment of Plotinus and Neoplatonism, see George L. Abernethy and Thomas A. Langford, *Introduction to Western Philosophy: Pre-Socratics to Mill* (Belmont, CA: Dickenson Publishing Co., 1970), 94–104, esp. 98–99.

In time, Neoplatonism developed a number of schools, of which two differed considerably in approach: one tended to minimize the series of emanations from the One to the visible world (as in Plotinus and Porphry); the other tended to maximize them (as in Proclus). The first was successfully Christianized by Augustine of Hippo (354–430), who limited the emanations to three—the One, Nous, and World Soul—concepts that formed the basis for his doctrine on the Trinity. Since the concept of "emanation" implies necessity and contradicts the doctrine of divine freedom, Augustine attributed the existence of all else in visible and invisible reality to God's free creative action. The second was successfully Christianized by Pseudo-Dionysius (c. 500), who distinguished between the created world and the emanations within the Godhead yet devoted more interest to the various visible and invisible hierarchies in the created universe. His work, inspired by the thought of Proclus, is distinguished by its exploration of the hierarchies that God has "built-into" the very nature of creation.[4]

Pseudo-Dionysius' spirituality, which focuses on both God and the created world, has three distinctive approaches: positive (cataphatic) theology, negative (apophatic) theology, and symbolic theology. The first two deal with what can and cannot be said about God; the third focuses on God's activity in creation. His four treatises develop these theologies. *The Divine Names* shows how God, the First Principle, can be *named* by such terms as the One, the True, the Good, the Beautiful. Although this "way of knowing" does not exhaust the nature of the Godhead, it offers authentic insights into the divine nature. *The Mystical Theology* explains the dimension of the Godhead beyond all names and concepts. This "way of unknowing" that proceeds by way of negation affirms only what God is not. *The Celestial Hierarchy* discusses divine activity in the intelligible world, especially its hierarchic triads and choirs of angels. *The Ecclesiastical*

---

4. For the various schools of Neoplatonism, see HP, 1: 476–85 [esp. Proclus, 478–81].

Hierarchy examines divine activity in the sensible world, especially in the holy sacraments, the priestly hierarchy, and those subject to them.[5]

It should be noted that for Pseudo-Dionysius, the ecclesiastical hierarchy reflects the celestial. He points out that just as there are three triads each with three angelic choirs, so too there are three sacraments of initiation (baptism, Eucharist, confirmation), three orders of sacred priesthood (bishops, priests, deacons), and three orders of the general faithful (monks, catechumens, penitents). His teaching on the sacraments falls under his symbolic theology, since it represents a visible reflection of the heavenly world. This symbolism is based on light which, according to fifth-century Neoplatonism, has both an intelligible and a sensible nature. In the ecclesiastical hierarchy, the sacraments are the source of light; the clergy spreads it; the laity receives it in order to be saved.[6]

Pseudo-Dionysius on the Eucharist

Pseudo-Dionysius' teaching on the Eucharist, which appears in chapter three of *The Ecclesiastical Hierarchy*, is divided into three parts: (1) The Rite of Synaxis, (2) The Mystery of the "Synaxis" or Communion, and (3) the Contemplation.[7]

In the first part the author situates the Eucharist with respect to the other sacraments and determines its proper role according to the names that it has received: "gathering" (*synaxis*), "communion" (*koinonia*), and "operation of grace"(*eucharistia*). The Eucharist is the "sacrament of sacraments"; the other sacraments depend upon it. Although the other sacraments also pass on the light of God,

---

5. See P. Sheldon-Williams, "*The Ecclesiastical Hierarchy of Pseudo-Dionysius*—Part I," *The Downside Review* 82 (1964): 294–95.
6. See P, 604; Sheldon-Williams, "*The Ecclesiastical Hierarchy of Pseudo-Dionysius*— Part I," 295–96.
7. Pseudo-Dionysius, *The Ecclesiastical Hierarchy* [424C-445C], trans. Colm Luibheid, *CWS* (New York: Mahwah, N.J., 1987), 209–24.

the Eucharist "first introduces the light and is the source of all divine illumination."[8]

The second part describes the Eucharistic ritual. He recalls only the most significant elements, which will be explained later in the "Contemplation." The bishop says a prayer at the altar, incenses the sacred space, and begins singing the sacred psalms as the rest of the assembly joins in. The deacons then begin reading the scriptures, after which the catechumens, penitents, and possessed are led out so that there remain only those entitled to the vision and communion of divine things. Some deacons guard the doors to keep proper order. The congregation sings the creed, then other deacons and priests prepare the divine altar and place on it the sacred bread and cup of blessing. The bishop then says a sacred prayer and bids everyone peace. After the exchange of the ritual kiss, the mystical reading of the sacred volumes draws to a close. After washing their hands, the bishop sits at the center of the altar surrounded by the priests and a few deacons. The bishop then praises God's sacred works, performs the divine action, and lifts the sacred symbols for all to see. He then receives communion and invites others to do the same. After distributing communion, he concludes with an act of thanksgiving. As the faithful look upon the divine symbols, the bishop is lifted by the Holy Spirit to the source of the sacramental mystery and is conformed to God in contemplation.[9]

The third part, the longest, explains the meaning of the ceremony in a commentary, directed first to the "imperfect" and then to the "perfect." The first explains things on the moral level. The second, more developed, explains the mystical character of the sacrament by examining the Cause from which the symbols have derived their unifying

---

8. See Pseudo-Dionysius, *The Ecclesiastical Hierarchy* [424C-425B], 209–10; E. Boularand, "L'Eucharistie d'après le pseudo-Denys l'Aréopagite," *Bulletin de littérature ecclésiastique* 58(1957) : 194–206.
9. See Pseudo-Dionysius, *The Ecclesiastical Hierarchy* [425C-428A], 210–11; Boularand, "L'Eucharistie d'après le pseudo-Denys l'Aréopagite," 194, 207–13

light. This two-tiered commentary reflects the capacity of the various audiences to which it is directed and gradually develops the deeper meanings of the Eucharistic liturgy.[10]

By the "imperfect," Pseudo-Dionysius refers to those not fully initiated into the Christian mysteries or who need purification (catechumens, penitents, the unclean [possessed]). To them he offers a moral (or "tropological") explanation of the Eucharist, pointing out that singing the psalms and reading Scripture teach the rules of virtuous living, the need to reject vice, and the purification of self from evil. He also points out that receiving Communion establishes another important moral and spiritual norm: "As we become worthy to receive the divine food, we receive the grace of assimilation and union with the divine mysteries."[11]

By the "perfect," Pseudo-Dionysius means those who have been fully initiated into the Christian mysteries yet still need illumination (the baptized, the absolved, the cleansed [exorcised]). With the sacred action of the priesthood, they penetrate the material dimension of the sacramental rituals and Scriptures, coming to a contemplative grasp of their mystical significance. With this newly awakened understanding, they can look beyond the material symbols of bread and wine to the holy, mystical realities that they represent. By receiving the sacramental mysteries, monks are said to have reached this mystical goal of contemplation and union with God. By doing so, they have left the symbolic world behind to live in the intelligible, mystical world that the sacramental mysteries reveal. The third part, the "Contemplation," affirms the unity of the meaning of the sacramental symbols involved in celebrating the Eucharist. It exhorts the "imperfect" to lead a life of purgation and the "perfect" to walk the way of illumination so as to receive

---

10. See Pseudo-Dionysius, *The Ecclesiastical Hierarchy* [428B-445C], 211–24; Boularand, "L'Eucharistie d'après le pseudo-Denys l'Aréopagite," 194, 213–17.
11. See P. Sheldon-Williams, "*The Ecclesiastical Hierarchy of Pseudo-Dionysius*—Part II," *The Downside Review* 83(1965): 22–23.

the transcendent gnosis by which individuals are deified and brought into union with God.[12]

Observations

Pseudo-Dionysius' view on the Eucharist invites a number of observations that will draw out some of the hidden implications of his thought.

Because the philosophical presuppositions underlying Pseudo-Dionysius' worldview differ from postmodern Western sensitivities, they can be difficult to grasp. His Christian Neoplatonism, with its vast system of participating hierarchies—created and uncreated, visible and invisible—appears strange and perhaps even unnecessary. The contemporary worldview has been shaped by vastly different philosophical forces, not the least of which is the famous principle of parsimony (i.e., Ockham's razor), that avoids unnecessary duplication and always opts for the simpler explanation. By way of contrast, Pseudo-Dionysius delights in the hierarchical pluralities upon which he believes the entire created universe, both visible and invisible, has been patterned. Contemporary thought prizes egalitarianism; he considers hierarchy to be fundamentally positive because it represents the underlying structure of reality and the means through which God has left a vestige of himself in creation.

Pseudo-Dionysius' Christian form of Neoplatonism offers a comprehensive philosophical (as opposed to theological) justification for a hierarchical priesthood. Western Christians might benefit from exploring the latent Neoplatonic roots of their present-day liturgy. Dionysius' Christian Neoplatonism, especially as it is expressed in the Eucharist, the "sacrament of sacraments," may help us appreciate the positive dimensions of the notion of hierarchy that for centuries have inspired both the Eastern *and* Western forms

---

12. Ibid., 23–25.

of Christianity. Although it has become muted and in the West usually is not mentioned, the notion of "hierarchical participation" remains an underlying philosophical presupposition in both traditions. Such appreciation might temper the more ambivalent (and even negative) attitudes concerning hierarchy among believing Christians, many of whom are influenced by postmodern relativism.

The Eucharistic celebration described in chapter three of The Ecclesiastical Hierarchy *closely resembles the Syriac-Antiochene liturgy (one of the reasons for suggesting that the author wrote from Syria)*[13] *and espouses a typically Eastern Christian liturgical mysticism.* Western Christianity can learn from Eastern Christianity's rich symbolism and appreciation for the mystical. Pope John Paul II's call for all Christians to breathe once more with both lungs of their Eastern and Western heritage challenges us to open our minds and hearts to all valid expressions and celebrations of the Christian mysteries.[14] Although they are difficult to grasp, Pseudo-Dionysius' writings on the Eucharist can help all Christians understand the source of their liturgy — the roots of Eastern traditions, and the symbolism and mysticism of the West.

Pseudo-Dionysius offers a twofold commentary: one moral (or tropological) and the other mystical. This twofold approach is based upon his distinction between the imperfect and the perfect, i.e., those not fully initiated into the Church who need purgation, and the fully initiated who need illumination. The common practice today of dismissing catechumens after the celebration of the Liturgy of the Word suggests the value of developing commentaries suited to the different capacities of the members of believing community.

---

13. See *P*, 606; Boularand, "L'Eucharistie d'après le pseudo-Denys l'Aréopagite," 209.
14. This theme was often emphasized by Pope John Paul II. See, for example, his reflection on his visit to Romania, *General Audience*, Wednesday, May 12, 1999 and his "Angelus," address on Friday, June 9, 2001.

A common theme in contemporary Catholic theological discourse is the connection between the moral and the spiritual aspects of life. Liturgical commentaries that distinguish between the two while emphasizing their close, intimate connection would help today's believers understand the meaning of *lex orandi, lex credendi, lex vivendi* ("the law of praying is the law of believing and the law of living").[15]

The various names by which Pseudo-Dionysius refers to the Eucharist—"gathering" (synaxis), *"communion"* (koinonia), *and "operation of grace"*(eucharistia)—*contribute to understanding the Eucharistic liturgy.* Each of these terms focuses on one dimension of the celebration. As a "gathering" or "reunion" of believers, the *synaxis* emphasizes our coming together as a body to celebrate the divine mysteries. The community of believers is not some vague, virtual reality but a church with a concrete, local membership that gathers often to retell and reflect on the Christian narrative and celebrate the symbols that lead them to choose God. As a "communion," or *koinonia*, the community recognizes that each member is bonded to the other through the love of Christ's Spirit, the same bond that unites Jesus to the Father and the Father to Jesus. The community recognizes that the liturgy, as an "operation of grace" or *eucharistia*, is a work of God made possible through the redemptive action of Christ's paschal mystery and the sanctifying power of the Spirit. These physical, spiritual, and transcendent dimensions demonstrate God's deep love for us and our need to express concretely our love for God and for neighbor.

---

15. For the relationship between spirituality and morality in contemporary Catholic theological discourse, see Dennis J. Billy and Donna Lynn Orsuto, eds., *Spirituality and Morality: Integrating Prayer and Action* (Mahwah, NJ: Paulist Press, 1996); Mark O'Keefe, *Becoming Good, Becoming Holy: On the Relationship of Christian Ethics and Spirituality* (New York/Mahwah, NJ: Paulist Press, 1995).

Conclusion

The author known as Pseudo-Dionysius is as enigmatic as his writings. Little is known of his identity and the provenance of his documents, and even less about why he chose the pseudonym that he did. Because of his familiarity with the Syriac-Antiochene liturgy and dependence on the Neoplatonic philosopher, Proclus, late-nineteenth century scholars concluded that he wrote from Syria at the turn of the sixth century A.D. His Dionysian identity, unquestioned for almost a thousand years, gave his writing an aura of sub-apostolic authority. As a result, it influenced greatly the Christian spiritual and mystical tradition, especially in the West, where it was widely read in Latin translation.

Pseudo-Dionysius' teaching on the Eucharist includes a symbolic theology that describes how hierarchies participate in the sensible world. It presents a vision in which everything in the visible realm has a proper role that reflects a corresponding heavenly reality. He presents the Eucharist as the "sacrament of sacraments," a "gathering," a "communion," and an "action of grace" that leads believers along the way of purgation and illumination to ultimate union with divine love. His two-tiered commentary on this sacred liturgy offers a moral interpretation for those who need purgation because they are not fully initiated into the Christian faith, and a mystical one for those moving toward illumination and union. He envisions a threefold sacramental initiation (baptism, Eucharist, confirmation), a three-tiered hierarchical priesthood (bishop, priests, and deacons), and a threefold grouping of the general faithful (monks, catechumens, penitents). These symbolic hierarchies of the visible world reflect the three triads of the angelic choirs of the invisible, heavenly sphere.

Contemporary Christians (especially those in the West) find Pseudo-Dionysius' teaching on the Eucharist esoteric and complicated. This mysterious and elusive character, however, challenges our attitudes (and possible prejudices) toward the nature and function of hierarchy in Christian life and worship. It also asks us to examine the moral and spiritual content of our descriptions and explanations of our Eucharistic celebrations. It invites us, moreover, to examine the mystical roots of our own liturgical tradition in order to appreciate the great gift that God has given us in the sacrament. Pseudo-Dionysius' teaching represents a valuable tool for appreciating the mystical roots of our liturgical traditions and rooting ourselves in the life-giving Spirit who prepares us for and leads us into union with the mystery of God's love.

Reflection Questions

- Why does Pseudo-Dionysius call the Eucharist the "sacrament of sacraments"? What makes it preeminent among sacraments? What is its relationship to the other sacraments? How does it bring about a person's sanctification?

- How do you understand Pseudo-Dionysius' description of the Eucharist as a "gathering," a "communion," and an "action of grace?" With which of these three actions do you identify most? To which are you most attracted?

- How do you understand Pseudo-Dionysius' explanation that the Eucharist leads us along the way of purgation, illumination, and ultimate union with divine love? Where are you in this spiritual journey to divine love?

Voice Two

John Damascene: Living Rule of Faith

> The Body is truly united to divinity, the Body which was from that of the Holy Virgin, not that the Body which was taken up comes back down from heaven, but that the bread itself and the wine are made over into the Body and Blood of God.
>
> *John Damascene*

Like Pseudo-Dionysius, our next voice, also from Eastern Christianity, had a deep impact on Western thinking concerning the Eucharist. He comes from the very end of the patristic age and the dawn of the Middle Ages, when Europe was declining after the collapse of the western Roman empire and Islam was ascendant throughout the ancient Near East and beyond. His capacity to synthesize Christian thought bequeathed to the Church a body of theological thought that was both comprehensive and orthodox. In him theologians and spiritual writers, Eastern and Western alike, found an accessible and trustworthy voice of authority in promoting and defending the faith. His teaching on the Eucharist consolidated the tradition and solidified the Church's response to external and internal threats.

Last of the Fathers

John Damascene (d. c.749), the "last Father of the Greek Church," was born in the late seventh century in the

Saracen-ruled city of Damascus. His father held an important position in the court of the caliph. Upon his father's death he inherited this post and served until 700, when the reigning caliph's hostility towards Christians forced his resignation. In 715, he withdrew to the monastery of St. Sabas near Jerusalem to lead a life of contemplation.

John Damascene is best remembered for his defense of sacred images during the Iconoclast controversy, as well as his magnum opus, *The Fountain of Knowledge*. This work contains three parts: a philosophical treatise, a history of the heresies, and *On the Orthodox Faith*, a summary of Christian doctrine.

Although John was not a theological innovator, Greek theology depended upon his extraordinary skills as a synthesizer and compiler of texts. *On the Orthodox Faith* was translated into Latin and is often cited in medieval scholastic treatises. His teaching on the Eucharist comes, in large part, from this important "Summa" of Greek theology, which is noted for its sacramental realism and strong adherence to the tradition of the Greek fathers.[1]

Damascene's Spirituality

John Damascene compiled and synthesized the traditions of Eastern Christianity, an important step in preserving the Greek theological tradition.

The first part of *The Fountain of Knowledge* describes his philosophical and theological method:

> Like a bee... I shall gather all that conforms to truth, even deriving help from the writings of our enemies.... I am not offering you my own conclusions, but those which were laboriously arrived at by the most eminent theologians, while I

---

1. See *CH*, 2: 87–88; *HD*, 3: 468–70; William J. McDonald, gen. ed., *The New Catholic Encyclopedia*, vol. 7 (New York: McGraw-Hill, 1967), "John Damascene, St.," by B. Kotter.

have merely collected them and summarized them, as far as possible, into one treatise.[2]

This approach echoes Benedictine monasticism, which sought to preserve the literary treasures of classical antiquity. It also resembles the early scholastic method, which gathered varying opinions to point out some of the underlying tensions between Sacred Scripture and theological texts of the Christian tradition.[3]

John was heavily influenced by Aristotelian and Neoplatonic philosophy, but did not feel bound to these traditions when they departed from the tenets of Christian orthodoxy. His theology was influenced by the Pseudo-Dionysius the Areopagite, (c. 500), Leontius of Byzantium (c. 485-c. 543), and Maximus the Confessor (c. 580–662), the great defender of the faith against Monothelitism. His main theological concern was to preserve the unity of the faith and help it resist attempts to compromise its truthfulness.[4]

John's theological outlook is illustrated through his role in the Iconoclast controversy. Claiming that images were false idols, the iconoclasts claimed it was sinful and even heretical to make or venerate them. The iconophiles, by way of contrast, drew a distinction between an image and what it represented. John, a great iconophile, identified an image as "a likeness, an illustration, and a representation of something, showing forth in itself that which is imaged."[5] Praying before an icon, he claimed, is not veneration of the image itself, but of the person or mystery it represents. The icon, in other words, points to something beyond itself and leads to the threshold of the sacred. Another way of putting it is that the "prototype" of a particular mystery is imprinted

---

2. John Damascene, *Dialectic, pr.* Cited in *CT*, 2: 136.
3. For a description of the monastic and scholastic approaches to learning, see *AMHT*, 52–57.
4. See *HD*, 3: 469–70.
5. John Damascene, *Orations on the Images*, 3.16. Cited in *CT*, 2:119.

into the image and leads to a close relationship but not an identification between the two.[6]

Iconoclasts maintained that the divine mysteries cannot be contained, but John responded that the doctrines of the incarnation and the real presence of Christ in the Eucharist already speak of a certain "circumscription" of the Word of God in becoming flesh and then bread and wine.[7] Icons, another application of this fundamental principle on another level, address the human need for tangible, sensible aids for prayer. Icons, in other words, stand for the unity of sound doctrine and authentic worship—as the Latins would put it, *lex orandi, lex credendi*. Iconoclasm contains a hidden Gnosticism that does not acknowledge the connection between the spiritual realm and the material. John's theology is permeated by a deep consciousness of the need to find a *via media* (middle road) between "the false spiritualism of the iconoclasts and the false materialism of the idolaters."[8] His teaching on the Eucharist illustrates this.

Damascene on the Eucharist

John does not explain his understanding of the Church or present a general treatment of the sacraments. His theology of Church and sacraments must be inferred from his larger literary corpus, especially his statements concerning individual sacraments. He clearly considers the Church to have been instituted by Christ as "the living rule of faith," free of secular authorities in both doctrinal and disciplinary concerns. The apostles alone have received the power to loose and bind, and Peter is the worthy leader appointed by Christ to guide the Church on earth. The sacraments, such as baptism, flow from the life of the Church and are "signs

---

6. See *CT*, 2:119–20.
7. Ibid., 2:134.
8. Ibid., 2:123.

of grace." They are, in other words, visible symbols of the spiritual.[9]

Concerning the Eucharist, John affirms Jesus' real presence in the consecrated species. At the Last Supper Jesus states clearly that the bread and wine are actually changed into his body and blood. Damascene admits that at times some Church fathers have referred to the bread and wine as "antitypes" of the Lord's body of blood, but insists that such terminology refers to the bread and wine before the consecration:

> The Bread and the Wine are not a type of the Body and Blood of Christ—perish the thought!—but the deified Body Itself of the Lord, since the Lord Himself has said: 'This is My Body.' He did not say a type of His Body, but His Body; nor a type of His Blood, but His Blood... If some have called the bread and wine antitypes of the Body and Blood of the Lord, as does the divinely inspired Basil, they said this not after the consecration but before the consecration, giving this name to the offering itself.[10]

John also notes that the sacraments themselves are sometimes described as "antitypes of future things," but attributes this claim to the belief that, through them, the faithful hope to share in Jesus' divinity. He insists that the term "antitype" does not undermine the doctrine of the real presence. He considers that Jesus' words at the Last Supper should be taken at face value and allowed to speak for themselves.[11]

When discussing *how* the bread and wine becomes Jesus' body and blood, John affirms God's power to do so through the movement of the Holy Spirit:

> If you inquire into the way in which this happens, let it suffice for you to hear that it is through the Holy Spirit, just as

---

9. See *HD*, 3: 489.
10. John Damascene, *The Fountain of Knowledge*, 3.4.13. Cited in *FEF*, 3: 339.
11. See *HD*, 3: 490–93.

it was through the Holy Spirit that the Lord took on Himself from the Holy Mother of God the flesh that subsisted in Himself. More than this, we do not know, except that the word of God is true and effective and powerful; but the manner [of the Eucharistic transformation] is inscrutable.[12]

John sees no need to explain the process by which bread and wine are transformed into Jesus' body and blood. He is content simply to acknowledge God's ability to do so. "For God all things are possible" (Mt 19:26), says the Gospel of Matthew. Human beings must not probe the divine mysteries too deeply lest they be emptied of the sacred by reducing them to rational theories that make logical sense but do not address the deepest concerns of the human heart, where God wishes to dwell.

Although John asserts the power of the Holy Spirit to transform the Eucharistic elements into Jesus' body and blood, he does use a metaphor to describe what takes place. By way of analogy, he likens the transformation of the Eucharistic elements to the transformation of those who consume them:

> Just as bread in the natural process of eating, and water and wine in drinking, are changed into the body and blood of the one eating and drinking, and do not become another body than his former body, so too the bread on the credence table, as also the wine and water, though the epiclesis and coming of the Holy Spirit, are supernaturally changed into the Body of Christ and into His Blood, and they are not two but one and the same.[13]

Interestingly, John attributes the transformation of the bread and wine into the body and blood of Christ to the power of the Holy Spirit invoked at the epiclesis, rather than to the words of institution. His earlier reference to St. Basil

---

12. John Damascene, *The Fountain of Knowledge*, 3.4.13. Cited in *FEF*, 3: 339.
13. Ibid.

and his use of the word "antitype" supports this claim. In the Divine Liturgy of St. Basil, the word "antitype" follows the words of institution ("This is my Body. This is my Blood"), but precedes the epiclesis.[14] For John, the transformation takes place not when the priest recites the words of institution over the bread and wine, for they are still "antitypes" of what is to come. It occurs instead at the epiclesis, when the priest invokes the power of the Holy Spirit to take the offering of bread and wine and turn them into the body and blood of the Divine Savior.

From this perspective, John's teaching on the Eucharist highlights how an element in the Greek Eucharistic practice differs from the Western tradition. Both traditions consider both the epiclesis and the words of institution to be important for the Eucharistic celebration. The West, however, has focused on the words of institution as the moment when the transformation takes place, while the East has looked more to the presence and power of the Holy Spirit present throughout the entire liturgy and, in a special way, when invoked at the epiclesis.

John also claims that the faithful participate in Christ's divinity precisely through their sharing in the Eucharist. The consecrated bread and wine are intimately united to the divine nature and elevate those who worthily partake of it.[15] As a result, those who receive it with the proper dispositions share in that nature and live in communion with God and one another:

> Participation [in the Eucharist] is spoken of, because through the Eucharist we participate in the divinity of Jesus. Communion is likewise spoken of, and it is real communion, because through the Eucharist we have communion with Christ and share in His flesh and in His divinity. We do indeed have such communion thereby, that we are united with each other.

---

14. See *HD*, 3: 492.
15. Ibid. 3:493.

For since we partake of one Bread we all become one body of Christ and one blood, and members of each other, since we become of one body with Christ.[16]

These words indicate John's deep consciousness of the Eucharist as a source of communion with both God and neighbor. The nature of this communion is an actual sharing in the divine nature, made possible by the transformed status of what has been received, and therefore is a source of communion with God and within the Church. For this reason, John opposes allowing those who do not share the same faith to receive the body and blood of Christ: "For if this union is truly with Christ and with each other, certainly we are voluntarily united also with all who partake along with us."[17] John's teaching on the Eucharist can inform contemporary understanding of who should and should not be allowed to receive the Eucharist. The bond of communion shared by those who receive the body and blood of Christ reflects shared doctrinal beliefs and ethical practices. It is a holy gift from God and a profession of what God's people believe.

Observations

John Damascene's views on the Eucharist invite a number of observations that will draw out some of the hidden implications of his thought.

John has a profound sense of humanity's limitations in scrutinizing the mysteries of the faith. He intuitively grasps that some elements of the Church's proclamation will never be fully understood; they can be explained only by God's true and effective power. The change of bread and wine into Jesus' body and blood is one such instance. Although analogies suggest how such a transformation might take place

---

16. John Damascene, *The Fountain of Knowledge*, 3.4.13. Cited in *FEF*, 3: 339.
17. Ibid, 3.4.14. Cited in *FEF*, 3: 339–40.

(e.g., how what is eaten becomes part of the one who eats), he concludes that it can only be explained by God's omnipotence. John is aware that unorthodox tendencies to overly "spiritualize" or "materialize" the divine mysteries must be avoided. His teaching on the Eucharist reflects this awareness and presents a balanced alternative to the extremes of Gnostic spiritualism and pagan idolatry.

John believes in the real presence of Christ and goes to great lengths to affirm its doctrinal validity. He takes Jesus' words of institution at face value and does not try to interpret them in a spiritual sense. This sacramental realism is key to his iconophile stance. Because the bread and wine are transformed into Jesus' body and blood, he can cite examples in scripture and the Church's tradition of the divine Logos being contained or circumscribed by matter. From this perspective, the Eucharist is the "icon" par excellence of the Church's living faith. To worship it is not idolatry, but a genuine expression of loving homage for the divine mysteries.

John teaches that the bread and wine are transformed into Jesus' body and blood through the power of the Holy Spirit, thus emphasizing the importance of the invocation of the Spirit or "epiclesis" in the Eucharistic celebration. By emphasizing the power of the Spirit, he reaffirms the tendency in Eastern Christianity to view the Divine Liturgy as a work of God performed "in the Spirit" by the believing community, both living and dead. He also highlights the underlying mystical quality of the Eucharistic celebration, a sacramental mystery in which bread and wine are transformed into the body and blood of Christ, as are the lives of believing Christians by being brought in direct contact with Christ's divinized nature. This emphasis on the Spirit, although present Latin theology, was not emphasized as it was in the East. Perhaps it should be retrieved by the West and highlighted with renewed vigor.

For John, to receive the Eucharist is to enter into a close communion with the divinized Christ. This intimate bond allows the one who receives with the proper dispositions to participate in the divine nature as an adopted son or daughter of God. To participate in the divine nature involves healing the wounds of sin and the sinner's subsequent elevation to a divinized status. By communing with Christ in the Eucharist, believers experience this twofold process, becoming more and more "Christ-like." John's teaching reminds us that to receive the Eucharist represents our willingness to enter into this process of divinization by leading a life of genuine and heartfelt conversion.

At a time when the Church is emphasizing the importance for all members of the faithful to practice a "spirituality of communion,"[18] John's teaching also highlights the Eucharistic roots of Christ's body, the Church. To participate in the Eucharist is to affirm one's unity with the body of believers in matters of faith and morals. John insists that the Eucharist not be administered to those who do not share in these beliefs because of his deep sense of the intimate sacramental union of Christ and the Church. As the "sacrament of communion," however, the Eucharist calls those who share in it to overcome the differences that divide Christians so as to resolve the "scandal of disunity" that compromises the Church's identity and mission. The "discipline of unity," in other words, requires Catholics to preserve the integrity of their faith, while at the same time reaching out to other Christian churches and faith communities in a spirit of fraternal love and dialogue.

Conclusion

For centuries, John Damascene's presentation of the Eastern Christian tradition, an important milestone in Greek

---

18. See, for example, *NMI*, nos. 43–45 (accessed April 23, 2012).

theological thought, has affected the theological landscape of both the Eastern and Western Churches. Although he was primarily a synthesizer and compiler, the brilliance of his own theological depth often shines through, as in his defense of the use of images during the Iconoclast controversy.

Rooted in the scriptures and the tradition of the Greek fathers, John's teaching on the Eucharist reflects the principles that underlie his iconophile position. Noted for its sacramental realism and its emphasis on the power of the Spirit to transform mere bread and wine into Jesus' body and blood, it emphasizes the divinizing effects of the Eucharist on those who receive it and the bond of communion it sustains among the members of Christ's body. The Eucharist, for John, is a visible expression of the invisible Logos, who has taken on human flesh in the Incarnation and becomes bread and wine in the sacramental mystery of the Lord's table. It is the icon par excellence of God's redemptive, transforming, and divinizing Word.

Today's community of believers can learn from John's teaching on the Eucharist. It reminds us of God's omnipotence and reaffirms our belief that whenever we gather to celebrate the sacrament, God enters our world anew. It also reminds us of the sacrament's transforming effects on those who receive it worthily and of the bonds of communion that it forges within the community of believers. The deep significance of this teaching challenges Christians from East and West, indeed, from all churches and faith communities, to overcome their divisions.

Reflection Questions

- Describe John Damascene's middle course between the tendencies to overly "spiritualize" or "materialize" the divine mysteries. What value would it have for you to live out this course in your attitude toward the Eucharist? How would it affect your reception of the sacrament?

- What images or analogies do you find most helpful in explaining this mysterious transformation of bread and wine into the body and blood of Christ? How are they limited in explaining what lies only in the power of God to do what otherwise would be impossible?

- Why does John Damascene believe in the central and transformative role played by the Spirit in the Liturgy? What role does the Holy Spirit play in your spiritual outlook? In your search for holiness? In your day-to-day activities?

Voice Three

Anselm of Canterbury: Faith Seeking Understanding

> Thank you for the good gift of this your holy Body and Blood, which I desire to receive, as a cleansing from sin, and for the defense against it. Lord, I acknowledge that I am far from worthy to approach and touch this sacrament; but I trust in that mercy which caused you to lay down your life for sinners that they might be justified, and because you gave yourself willingly as a holy sacrifice to the Father.
>
> *Anselm of Canterbury*

Our next voice on the Eucharist, from the Latin West, represents the period when Western Europe was emerging from a period of decline (the so-called Dark Ages) and beginning to re-assert itself intellectually, economically, and politically. The re-awakening of this period produced the market economy, scholasticism, the universities, the Crusades, and Europe's great cathedrals. Anselm, a Benedictine monk who later was named bishop of Canterbury, England, continues the patristic tradition (especially the thought of St. Augustine), yet represents a shift in the theory and practice of theology. He defined theology as *fides quaerens intellectum* ("faith seeking understanding") and was among the first to use logic or "dialectics" to clarify Christian revelation. This innovative approach had a deep impact on Western thinking in general, particularly in the understanding of the Eucharist. Anselm sets a direction that Western philosophy and theology would travel for centuries.

Father of Scholasticism

Anselm of Canterbury (1033/34–1109), one of the great intellects of the medieval world, is known as the "Father of Scholasticism." Born at Aosta, in what is now northwestern Italy, in 1160 he entered the Benedictine monastery of Bec in Normandy, where he studied under the great Lanfranc. He became Prior of the abbey in 1063 and its abbot in 1078.

In 1093, Anselm was summoned to succeed his mentor Lanfranc as Archbishop of Canterbury and Primate of England. In that capacity, Anselm struggled with King William Rufus and his successor Henry I over the Church's property. Their attempts to exert royal jurisdiction over church affairs forced Anselm into exile from 1097–1100 and again from 1103–1107. These periods gave him time for prayer, reading, and writing. He returned from exile just two years before his death.

Anselm's most famous works are the *Monologium* (1076), the *Proslogium* (1077–78), and the *Cur Deus homo* (*Why the God-Man*, ca. 1098). Although noted for his contributions to scholastic method, Christian soteriology, and his ontological proof for the existence of God, he also offers important insights concerning the Eucharist, particularly regarding the use of unleavened bread for celebrating the sacrament. He demonstrates his devotion to the Eucharist in meditations filled with heartfelt sentiments that were unique for their time.[1]

Anselm's Spirituality

Anselm bridged the patristic and scholastic approaches to theology, a movement from the sapiential to the dialectic, from the search for wisdom to identifying and systematizing

---

1. See *IPMT*, 183; *CH*, 2:243–45.

the content of revelation. Rooted in monastic love of learning and desire for God, an approach to truth that continued the tradition of the Church fathers, he departed from ways of the cloister by using dialectic (i.e., rational argument) rather than grammar to explore human knowledge of the divine. Anselm trusted the capacity of human reason to arrive at truth and used logical argument to assess it. Theology, he believed, was *fides quaerens intellectum* ("faith seeking understanding")—faith's active search to make sense of the truths of Christian revelation. Although reason could not exhaust the divine mysteries, it had some capacity of understand them. In other words, humanity's fall from grace weakened but did not extinguish reason's capacity to ascertain truth. Guided by faith, human reason can probe the divine mysteries and reach concrete conclusions about them. Anselm's use of rational argument to ponder the mysteries of the Christian faith contributed to the scholastic method and set theological inquiry on a path that Christian thought would follow for centuries.[2] Two of his more creative uses of rational argument appear in his ontological argument for the existence of God and his satisfaction theory of the redemption.

The ontological argument he made in the *Proslogion* has been discussed by philosophers ever since. Starting with the premise that God is "something than which nothing greater can be thought,"[3] Anselm argued that this being *must* exist because, if it did not, one would be able to think of a still greater being, namely, one that did exist. Although many think that the argument posits too fluid a transition from mind to reality, it should be understood in the context of its underlying Christian Neoplatonic presuppositions. These

---

2. For the monastic love of learning and desire for God, see *LLDG*, 191–235. For Anselm's method, see *IPMT*, 183–83; *HPMA*, 128–30.
3. Anselm of Canterbury, *Proslogion*, chap. 2 in *Complete Philosophical and Theological Treatises of Anselm of Canterbury*, trans. Jasper Hopkins and Herbert Richardson (Minneapolis: The Arthur J. Banning Press, 2000), 93.

underpinnings affirm universal "Ideas" in the mind of God as the ultimate reality, to which human beings are granted access through their participation in Eternal Reason. For Anselm, thought and reality, although distinct, are also intimately intertwined. Given his philosophical outlook, the leap from one to the other was reasonable. His argument is acceptable, however, only if judged according to the foundation upon which it is based. If examined from other philosophical perspectives, it loses much of its cohesiveness.[4]

His satisfaction theory of redemption had a greater influence on Christian thought. Reacting to the prevalent theory of his day, which held that Christ became man and died on the cross in order to ransom humanity from Satan, Anselm explained redemption without referring to the devil. He argued in *Cur Deus homo* that in Adam's sin humanity committed an offense of infinite proportions against God's justice, one that demanded an act of infinite satisfaction. Because of its weakened and finite condition, however, humanity could not make such satisfaction. Anselm's theory reveals a drama within the Godhead. Moved by compassion and love for humanity, God himself accomplished this act by becoming man and dying on the cross. Divine compassion thus satisfied divine justice. Released from the snares of Satan, men and women could once more walk with God and share in the divine life. Anselm's explanation eventually became the dominant theory of redemption and has had a lasting effect on Catholic theology. Despite its shortcomings, it advanced human understanding of Christ's redemptive mission.[5]

---

4. According to G. R. Evans, however, "his [Anselm's] argument has never been decisively refuted, because it has proved impossible to determine on exactly what it turns. It is of some importance here that it hangs upon precisely the question of that intersection between thought and reality which was central to medieval work on epistemology and language." See *Philosophy and Theology in the Middle Ages* (London: Routledge, 1993), 54.
5. For the difference between Anselm's satisfaction theory and what preceded it, see R.

Anselm made many other contributions to Christian spirituality, but his ontological proof for the existence of God and his satisfaction theory of redemption provide a general sense of his conceptual universe, his theology, and his method of argumentation. They also provide a backdrop for his ideas on the Eucharist.

Anselm on the Eucharist

In a letter written before December, 1105 to bishop Walram of Naurburg, Anselm addresses the criticisms of the Latin tradition by the Greeks, who celebrate Eucharist with leavened instead of unleavened bread.[6] He demonstrates through logic not only that the Greeks were wrong to look down upon the Latins, but that the Latin practice is actually preferable. He begins by pointing out that the Greek practice is not contrary to the Christian faith, since both "leavened and unleavened bread do not differ in *substance*" (italics mine).[7] At the same time, he mentions that because Jesus almost certainly used unleavened bread when he celebrated his last supper with his disciples, the Latin practice follows Jesus' action more faithfully. Nevertheless, he points out that Jesus himself never specifically mentioned whether to use unleavened or leavened bread.

To the accusation that Jesus used unleavened bread only to fulfill a precept of the Old Law, which his death and resurrection surpass, Anselm responds that the Latins consecrate with unleavened bread not to fulfill a precept of the Old Covenant, but to perform the commemorative action as Jesus himself did. If the Greeks accuse the Latins

---

W. Southern, *The Making of the Middle Ages* (New Haven: Yale University Press, 1953; 27th printing), 234–40. For some of the shortcomings of Anselm's theory, see *IPMT*, 189; Gustaf Aulén, *Christus Victor: An Historical Study of the Three Main Types of the Idea of the Atonement* (New York: Macmillan, 1969), 93–95.

6. See Anselm of Canterbury, "The Sacrifice of Unleavened and Leavened Bread," in *Complete Philosophical and Theological Treatises of Anselm of Canterbury*, 515–22.
7. Ibid., 515.

of being Judaizers, then they must also accuse Jesus. There is nothing wrong with following Jesus' example, especially when it concerns a sacred action such as the celebration of the Eucharist. Moreover, to the accusation that Latins' use of unleavened bread reflects a Jewish symbolism unfit for Christians, he responds: "We do not signify that the Messiah is going to come without the leaven of sin, as do the Jews; rather, as do Christians, we indicate that He has already come without sin."[8] He continues that the Greek practice itself is symbolic, reflecting, if truth be told, neither what Jews nor Christians intend but what pagans do, "who think that Jesus was leavened by sin, as are other men."[9] Moreover, he responds to the Greek accusation that Latins should not take Jesus' action literally because "the letter kills, but the Spirit gives life" (2 Cor 3:6).[10] He points out that the letter kills only without the assistance of grace. He concludes that the Greeks have no valid arguments against the use of unleavened bread in the celebration of the Eucharist: "Either we alone act rightly, and they act wrongly, or else if they act rightly we act more rightly and more correctly."[11] It bears noting that Anselm's primary aim is to defend against unjust criticism the Latin use of consecrating unleavened bread. He recognizes the Greek practice as legitimate, but warns detractors of the Latin practice that their own arguments can be used against them.

Anselm uses rational argument to defend aspects of his Eucharistic belief, but he also demonstrates his warm, heartfelt devotion to the sacrament. His prayers and meditations reveal a rich interior life, in which he shares with God his deepest feelings. One in particular concerns his deep Eucharistic devotion.[12] He addresses a prayer to his Lord

---

8. Ibid., 518.
9. Ibid.
10. Ibid., 520
11. Ibid., 519.
12. See *RPA*, 78–80. See also *The Prayers and Meditations of Saint Anselm* (Harmondsworth, England: Penguin Books, 1988), 100ff.

Jesus Christ, who freely offered his life on the cross and "mercifully redeemed the world from sin and everlasting death."[13] He venerates and adores Jesus, thanking him for the gift of his body and blood, even while acknowledging the coldness and poverty of his own love and devotion. Although unworthy to approach the altar and to receive the sacrament, he trusts in Jesus' mercy to cleanse him from sin and to defend against it. His hope for justification lies solely in Jesus' willingness to offer himself "as a holy sacrifice to the Father."[14] Unworthy as he is, Anselm presumes to receive the gifts of Jesus' body and blood so that he may be justified by them. He asks that his reception of the sacrament, given for the cleansing of sins, may be an occasion not for an increase of sin but of forgiveness and protection. He then asks Jesus to use the sacrament to root him firmly in the mystery of Christ's death and resurrection, by which the "old man" will be mortified and he will be renewed so he might lead a life of righteousness. He also asks Jesus to make him worthy to be incorporated in his body, the Church, to be a member of that body which has Christ as its head, for he wishes only to remain in Christ and Christ in him. He ends his prayer looking forward to the resurrection of the dead, when his body will be refashioned according to Christ's glorious body and he will be able to give glory to God and rejoice forever in Christ who reigns with the Father and the Holy Spirit forever. Anselm's prayer, well written and carefully crafted, has a heartfelt freshness and spontaneity rooted in personal experience.

Observations

Anselm's views on the Eucharist invite an exploration of the implications of his method and the content of his teaching.

---

13. *RPA*, 79.
14. Ibid.

Anselm's approach to the Eucharist reflects both scholastic rational argument and monastic experience. The two documents considered in this chapter demonstrate Anselm's willingness to subject even the sacrament of the Eucharist to critical analysis and his desire to open his heart to God in deep, affectionate prayer. He was a scholastic *and* a monk and, unlike some theologians who followed him, did not see a contradiction between the two. For him, God could be the object of rational reflection *and* a divine subject to be engaged in intimate conversation. As a result, he was able to apply critical analysis to the important concerns of his day regarding the Eucharist without compromising his devotional life. To understand Anselm fully, both of these dimensions of his life must be taken into account.[15]

Placed side by side, Anselm's letter and prayer show that, for him, "faith seeking understanding" involves not just identifying the objective content of the faith (as scholastic theology would have it), but also the sapiential knowledge that accompanies a personal experience of God (as monastic theology prefers). In his letter to bishop Walram, Anselm uses scholastic argument to resolve the controversy over using leavened or unleavened bread at Eucharist, concluding that both adhere to Christian practice because they share the same "substance."[16] In his prayer to Jesus, however, he asks his Lord "to perceive with lips and heart and know by faith and love,"[17] terms more consistent with his monastic background. In this light, Anselm's understanding of "faith" transcends what scholastic method or monastic experience might reveal. Because he embraced these seemingly

---

15. For a comparison between monastic and scholastic theology, see *AMHT*, 52–57. For the tension between these theologies in later centuries, see Jean Leclercq, "Monastic and Scholastic Theology in the Reformers of the Fourteenth to Sixteenth Century," in *From Cloister to Classroom: Monastic and Scholastic Approaches to Truth* (Kalamazoo, MI: Cistercian Publications, 1986), 178–201.
16. Anselm of Canterbury, "The Sacrifice of Unleavened and Leavened Bread," 515.
17. *RPA*, 79

opposing approaches, he expanded the horizons of theological knowledge as well as his own monastic vocation.

Anselm's contribution to developing the scholastic method grew out of his monastic vocation and, in his view, always remained a part of it. His training in the Benedictine monastery at Bec gave Anselm the tools with which he could excel in both rational argument and theological method. The same can be said concerning his understanding of and approach to the Eucharist. Anselm believed in Jesus' real presence in the consecrated bread and wine and throughout his life maintained a deep love and veneration of the sacrament. Because of this, he saw the need to clarify controversies concerning the Eucharist, in this case whether to use leavened or unleavened bread. In this instance, Anselm's monasticism supersedes his scholastic dialectic. His heartfelt love for the Eucharist compelled him to enter into controversy and clarify certain truths pertaining to the sacrament.

Anselm's letter to bishop Walram reveals the distinction between dialectic and the usual means of argument in his time, such as an appeal to scripture or authority. To each objection concerning the Latin practice of using unleavened bread, Anselm reasons why it should be dismissed or overturned. His respect for both the sacrament and his opponents prevents him from overstepping the bounds of reason. He uses rational argument to defend the Latin practice and to point out weaknesses in the Greek objections. Moreover, at the outset of his letter he states clearly that many consider the Greek practice to be in keeping with the Christian faith. Anselm does not seek to disprove the Greek practice, but to recognize the legitimacy of both because leavened and unleavened bread share the same "substance." Through scholastic dialectic and categories he argues in favor of the Latin practice and suggests that, of the two, it is the more fitting way to celebrate the sacrament.

Anselm's satisfaction theory explains redemption without recourse to Satan and how Jesus' sacrificial self-offering on the cross put humanity back in touch with God. Through Jesus' death, human beings are reconciled to God and once again able to converse face-to-face. Anselm's heartfelt prayer reflects this change in medieval spirituality. He speaks to Jesus not as a passive onlooker, but as someone actively and intimately conversing with God. It is a prayer of someone who stands before the threshold of the divine, deeply conscious of God's compassionate love for humanity. Anselm recognizes the Eucharist as a gift that enables us to receive the body and blood of Christ and share in his paschal mystery. Because of this participation in Jesus' death and resurrection, Anselm hopes to be conformed more and more unto his likeness. The Eucharist, for Anselm, brings Christ's redemption into the present moment. It fosters in those who receive it eschatological hope in the coming reign of God's kingdom.[18]

By removing Satan from the drama of Christ's redemptive activity and putting humanity face-to-face with God, Anselm's satisfaction theory focuses on humanity's sinful limitations rather than the struggle between Christ and the forces of evil. This change of emphasis brought about a deeper sense of the need for repentance, conversion, and penitential practice in the life of the believer. Anselm's theory of redemption, one might say, helped shift medieval piety from a baptismal to a eucharistic-penitential spirituality.[19] This change is reflected in Anselm's prayer to Christ, in which receiving the body and blood of Christ becomes an occasion for being cleansed from sin and being protected

---

18. For the close relationship between Anselm's satisfaction theory of redemption and his approach to meditation, see Dennis J. Billy, *"Anselm of Canterbury's Meditatio Redemptionis Humanae," Studia moralia* 42 (2004): 391–410.
19. For the influence of Anselm's satisfaction theory on the development of Church penitential and Eucharistic practice, see G. H. Williams, *Anselm: Communion and Atonement* (Saint Louis: Concordia, 1980).

from it. Since Christ is the expression of God's mercy *par excellence*, it follows that receiving him in the Eucharist would be a major way of receiving forgiveness for one's sins. This perspective highlights the bond between the sacrament of reconciliation and the Eucharist. Confessing one's sins prepares a person to receive Christ's body and blood, which in turn deepens his or her awareness of God's mercy and a life of conversion.

Finally, Anselm's understanding of the Eucharist has a strong ecclesiological dimension. For him, receiving the body and blood of Christ is not an individual act or private devotion, but an action with ramifications throughout Christ's body, the Church. He receives the Eucharist because he hopes to be incorporated more deeply into that body as a living member with Christ as his head. Anselm wishes only to remain in Christ and Christ in him. For this to happen, he must be planted in the likeness of Christ's death and resurrection. Doing so will enable him to mortify the old self and live a life of righteousness. For Anselm, the Church is closely tied to the Eucharist. This sacrament nourishes the whole of Christ's body, not just its individual members. It not only strengthens this body in faith, hope, and love, but also gives those who partake of it a foretaste of the heavenly glory that one day they hope to share fully with Christ.

Conclusion

Anselm of Canterbury was an original monastic thinker who laid important groundwork for the scholastic method. As such, he was a forerunner of developments in Christian thought that would eventually revolutionize the entire theological enterprise. In his day he made unprecedented contributions to the method, content, and scope of theology and for this came to be known as "Father of Scholasticism."

Although he contributed to scholastic thought, at heart Anselm was a monk. His experience at the Benedictine monastery at Bec shaped his outlook and fostered in him a love for learning and a deep yearning for God. His contributions to scholasticism must be understood in the larger context of his monastic vocation. For him, the experience of God did not contradict using reason to clarify the objective content of faith. What theologians of later centuries would consider opposing forces, he understood as sides of the same coin, two parts of the one search for truth.

These dimensions of Anselm's life are reflected in his approach to the Eucharist. In his life of prayer, he opened his heart to Jesus and thanked him for the gift of his body and blood. His prayer reveals a deep love for Jesus and a longing to be molded unto his likeness. It also reveals his desire to be a living member of Jesus' body, the Church, and a yearning to share in the glory of Jesus' resurrection. Such sincere and heartfelt sharing, however, did not prevent Anselm from using to tools of dialectic to defend his beliefs. As seen in his argument concerning the propriety of unleavened bread, he was willing to submit his beliefs and practices to scrutiny. For him, reason did not oppose faith, but with judicious use strengthened it. Such an approach to the Eucharist reflects his conviction that as "faith seeking understanding," theology could probe not only the mysteries of God, but also the deepest corridors of the human heart.

Reflection Questions

- Anselm approached God through both mind and heart. Where does your knowledge of God come from? How has he revealed himself to you?
- How does your love for the Eucharist relate to your belief in the real presence? How would you describe what takes place at Mass?
- For Anselm, receiving the Eucharist was a communal act. Why is it important to celebrate the Eucharist together? How has the Eucharist shaped your understanding of Church? How has it shaped the way you relate to the community of believers?

Voice Four

Bernard of Clairvaux: Food for the Heart

> There are some things to eat that yield their savor on the spot, whereas with others you must work to get at it. It is the same with spiritual foods; the open, obvious ones require no explanation, but the closed ones do. A mother does not give a whole nut to her little child; she cracks it open and gives him the kernel. And in the same way, brethren most beloved, I ought to open the closed sacraments to you; but, as I am not equal to the task, let us beseech Wisdom, our mother, to crack these nuts for you and me alike.
>
> *Bernard of Clairvaux*

Our next voice on the Eucharist united himself with the patristic tradition, so much so that he is sometimes referred to as the last of the Latin Fathers. He exerted enormous influence in his day on nearly every level of Church life and enjoyed a great reputation for sanctity. In an age when the scholastic method was on the rise, he opted instead to explore the sapiential approach of his monastic heritage rooted in a meditative reading of Scripture and a deep sensitivity to its spiritual senses. This approach led him to write many commentaries on Scripture and treatises on mystical experience. He emphasized the experiential knowledge of God through love, especially through the spiritual and life-giving nourishment of the Eucharist.

Spiritual Master

Bernard of Clairvaux (1090–1153) was a master of the spiritual life and a great churchman. He entered the Cistercian Order in 1112 with a group of thirty noble companions; in time, he oversaw a remarkable expansion of the order. He became abbot of the monastery of Clairvaux, France and is known as the order's second founder.

The Cistercians, a reform of Benedictine monasticism, were founded at Citeaux (Burgundy) in 1098 by Robert of Molesme. They followed the Benedictine Rule to the letter, doing away with certain monastic practices that had been added since the time of Benedict five hundred years before. In true Benedictine spirit, to restore the balance between work and prayer so highly regarded in the Rule, they made each day sacred by praying the psalms in common, spiritual reading, and manual labor. They settled in remote places, wore habits of un-dyed wool, and cultivated the land. They transformed the interior landscape of medieval Europe, turning heavily forested areas into productive farms and meadows for grazing sheep and cattle.

In the first half of the twelfth century, Bernard was the leader and main theological spokesman of this monastic reform movement. A gifted preacher who could move hearts by drawing out the deep spiritual senses of the Scriptures, he wrote *On the Steps of Humility and Pride* (1125–26), *On Loving God* (1127–35), and *Sermons on the Song of Songs* (1135–53). He promoted monastic theology, an extension of the patristic tradition that highlighted the importance of compunction, the desire of heaven, and the wisdom gained from a true Christian gnosis. These and other spiritual concerns also surfaced in his teaching on the Eucharist.[1]

---

1. See C. H. Lawrence, *Medieval Monasticism: Forms of Religious Life in Western*

Bernard's Spirituality

In his writings, especially *Sermons on the* Song of Songs, Bernard's emphasized monastic spirituality, particularly a personal knowledge of God. He explained to his readers and listeners how the symbols in creation, scripture, and the liturgy lead to the contemplation of the divine mysteries. He appreciated their mystery and resisted making them more rational and systematic. He recognized that love's power to unite heightens the monk's desire for God and brings about a connatural knowledge of the divine. He was apprehensive that reason's concern for clarity might move spiritual experience to the periphery of theological thought and impede theology's essential purpose of union with God. Among other things, these concerns explain Bernard's strong mystical leanings, preference for the spiritual senses of scripture, conservative interpretation of Benedictine monasticism, distrust of secular sources, and heated criticism of Peter Abelard (1079–1142) for using dialectic to explore the mysteries of the Christian faith.[2]

Bernard's spirituality was rooted in and influenced by the scriptures, Church fathers, and the divine liturgy. His monastic vocation taught him that through meditative reading of God's revealed Word a person could achieve an intimate, deeply personal experience of God. Using *lectio divina*, he meditated upon the sacred words and waited for the Spirit to reveal their deep, hidden meanings. Bernard looked to the fathers of the Church, especially Origen, St. Augustine, St. Ambrose, and St. Gregory of Nyssa, for their insights into scripture. He was also moved by reciting or chanting the psalms during the Divine Office and by Sacrifice of the Mass, permeated throughout by scripture. These sources fed

---

Europe in the Middle Ages, 2nd ed. (London/New York: Longman, 1989), 174–205; *WSCMA*, 254.

2. For a summary of these and other themes in Bernard, see Jean Leclercq, "Introduction" to *Bernard of Clairvaux: Selected Works*, trans., G. R. Evans (New York/Mahwah, NJ: Paulist Press, 1987), 13–57.

him spiritually, giving him unique insights into the divine mysteries. Bernard looked for the hidden order and beauty in things. He was a poet who expressed through imagery and metaphor the intuitive knowledge concerning beauty that was revealed to him through prayer. His polished Latin style reflects his appreciation of the power of language to both reveal and conceal. He put his gifts at the service of Christ and his Church so that sinful human beings might experience God's salvific love.[3]

Bernard's teaching revolved around three central themes: humanity's sinfulness, Christ, and the Church.[4] Although he knew that human beings are created in the image and likeness of God, he recognized the division between the divine and the human caused by sin. Adam and Eve's fall from grace did not destroy humanity's likeness to God; its restoration would require a long spiritual journey. Bernard's spiritual theology outlines the steps of purification and illumination which the soul must take to restore union with God. For sinful human beings to regain their understanding of union with Christ, their self-centeredness must be transformed by grace. Bernard's spirituality centered on the mystery of the Incarnation, by which Jesus Christ, the Word-made-flesh, the embodiment of divine mercy, restored humanity. We are healed by Christ assuming our human nature and experiencing the misery of the human condition. Through the Incarnation and all that flowed from it, Jesus reestablished the bond of love between God and humanity. Bernard saw the Church as the place where sinful humanity came face to face with Christ the Savior. It is the City of God, a society dedicated to holiness, to becoming one with Christ. To participate in this mystery, human beings—as individuals and as a community—must return to the Father through Christ, and in the Spirit through a process of

---

3. See Jean Leclercq, *Bernard of Clairvaux and the Cistercian Spirit* (Kalamazoo, MI: Cistercian Studies, 1976), 12–34.
4. Ibid., 75.

conversion. We undertake this process by meditating on the scriptures and by partaking of the sacraments.[5]

Bernard explained how grace flowed through the sacraments as a result of a covenant made by God. They are sacred signs or mysteries that confer a particular benefit determined by God. They are efficacious, in other words, not because of anything intrinsic in them, but because God wills them so. Because Christ instituted these symbolic actions, they bring about what they signify when properly performed and faithfully received. In later centuries, his position would be interpreted in various ways, often in connection with *sine qua non* causality, the theory that the sacraments are work not intrinsically in themselves but only to the extent that Christ *ascribed* a certain value to them. Nevertheless, we must remember that at heart Bernard was a monastic theologian who wrote a full century before scholastic theologians battled over questions of sacramental efficacy. In the context of his times, he clearly believed that ascribed virtue could be equally effective as inherent virtue and did not wish to denigrate the sacraments in any way. For this reason, he should be viewed as one of the first theologians to deal with the question of sacramental causality, someone who developed a creative and persuasive explanation for it. Equally imaginative are his views on the Eucharist.[6]

Bernard on the Eucharist

Bernard discusses the Eucharist at various times. His *Sermon for Holy Thursday* and *Third Sermon for Palm Sunday* in particular present Bernard's understanding of the

---

5. Ibid., 75–93.
6. For a balanced treatment of Bernard's presentation on sacramental efficacy and how it was later interpreted, see William Courtenay, "Sacrament, Symbol and Causality in Bernard of Clairvaux," in *Bernard of Clairvaux: Studies Presented to Dom Jean Leclercq* (Washington, D.C.: Cistercian Publications, 1973), 111–22.

effects of the sacraments, especially the Eucharist as "food of the heart."[7]

In the Holy Thursday sermon, using the notion of sacramental causality discussed above, he demonstrates the effects of Baptism, Holy Communion, and the sacramental gesture of the washing of feet (performed on Holy Thursday). Through God's covenantal design each of these sacred actions achieves a different end. Baptism washes away "the sin which we all contracted from our first parents."[8] Holy Communion has two effects: "It weakens the force of concupiscence in the lesser things and keeps us from consenting in more serious matters."[9] Christ instituted the washing of feet for "the remission of our daily venial faults."[10] God, in other words, invested each "sacred sign" with a specific end.[11] Baptism cleanses us from original sin; the Eucharist heals our inordinate concupiscence and strengthens us in the face of serious temptation; the washing of feet brings about the forgiveness of venial (i.e., lesser) sins. Bernard uses the rite of investiture as an analogy to explain how each sacrament achieves such a different effect:

> There are various kinds of investiture differing one from another according to the variety of the offices or dignities, wherewith men are invested with a book being used in the investiture of canons, a crosier in the investiture of abbots, and a ring with the crosier in the investiture of bishops — so in things spiritual 'diversities of graces' (cf. 1Cor 12:4) are communicated in different sacraments.[12]

---

7. See Bernard of Clairvaux, *Sermons for the Seasons and Principal Festivals of the Year*, trans., A priest of Mount Melleray, vol. 2 (Westminster, MD: The Carroll Press, 1950), 126–33, 154–61.
8. Ibid., 157.
9. Ibid., 158.
10. Ibid.
11. Ibid., 155.
12. Ibid., 156.

Although a book, a crosier, or a ring itself does not affect what it signifies, each of them does so because particular powers of office have been specifically ascribed to them. In a similar way, God has assigned specific ends to the waters of Baptism, the Eucharist, the ritual of the washing of feet, brought about when properly performed and faithfully received. They have been empowered by God's Word and God's Word does not return in vain. In the context of God's design, the sacrament of Holy Communion has the special functions of healing and strengthening.[13]

In his *Third Sermon for Palm Sunday*, Bernard discusses the Eucharist from a different perspective. Instead of considering its sacramental effects, he examines it in the context of events in Jesus' earthly life. He discusses five in particular: the procession into Jerusalem, the Last Supper, Jesus' passion and death, his time in the tomb, and his resurrection.[14]

Each of these has special significance for those who follow Christ, for they display respectively the transient nature of human glory, Jesus' fatherly concern to feed his family, the suffering he endured for that family, the peaceful rest of all who die in the Lord, and the glorification of the body they one day will experience. Concerning the Eucharist, Bernard points out that at the Last Supper Jesus fed his family with five different "loaves": (1) He gave example and strengthened their consciences to do God's will. (2) He exhorted his followers to receive his cleansing action or else have nothing to do with him. (3) He gave them many promises concerning the resurrection, the coming of the Holy Spirit, their own faith, and their final return to him. (4) He prayed for them, weeping for them with the eyes of the Church. (5) He gave them the sacrament of his body and blood, and

---

13. See William Courtenay, "Sacrament, Symbol and Causality in Bernard of Clairvaux," 113–14.
14. See Bernard of Clairvaux, *Sermons for the Seasons and Principal Festivals of the Year*, 126.

asked them to partake of it frequently.[15] These "loaves" are "food of the heart" for they strengthen the "stomach of the soul" and help us to carry out God's will.[16] The Eucharist, Bernard says, teaches us to imitate Jesus, exhorts us to follow his instructions, promises us the riches of the kingdom, enables us to pray and to weep with Christ and his mystical body, and gives us Jesus' body and blood for nourishment. This sacred action that Jesus performed in his own life has been an event in the life of the entire Church, from its earliest days.

Observations

The following remarks will draw out some of the hidden implications of Bernard's method and the content of his teaching from a variety of perspectives.

Bernard's definition of a sacrament as "a sacred sign or sacred mystery"[17] offers a wide view of sacramentality that enables him to include a ritual such as the washing of feet. In the first half of the twelfth century, the Church had not yet limited the number of sacraments to seven and theologians and spiritual writers commonly extended the term to other sacred rituals and Church practices. Although the washing of feet today falls under the theological category of "sacramental," in his day Bernard was doing nothing out of the ordinary by calling it a "sacrament" and by treating it in conjunction with Baptism and Holy Communion.

Bernard presents his views on the effects of the Eucharist in the context of other sacred rituals, specifically in conjunction with Baptism and Holy Thursday's ritual action of the washing of feet. In doing so, he demonstrates their interconnected nature in God's redemptive plan for

---
15. Ibid., 129–32.
16. Ibid., 130.
17. Ibid., 155.

humanity. Each sacrament was instituted by Christ for a specific reason and plays a specific role in mediating God's redemptive grace. The limited scope of this study does not permit a discussion here, but interestingly enough Bernard does relate the washing of feet to the sacramental practice of auricular confession.

The interconnected nature of the sacred mysteries reflects their relationship to Christ's mystical body, the Church. As mentioned earlier, Bernard focuses on three central themes: humanity's sinfulness, Christ the Savior, and the Church. He considers the Church to be Christ's mystical body, the point of encounter between Christ and humanity. Through it, humanity is lifted up into Christ's humanity and made whole. Through the sacraments, humanity's sinful nature is cleansed, healed, and restored to the divine likeness. When seen in this light, the Eucharist's role in the daily life of the Church is to calm the passions and strengthen those who receive it to live a life of virtue.

By assigning both restorative and fortifying functions to the Eucharist, Bernard distinguishes a twofold grace in the sacrament that is closely associated with its nourishing qualities. Just as natural food restores the body and strengthens it for the tasks of daily life, the spiritual food of the Eucharist heals the soul of its wounds and gives it strength to face and overcome its daily spiritual challenges. Healing and restoring the soul does more than merely cleanse it from sin. It treats the effects of sin that weaken the soul and allow it to stand firm in the face of future temptations. This essential spiritual food affirms the hope of completing life's pilgrimage.

By examining the Eucharist in the context of other significant events in Jesus' earthly life, Bernard strengthens the important scriptural link with the sacrament, as well as the continuity of what today we would call the Jesus of history and the Christ of faith. The Last Supper, in other words, was not an isolated event in Jesus' life, but a sacred action closely linked with his entire earthly and post-earthly life. In this respect, it points both to Jesus' earthly ministry, to his passion and death, and also to his glorified existence after death. Because Bernard views the Church as Christ's mystical body, he connects the significance of the Eucharist for our own lives, earthly and post-earthly.

At one point, Bernard likens Jesus instituting the Eucharist at the Last Supper to an affectionate father providing nourishment for his family.[18] The Fatherhood of Jesus stems from his relationship to his Father in heaven, but has special significance for his position as head of his mystical body, the Church. Jesus is the head of a mystical family, one incorporated into his humanity and divinized by the graces poured out by virtue of his Incarnation and Paschal Mystery. As head of the Church, he provides the members of his body with all that they need to be active and vibrant participants in the divine plan. The Eucharist is but one of many manifestations of Jesus' fatherly concern for his people.

Finally, Bernard's presentation of the Eucharist as "spiritual food for the stomach of the soul" and his development of the five different "loaves" presented to the apostles at the Last Supper reflect his fondness for the spiritual senses of scripture and his desire to discover the deepest meaning possible in this important symbolic event in Jesus' life and ministry. At the Last Supper, Jesus gave his apostles example, exhortation, promises, prayers, and his own body and blood. Each of these "loaves" is related to the others and suggests how the moral, spiritual, and doctrinal dimensions of the Church's teaching are intimately intertwined in each believer's life.

---

18. Ibid., 129.

Conclusion

Bernard of Clairvaux is a great spiritual and theological voice. A major exponent of the monastic approach to theology, his sermons and spiritual treatises elaborated upon human sinfulness, the need for conversion, and the possibility of personal experience of the divine through Christ and his mystical body, the Church. He persuaded his audiences of the truth of these themes by using scriptural, patristic, and liturgical sources and a polished literary style too. Because of his rhetorical skills and his ability to convince his listeners of their need for God he became known as, *Doctor Melifluus* ("The Golden-voiced Doctor").

Bernard's teaching on the sacraments flowed from his teaching on Christ and the Church. He held with a wide notion of sacrament, one that embraced Baptism and Eucharist, as well as the liturgical washing of feet on Holy Thursday. These and other "sacred signs" administered by the Church gave believers access to Christ's redemptive grace. Bernard was among the first to examine how the sacraments actually conveyed grace, arriving at a covenantal understanding of sacramental efficacy. Through the power of his Word, God ascribes redemptive grace to a particular ritualistic action. Although scholastic theologians of the succeeding centuries would interpret Bernard's position in various ways , he clearly considered this covenantal explanation to be fully efficacious.

Bernard's teaching on the Eucharist should be understood against the backdrop of his views on Christ, the Church, and sacramental efficacy. In his *Sermon for Holy Thursday*, he describes how the Eucharist heals and strengthens believers. His *Third Sermon for Palm Sunday* describes it as "food of the heart" and enumerates the ways in which Jesus nourishes believers through the sacrament. Bernard emphasizes the Eucharist's curative and restorative properties, as well as the ways by which Jesus nourishes the members of his body through it. He considered the sacrament to be the primary means by which Christ's redeeming and transforming grace touches the lives of believers.

Reflection Questions

- Bernard considers the Eucharist to be "food of the heart" which strengthens the "stomach of the soul" to carry out God's will. How has the Eucharist restored and then nourished your soul? How has it strengthened the "stomach of your soul" and enabled you to do God's will? Can you point to any concrete examples?

- Bernard says that, at the Last Supper, Jesus gave his apostles example, exhortation, promises, prayers, and his own body and blood. Which of these five gifts is most important? Which, in your mind, is the least important? What does Jesus give you when you attend Mass and receive Holy Communion?

- Bernard sees the Eucharist as one of many manifestations of Jesus' fatherly concern for his people. How is Jesus' headship and fatherhood of the Mystical Body, the Church, rooted in his relationship to his Father in heaven? What does his fatherhood of us mean for our relationship to God? What does it mean for our relationship to each other?

Voice Five

Hildegard of Bingen: Saving Souls

> For, as the goldsmith first unites his gold by melting it in the fire, and then divides it when it is united, so I, the Father, first glorify the body and blood of My Son by the sanctification of the Holy Spirit when it is offered, and then, when it is glorified, distribute it to the faithful for their salvation.
>
> *Hildegard of Bingen*

Our next figure brings an important feminine voice to the discussion. From a time when women generally had limited access to learning, she stands out as a great literary light. A prolific author known for her expansive knowledge and deep spiritual sensitivities, she saw what others could not. Through her power of imagination, moreover, she expressed deep visionary experiences in a way that still captures the Catholic imagination. Her profound mystical life was nurtured by her deep devotion to the Eucharist and loyalty to the Church.

Medieval Visionary

Hildegard of Bingen (1098–1179), Doctor of the Church, often called the "Sibyl of the Rhineland," was a Benedictine abbess, mystic, and visionary. She is considered the first great woman Christian theologian, someone whose breadth of knowledge was surpassed only by her capacity to delve beneath appearances and express inner truths through vivid words and images.

Born to a noble family in Rhine-Hesse, as a child Hildegard was sickly. At the age of eight she was entrusted to a holy anchoress, Blessed Jutta, at the small monastery of Disibodenberg, where at fifteen she took the Benedictine habit. After Jutta's death, in 1136, Hildegard became the abbess and eleven years later left with eighteen sisters to establish a monastery at Rupertsberg near Bingen, a site revealed to her in a vision.

Hildegard, a prolific author, wrote in many literary genres about a variety of topics (e.g., hymns, morality plays, homilies, letters, natural history, medicine). She is most remembered for *Scivias*, a collection of twenty-six visions received during a ten-year period (1141–51) that present clear symbolic pictures and interpretations of many major Christian themes. These include God and man, creation and redemption, Christ and the Church, the sacraments, the devil, and end times. Her teaching on the Eucharist, in the Sixth Vision of Book Two, is an important aspect of her theological outlook.[1]

Hildegard's Spirituality

From childhood, Hildegard received instruction in the religious life, psalmody, and manual labor suited to women contemplatives. Although physically frail, she had keen intuitive insight, a probing intellect, and a capacity for vivid interior visions that she experienced even during childhood. She did have authentic mystical experiences, but her prophetic visions were filled with imagery and figures of speech reminiscent of Ezekiel and the Book of Revelations. These urgent, apocalyptic visions make her seem more a prophetic reformer than a mystic with immediate face-to-

---

1. The information in this section comes from *CII*, 252–53, Evelyn Underhill, *Mystics of the Church* (Cambridge: James Clark & Co., 1925; reprinted. 1975), 74–79; *NCE* 2, s.v. "Hildegard of Bingen, St," by M.D. Barry.

face encounters with the divine. In the words of Bernard McGinn, "Hildegard, poised between two worlds, is a major theological voice, but less a mystic than a prophetic teacher."[2]

Hildegard conveys her spiritual insights in a twofold fashion—she describes the vision itself and then offers a spiritual commentary on it. Her visions were unique. Traditional Christian visionaries received dreams or visions in a state of rapture or ecstasy. She usually had these experiences while fully conscious of what was going on around her. She seems to have experienced them internally, through memory and imagination rather than through her external senses of hearing, sight, touch, taste, and smell, and describes her profound spiritual intuitions through vivid imagery and sounds. Her theological skill lies in her ability to describe these visions in rich symbols and imagery while offering an in-depth spiritual explanation of what she saw. Her imaginative description and her intellectual grasp of their inner spiritual significance enhanced her spiritual intuitions. Hildegard herself describes this process in terms of her visions being accompanied by a twofold light:

> "...the shadow of the living brightness" (*umbra viventis lucis*) corresponds to her descriptions of her visions; 'the living light' (*lux vivens*) corresponds to her spiritual commentary on them.[3]

Hildegard's spiritual outlook is rooted in the mystery of the Incarnation, the Church as the Mystical Body of Christ, and the sacraments. Her prophetic sensibilities brought to her theology a strong eschatological dimension by which her readers were exhorted to view the present in the light of the glories to come. In her theory of redemption she creatively synthesized the major theories of her day, opening

---

2. *PG*, 2: 336. See also *CH*, 2:252–53.
3. *PG*, 2:334–35; Peter Dronke, *Women Writers of the Middle Ages* (Cambridge: Cambridge University Press, 1984), 168–69.

new paths into the meaning of Christ's vicarious suffering. She does so by highlighting the spousal covenant between Christ and the Church, a bond that guarantees the lasting effects of Christ's salvific action down through the ages. For Hildegard, Christ in his passion and death has endowed the Church with a treasury of spiritual blessings. The Church, in turn, offers humanity these blessings for the sake of its salvation.[4]

As a representative of the medieval monastic tradition, Hildegard does not engage in dialectical argumentation, nor does she specifically intend her writings to clarify the content of the deposit of faith. In contrast to that tradition, however, she does not appeal to the Fathers and other revered authorities of the Christian tradition, but to her own visionary experience as interpreted in the light of the Scriptures and the Spirit's guiding inspiration. Her teaching on the Eucharist, which flows from this experience, presents the sacrament as a primary means through which the faithful gain access to the divine.

Hildegard on the Eucharist

Hildegard's teaching on the Eucharist appears in the Sixth Vision of Book Two of her *Scivias*. By far the longest and most developed section of her work, this vision appears in a section that covers a range of topics under six main headings: "Eucharistic theology, liturgical practice, communion, requirements for the priesthood, sexual ethics, and penance."[5] We will focus on the relationship between the crucifixion and the Church, the importance of the virgin birth for the priesthood, and the various kinds of people who receive communion.

---

4. See *DES*, s.v. "Ildegarda di bingen," by Giovanna della Croce. For more on Hildegard's theological vision, see Dennis J. Billy, "Redemption in Hildegard of Bingen's *Scivias*," American Benedictine Review 44 (1997): 361–71.
5. Barbara J. Newman, "Introduction," in Hildegard of Bingen, *Scivias*, trans. Mother Columba Hart and Jane Bishop (New York/Mahwah, NJ: Paulist Press, 1990), 33.

Hildegard depicts the relationship between Jesus' crucifixion and the Church as a spiritual betrothal and marriage. Her vision reads:

> I saw the Son of God hanging on the cross, and the aforementioned image of a woman coming forth like a bright radiance from the ancient counsel. By divine power she was led to Him, and raised herself upward so that she was sprinkled by the blood from His side; and thus, by the will of the Heavenly Father, she was joined with Him in happy betrothal and nobly dowered with His body and blood.[6]

This section's commentary on her vision presents the Church as the bride of Christ and his sacred blood as her dowry. At the moment of Jesus' death, the Church appears in heaven, comes down to be at his side, becomes his bride, and receives as her dowry his body and blood. From that moment, the salvation of souls becomes possible and she is charged with distributing to her children the graces derived from receiving his life-giving body and blood. Hildegard's imagery of spiritual betrothal and marriage lies at the heart of how she understands the Church as the Mystical Body of Christ. Through Jesus' passion and death the Church has become "one flesh," with her Lord and through her Jesus manifests and applies his redemptive action.[7]

Hildegard presents the Blessed Virgin Mary as a model for priests. In most of her visions a twofold light appears at the Eucharist—first, "a great calm light" when the priest first approaches the altar, and then a light of "inestimable brilliance" during the Eucharistic canon, especially at the moment of consecration.[8]

She describes the moment of consecration: "The offering was made true flesh and true blood. Although in human sight it looked like bread and wine."[9] Commenting on these

---

6. Hildegard of Bingen, *Scivias*, 237.
7. Ibid., 238–39.
8. Ibid., 237.
9. Ibid.

words, she compares the priesthood and Mary. Just as Jesus came forth from the womb of the Blessed Virgin, so now does he arise upon the altar at the Eucharistic assembly. Just as Mary manifested her belief in the angel's words by pronouncing her *fiat*, so too do priests bring Christ into the world when they pronounce the words of consecration. Mary, therefore, is mother of the Church and of the priesthood. What happened in her womb through her divine *fiat* reoccurs on the altar when the priest utters the *fiat* of Jesus' New Covenant.[10]

At one point in her vision, Hildegard describes the people who receive the sacrament:

> I noticed five modes of being in them. For some were bright of body and fiery of soul, and others seemed pale of body and shadowed of soul; some were hairy of body and seemed dirty of soul, because it was pervaded with unclean human pollution; others were surrounded in body by sharp thorns and leprous of soul; and others appeared bloody of body and foul as a decayed corpse in soul. And all these received the same sacraments; and as they did, some were bathed in fiery brilliance, but the others were overshadowed by a dark cloud.[11]

These figures, she says, are "faithful believers, doubters, the unchaste and lustful, the malicious and envious, the warlike and oppressive."[12] In her commentary, Hildegard emphasizes the importance of a person's interior disposition when receiving the Eucharist. The fiery light of Christ's redeeming grace bathes those who approach the sacrament worthily; darkness and the force of divine justice overshadow those who receive it unworthily. To support the authenticity of this vision and her interpretation of it, she invokes the apostle Paul: "Whoever, therefore, eats the bread or drinks the cup of the Lord in an unworthy manner will be answerable for the body and blood of the Lord"

---

10. Ibid., 246.
11. Ibid., 238.
12. Newman, "Introduction," 34.

(1 Cor 11:27).[13] Although God's mercy knows no bounds, his justice will not suffer those who take it for granted and refuse to reform their lives.

Observations

These points, only a small part of Hildegard's teaching on the Eucharist, have been selected because of their originality and capacity to stir the imagination. The following observations seek to draw out some of the implications of her teaching.

Hildegard uses spousal imagery to connect Christ, the Church, and the Eucharist. According to her vision, at the crucifixion a marriage took place when the Church, sprinkled with blood from Christ's side, was made one with his body and blood. This covenantal action made the Church the spouse of Christ and, at that moment, his widow as well. As a lasting inheritance for this spousal relationship, she received Christ's body and blood to sustain herself and others. The Eucharist, we might say, is both the Church's bridal dowry and her widow's dower. As its bridal dowry, the Church presents the Eucharist to Christ as a heartfelt offering of love. As its widow's dower, it is the gift Christ gives to the Church so that she can bring salvation and the promise of eternal life to those who see with the eyes of faith.

Hildegard's spousal imagery reflects feudal practices (betrothal, bridal dowry, widow's dower) that contemporary believers might not understand or even find irrelevant. To her credit, however, her concrete imagery, rooted in the experience of her day, ties Christ's paschal mystery to Church and sacrament in an intimate way. Contemporary believers can benefit from understanding these same intimate ties between Christ, Church, and sacrament through similar imaginative attempts rooted in their own experience.

---

13. Hildegard of Bingen, *Scivias*, 268.

Hildegard's description of Mary as the model of the priesthood draws out the close relationship between priests and Mary, the Mother of God and the Mother of the Church. Mary's courageous response to the angel reminds priests that their dedication and service to Christ and his Church should be rooted in their desire to discern and carry out God's will. As Mary brought Christ into world through her humble *fiat*, so priests bring him into the world through their humble recitation of the words of institution. Through Mary, the mystery of the Incarnation took place and was revealed to the world at a specific moment in time. Through the priesthood, Christ's paschal mystery and Eucharistic body and blood are remembered, celebrated, and revealed to the world throughout history. It would be a mistake to interpret Hildegard's description of Mary as a priestly model as a hidden (perhaps even unconscious) argument for women priests. Elsewhere in her visions, Hildegard makes it clear that men and women have specific vocations within the Church and that the priesthood is only for men.[14] Nevertheless, she sees Mary's role in the mystery of Redemption so closely tied to her Son's that she shares in his priestly duties. Although Hildegard's prophetic visions were meant to spur the imagination and deepen faith, the theology of the Eucharist that they present is completely consistent with the Church's teaching. St. Bernard of Clairvaux (1090–1153), probably the most revered defender of Catholic orthodoxy of his day, accepted her visions and at his suggestion they received papal approval.

Hildegard explains how the interior dispositions of those receiving the Eucharist determine the sacrament's efficacy as an instrument of grace. As scholastic theologians would point out hundreds of years after Hildegard's time, the Eucharist has both objective and subjective qualities. On the one hand, it makes the body and blood of Christ really

---
14. Ibid., 278.

present in the species of bread and wine simply from the action performed (*ex opere operato*). On the other hand, the grace received depends on the communicant's internal state (*ex opere operantis*). Although Hildegard does not use such terms, her vision of the various kinds of people who approach the priest to receive the sacrament and her commentary on them demonstrates that the state of a person's soul determines the sacrament's salvific efficacy. The Eucharist is not a magic pill that will miraculously heal spiritual ills, regardless of a person's interior disposition of faith. To receive the full grace of the sacrament, a communicant must believe in what it stands for and be free of the deadly effects of serious sin. Her unsettling vision highlights the close bond between the Eucharist and sacramental reconciliation, and emphasizes the need for repentance and conversion of life. It is a stark warning that communicants must approach the altar worthily, with the proper interior dispositions of faith.

Hildegard praises those who receive the Eucharist worthily. "Bright of body and fiery of soul," their faith in the real presence of Jesus' body and blood in the consecrated species frees them from all doubt. Their transparent faith affects them both physically and spiritually. The mystery of the sacrament fortifies and sanctifies their bodies and at the resurrection of the dead they will appear strong and holy. The fire of the Holy Spirit will so transform and enlighten their souls that they will abandon the things of the earth and yearn for the things of heaven. She likens the Holy Spirit to a powerful wind. Like a flame fanned by the wind, the souls of the faithful burn with a deep longing and love for God.[15]

Hildegard assigns both physical and spiritual effects to worthy reception of the sacrament. For her, the Eucharist enkindles hope and actually leads to the life of the resurrection. The Holy Spirit's sanctifying and transforming role gives the sacrament its eschatological character. By working

---

15. Ibid., 266.

on communicants' anthropological dimensions they are readied for life in the hereafter. Hildegard's vision of the Eucharist embraces the entire paschal mystery—Christ's suffering, death, *and* resurrection—and emphasizes its concrete effects on believers. Her vision suggests the need for a comprehensive approach to the sacrament that balances sound doctrine with authentic human anthropology.

The twofold light characteristic of Hildegard's visions appears in her vision of the Eucharist: "a great calm light" when the vested priest first approaches the altar; and "a fiery and inestimable brilliance" when he sings the Sanctus and recites the canon. The first corresponds to what she refers to as "the shadow of the living brightness" (*umbra viventis lucis*); the second, to "the living light" (*lux vivens*).[16]

In a Eucharistic context, this twofold light delineates different levels of the sacred. As the priest dons his vestments and moves toward the altar, he moves out of the ordinary and onto the threshold of the divine presence. Once he moves into the central, most important part of the Mass, however, "the great calm light" changes to "fiery and inestimable brilliance." This fiery brilliance does not merely remain over the altar; it intensifies and changes. As the Mass continues and the participants receive Holy Communion, those who receive worthily are enflamed by "the fiery gift of the Spirit" and "burn with celestial love."[17] The twofold light, in other words, moves from an altar of stone to the altar of the human soul, transforming communicants, setting them ablaze with love for God. In this way, the Eucharist mediates between the human and the divine. The sacrament's intermediary role has been obscured, but Hildegard's imagery of transforming light can help to restore its primacy in the imagination of the faithful.

---

16. See above n. 2.
17. Ibid.

Conclusion

Hildegard of Bingen, a twelfth-century monastic leader and prophetic visionary, influenced the Church in her time, and continues to do so even to this day. She made strongly apocalyptic revelations, and almost certainly experienced immediate, face-to-face encounter with the divine. As a Benedictine abbess, mystic, visionary, and theological innovator, her authority transcended that of most women during her era. She used that authority to build up the Church and protect it from harm.

Although Hildegard had many interests and wrote in a variety of fields, her most memorable works are the twenty-six prophetic visions of her *Scivias*, an innovative and unparalleled religious text in which vivid imagery combines with sound theology. Her visions received ecclesiastical approval while she was still alive, confirming her reputation as a woman of deep wisdom and far-reaching prophetic vision. Her visions and accompanying commentaries present a comprehensive account of major themes: creation, redemption, and salvation history. Intimately tied to her visions, her distinctive theology, including her doctrine on the Eucharist, is uniquely her own.

This teaching, which appears in the sixth vision of Book Two, covers a range of topics associated with the sacrament. Some reflect the sensitivities of medieval monastic culture; others have currency even in the present day. Although not exhaustive, the teaching developed in this essay reflects her theological conservatism regarding the sacrament as well as her ability to present Catholic doctrine in an imaginative, innovative way. Hildegard was a loyal daughter of the Church, an intellectual genius, a woman blessed with probing private revelations. Her prophetic witness challenges contemporary believers to foster a spirit of contemplation, an attitude of creative fidelity to the teachings of the Church, and a deep love and devotion to the holy sacrament and sacrifice of the altar.

Reflection Questions

- How do you understand Hildegard's belief that, as a result of the Lord's passion and death, the Church has become "one flesh" with Christ? How is this unity manifested in the Church's daily life? How is this unity manifested in your own life?

- Explain Hildegard's notion of a special bond between Mary and priests. Why would the Blessed Mother have a special love for priests? What can priests do to deepen their bond with her? What can you do to deepen it? In what sense is Mary a model for all Christians?

- Hildegard describes five types of people who receive the Eucharist: "faithful believers, doubters, the unchaste and lustful, the malicious and envious, the warlike and oppressive." Which of these categories describes you?

Voice Six

Aelred of Rievaulx: Sabbath of Sabbaths

> You have said, kind Lord, that it is not a good thing for the bread of your sons to be thrown to dogs, but nonetheless the dogs were in fact allowed to eat up the scraps that were thrown to them, and so I know that bread will be broken even for me. And when the bread is too hard for me, you break it into crumbs.
>
> *Aelred of Rievaulx*

Our next voice on the Eucharist, a monastic author from the British Isles, sought practical ways to foster the experience of God. Noted for his profound spiritual insights and eloquent Latin style, he places the Eucharist at the center in healing hearts and growing in the Spirit. A strong proponent of Cistercian spirituality, his writings hold an important place in Christian spirituality and are still read widely.

"Bernard of the North"

Aelred of Rievaulx (1110–67) was known for his work on the nature of Christian friendship. He was born in Hexham, in Northumberland near the border with Scotland, to a learned family with strong ties to the noble class. While still young, he was sent to the court of King David I of Scotland to further his education. In 1134, just two years after it was founded by the monks of Citeaux, he visited the newly established Cistercian monastery of Rievaulx. Impressed with what he saw there, just days afterwards he returned seeking admission.

Aelred spent his early years in Rievaulx as a novice and professed monk. In 1142 he went to Rome on behalf of his abbot to present the monastery's position concerning the elected successor of the archbishop of York. Upon his return he became novice master and soon was chosen to lead a group of monks to establish a new monastery at Revesby. In 1147 he became abbot of Rievaulx, a position he held for twenty years, until his death.

Because of his profound spiritual wisdom some of his contemporaries called Aelred the "Bernard of the North." His best-known treaties are *The Mirror of Charity* (*Speculum caritatis*, ca. 1142), *Jesus as a Boy of Twelve* (*De Iesu puero duodenni*, 1160–62), and *On Spiritual Friendship* (*De spiritali amicitia*, 1164–67). His teaching on the Eucharist reflects his depth of insight and fervor for the spiritual life.[1]

Aelred's Spirituality

Aelred's spiritual outlook relates closely to his Cistercian vocation. Because they were monastic rigorists, Cistercians interpreted the Rule of Benedict to the letter. They wore exactly what the Rule explicitly stated: a wool tunic and cowl, and a scapular. They slept on mats with only a pillow and a wool blanket. Their daily lives centered on common prayer, private devotion, and manual labor. The Cistercians wanted to base their private spiritual lives, their worship, and their

---

1. The information in this section comes from Douglass Roby, "Introduction," in Aelred of Rievaulx, *Spiritual Friendship* Cistercian Fathers Series, no. 5, trans. Mary Eugenia Laker (Kalamazoo, MI: Cistercian Publications, 1977), 3–14; Charles Dumont, "Introduction," in Aelred of Rievaulx, Mirror of Charity, CF 15, trans. Elizabeth Connor (Kalamazoo, MI: Cistercian Publications, 1990), 11–67; Aelred Squire, *Aelred of Rievaulx: A Study*, CS 50 (Kalamazoo, MI: Cistercian Publications, 1981), 1–71; John R. Sommerfeldt, *Aelred of Rievaulx: Pursuing Perfect Happiness* (New York/Mahwah, NJ: The Newman Press, 2005), 1–4; *The New Catholic Encyclopedia*, 2nd edition, vol. 1 (Detroit: Thomson-Gale, 2003), s.v. "Aelred (Ailred), St." by A. Hoste.

source of revenue on the text of the Rule, particularly the balance of work and prayer that it regarded so highly. In their liturgy, work, prayer, even their legislation they sought to preserve as best they could the letter of the Rule.[2]

The Cistercians were also deeply influenced by the five major characteristics of the monastic approach to theology. In the first place, it is *experiential*. The monk desires a personal knowledge of God and uses learning to achieve it. For this reason, prayer and study are linked to one another. Through them, the monk comes to a deeper understanding of himself and thus can give greater praise and glory to God. By contemplating the mysteries contained in scripture, creation, and the human soul, the monk seeks a close affective union with his creator.

Secondly, monastic theology is *symbolic*. Because of the Neoplatonic background of monastic thought, the cloister dweller can view all of reality as a visible reflection of God's glory. Everything functions as a symbol of another reality and expresses both a similarity to and a difference from its transcendent referent. The non-demonstrative method of monastic theology is closely linked with *meditatio* and *allegoria* (literally, "to say something other"). The symbols discovered in creation, scripture, and the liturgy (not to mention the human soul) carry the monk toward contemplation of the divine mysteries.

Third, monastic theology has a *traditionalist* nature. It maintains a symbolic system by which the monk is led to an experience of and ultimate union with the divine. This does not mean that the monk holds a static view of the past or that he cannot think progressively in concrete situations. It does mean, however, that he is wary of novelty for novelty's sake, especially in formulations concerning the divine mysteries. Because the monk uses the symbols of theology *to lead him*

---

2. See *Exordium parvum*, nos. 15–17 in *Nomasticon Cisterciense seu antiquiores ordinis Cisterciensis constitutions*, eds. Juliano Paris and Hugone Séjalon (Solesme : E Typographeo Sancti Petri, 1892), 62–64; Squire, *Aelred of Rievaulx*, 28.

to an experience of God, he hesitates changing them simply to make them more rational and systematic.

Fourth, monastic theology emphasizes *the epistemological role of love.* Love's power to unite heightens the monk's desire for God and brings about in him a connatural knowledge of the divine. This intuitive knowledge brings with it moments of intense insight that reveal a deep sharing in divine life. These insights come to the individual by the inner illuminating light of God and contribute to his interior, spiritual growth. The affective life of the monk is thus intimately tied to his intellectual activity. Reason and will work together; love can understand what the mind often cannot even begin to comprehend.

Finally, monastic theology places *limits on reason and secular learning.* Reason, it was thought, can obstruct theology's clearly stated purpose of union with God. Vain curiosity can distract the monk from prayer. The concern for clarity can move spiritual experience to the periphery of theological thought. Argument and speculation can replace growth in charity as the purpose of learning. For such reasons, secular knowledge was thought to have little value in itself and was considered useful only if it helped the monk along his spiritual journey. It was to be used cautiously and, at all times, submitted to the traditional judgments of faith.[3]

Aelred's spiritual vision, which represents the highest form of Cistercian and monastic theology, flows into his vision of the cosmos, Church, and society. He considered the universe and everything in it the hierarchical creation of a loving and caring God. Because the human being is a microcosm of this cosmos, the fall from grace had repercussions throughout the whole created order. This great disfigurement of sin is rectified by the refigurement of grace made possible through Christ's redeeming action. As a result

---

3. These five characteristics are treated in an expanded form in *AMHT,* 9–51. See also Dennis J. Billy, "Monastic Theology and Renewal of Catholic Moral Discourse: An Experiment in Historical Correlation," *Inter Fratres* 44 (2004): 30–31.

of this action, the wounds of human nature are healed and people are able to move away from their self-centeredness and walk once more in a humble, loving relationship with God and one another.[4]

For Aelred, the monastery was a beacon in a world immersed in shadow and darkness. It pointed to a world yet to come, but already present. This eschatological "already-but-not-yet" character of monastic life permeates his writing, especially his treatise on friendship. In the greenhouse of the cloister, the seeds of the kingdom can swell, sprout, and reach fruition. Within its walls, true friendship in Christ can take root, deepen, and mature. These intimate bonds demonstrate God's loving presence in the world and mirror those in the world to come. The Eucharist, for Aelred, was another such sign.

Aelred on the Eucharist

Aelred emphasizes the Eucharist is his treatise on love, *The Mirror of Charity*, written at the request of Bernard of Clairvaux to introduce novices to the fundamentals of Cistercian spirituality. In it, Aelred explores how God's love can purify and elevate the range of sentiments involved in human experience. The Eucharist, he maintains, is an important means for accomplishing this.

"If we wish to love ourselves in the way God wants us to love ourselves," Aelred writes, "we must not be corrupted by the pleasures of the flesh."[5] Because of humanity's fall from grace, our passions have rebelled against reason, becoming wild and unwieldy forces within the soul. Although we all have been redeemed by Christ's sacrificial death on the cross, each of us must reach out personally for the fruits

---

4. See John R. Sommerfeldt, Aelred of Rievaulx, *On Love and Order in the World and Church* (New York/Mahwah, NJ: The Newman Press, 2006), 1–27. For Aelred's teaching on humanity's creation, fall, and redemption, see Sommerfeldt, *Aelred of Rievaulx: Pursuing Perfect Happiness*, 10–40.
5. Aelred of Rievaulx, *The Mirror of Charity*, 3.5 in *RPA*, 86.

of this redemptive self-offering. For Aelred, the Eucharist is the primary means for overcoming our passions and taming them: "The remedy is to turn all our love of the flesh to the flesh of Our Blessed Lord."[6] God's love manifests itself in us when we take to heart even our enemies. We can remain in a state of grace if we think of Christ's patience (i.e., suffering in the present moment) in his passion and death.

Love for Christ in the Eucharist calms our passions and makes us long to be held by him. At one point, Aelred offers a beautiful description of someone who visits Jesus in the sacrament:

> When we have been purified by the twofold love of which we have just treated, we can find our way into God's own sanctuary and be embraced by Him there. Our longing breaks through the limitations of our flesh, and there we see Jesus Christ as God. We are drawn into His glorious light, and lost in His unbelievable joy. Everything that belongs to our human nature, everything fleshly and perceptible and transitory is stilled. All we can do is to gaze on the One who is forever changeless, and as we gaze on Him, we are perfectly at rest; so great is the delight we find in His embrace that this is indeed the Sabbath of all Sabbaths.[7]

When we turn to the Eucharist in this way, Christ embraces us and leads to see his divinity. As we enter into his light, we experience his profound joy and share in a peace that calms all human cares and anxieties. We wish only to gaze upon Our Lord and rest in his presence. The Eucharist, Aelred says, purifies our souls, gives us light, and enables us to enter into union with the divine. It also provides us with food for our spiritual journey of purgation, illumination, and union. It is the "Sabbath of all Sabbaths," a "mirror of charity" reflecting complete rest and perfect peace.

---

6. Ibid.
7. Ibid., 3.6 (p. 86).

Aelred goes on to assert that we now have only a foretaste of this "Sabbath of Sabbaths," and that the Eucharist points to a royal feast of which we one day hope to partake. When we approach the table of the Lord, we should humbly ask the Lord for the crumbs of this banquet by which we may feel the warmth of his love and allow the light of reason to show us the way. Aelred laments that many bishops fail in this regard:

> Do we not find bishops and even abbots whose houses give us an impression of Sodom and Gomorrah when we go in? There they have about them a host of young relatives, whose vices they make no attempt to correct, in no wise drawing them away from worldly vanity and pleasure, but even indulging their depraved tastes and paying for them with the price of Christ's blood.[8]

He wonders why the Lord remains silent when his sacrifice takes place among people who by oppressing the poor show their contempt for his scourging and crucifixion. It is inexcusable that some bishops and priests seek the pleasures of the world, "go[ing] about hawking and hunting on hard-driven horses."[9] He lists behaviors that are unacceptable in church or at certain times of the liturgical year. These include conducting worldly affairs during times specifically set aside for hearing the Word of God, wearing fine clothes during solemn penitential seasons, doing business or having sexual intercourse in church, and not refraining from common food and drink before receiving the Eucharist.[10] All God's people—clergy, monks, and laity alike—should show deep reverence and devotion when Mass is celebrated and the body of Our Lord comes into our midst and is presented to the Father.

---

8. Ibid., 3.24 (p. 87).
9. Ibid.
10. Ibid., 3.29 (p. 87).

Observations

Aelred's views on the Eucharist, which reflect his deep love for the sacrament, invite a number of observations.

Aelred's teaching on the Eucharist presupposes his theological vision, especially his views on humanity's fall and subsequent redemption by Christ's sacrifice on the cross. The sacrament is the primary means by which a person experiences the fruits of Christ's redemptive self-offering. Like most monastic writers of his day, at heart Aelred is an Augustinian and considers the inordinate passions of the soul to be a direct consequence of Adam's fall. Grace alone can heal the soul of such deep spiritual wounds, through the concrete remedy of the sacraments. Since the Eucharist unites us with the Body of Christ, it tames and ultimately transforms our inordinate passions.

Aelred associates the Eucharist with the spiritual itinerary of purgation, illumination, and union. In doing so, he highlights its value for a person's spiritual development and underscores the Eucharist's importance as food for the pilgrim journey. Since at any moment people can be at different points of their journey, they will likely relate to the sacrament and to one another in different ways. At the same time, the Eucharist remains a great unifying force in a person's spiritual journey. It offers believers an orientation for their lives, a window through which they can see their destiny, and an experience of communion that brings them into close, living contact with their compassionate and merciful God.

In addition to anchoring the Eucharist in the purgative, illuminative, and unitive ways, by using the language of "the visit" Aelred offers a concrete way to demonstrate and practice our love and devotion for Christ in daily life. By encouraging us to "find our way into God's own sanctuary" where we can gaze upon him, be embraced by him, and rest in him, he connects a person's spiritual journey to God with the practice of visiting Jesus in the Blessed Sacrament. "God's sanctuary" refers to the inner sanctum of the soul where God dwells as well as the physical sanctuary where the Body of Our Lord is reserved in the tabernacle. In other words, Aelred shows how a person can connect his or her inner and outer pilgrimage by visiting the holy place where Jesus' Body rests, imparting rest to those who visit him.

Aelred describes being "at perfect rest" while in the presence of Jesus' Body and describes the Eucharist as the "Sabbath of Sabbaths." In the present life, where we are accustomed to the "Sabbath of days and the Sabbath of years," we have only a foretaste of the true "Sabbath of Sabbaths," the heavenly banquet in the New Jerusalem. Aelred suggests that the Eucharist provides a foretaste of this heavenly banquet while already embodying it. It possesses, in other words, an eschatological (already-but-not-yet) quality that makes what we hope for present. The Eucharist is the "Sabbath of Sabbaths" because it makes the "Sabbath of Sabbaths" present in our midst, giving us a foretaste of what is still to come.

Because of his deep love for the Eucharist, Aelred realizes the importance of approaching it with great respect and devotion. The many ways it has been abused by God's people, especially by bishops and other high-ranking clerics, sadden him. His list of abuses to be avoided indicates the excesses that existed in his day. He pleads that people not give in to their passions, but allow the "warmth of love" and the "light of reason" to lead them to a respectful and dignified celebration of Christ's holy sacrifice. He laments abuses within the Church, but expresses hope that strong leaders will arise to end them and make appropriate reforms.

Conclusion

Aelred of Rievaulx gave up a promising career in the royal Scottish court to join one of the most rigorous monastic orders of his day. As a Cistercian, he followed the Rule of Benedict to the letter, dedicating himself to the pursuit of holiness through liturgical worship, spiritual reading, and manual labor. His many treatises on the spiritual life established him as one of the great spiritual authors of his day.

Aelred's writings reflect his monastic vocation and his intense desire to know the divine through experience. He explored the interior regions of the soul, seeking to calm the unruly forces within it and bring them under the gentle sway of reason's rule. For him, the warmth of love and the light of reason are not opposite but complementary dimensions of human existence. The passions, he believes, should not oppose the other dimensions of the soul, but act with them.

For Aelred, Christ's redemptive self-offering on the cross heals the soul of its inordinate concupiscence. Through the Eucharist, each individual receives the fruits of this sacrifice. He presents the sacrament as a reflection of a person's purgative, illuminative, and unitive journey and emphasizes the importance of expressing one's inner journey by visiting Christ in the sacrament. The Eucharist, an experience of holy rest, is an eschatological manifestation of the "Sabbath of Sabbaths." Because of his love and devotion for the Sacrament, he laments others' abuse of it in the past and hopes that they deepen their awareness of its importance for their growth in the spiritual life. The Eucharist offers a remedy for sin, food and light for the journey to God, and a mystical bond of communion with the Lord of the Sabbath, the Lord of Holy Rest.

Reflection Questions

- Through the Eucharist, how do we overcome our passions and tame them? How have you struggled with your passions and unruly appetites? Do they flare up at times with overwhelming force? How can you control them?
- What does Aelred mean by calling the Eucharist a "mirror of charity" that enables us to enter into union with the divine? How have you found deep, intimate contact with Christ through the Eucharist? When has it calmed your fears and anxieties? How has the Eucharist helped you in your spiritual journey?
- When have you, like Aelred, considered Jesus a close, intimate friend? Which of your deepest, innermost thoughts do you share with him? When have you rested in his presence? What evidence in your life indicates that you are a friend and disciple of Jesus? How is the Eucharist the sacrament of divine friendship?

Voice Seven

Albert the Great: Infinite Delight

There is nothing more delightful we could do. What could be more delightful than that in which God offers us infinite delight? "Without their toil you supplied them with bread from heaven ready to eat, providing every pleasure and suited to every taste. For your sustenance manifested your loving kindness towards your children; and the bread, ministering to the desire of the one who took it, was changed to whatever each one desired."

Albert the Great

Our next voice on the Eucharist is known for his vast learning and his desire to expand the frontiers' human knowledge. His inquisitive mind led him into areas that other scholars of his day either hesitated or refused to enter. His assimilation of Aristotelian thought set the groundwork for the great synthesis of Christian philosophy and theology completed by his Dominican confrere and pupil, Thomas Aquinas. Linking faith to reason, he applied his intellectual prowess to the mysteries of Christian faith, particularly the Eucharist.

"Universal Doctor"

Albert the Great (c. 1200–1280), a Dominican friar, scholastic theologian, and Christian mystic, was born to a noble family at Lauingen on the Danube in Swabia. He studied at Padua and Cologne, and became a Dominican in 1223. In 1245, he received the title of *Magister* and lectured in theology at Paris. He established a *studium generale* for his order at Cologne in 1248 and later became provincial of its German province. In 1260, he became bishop of Regensburg, later serving as papal legate and preacher of the Crusade in Germany and Bohemia. In time he resigned his ecclesiastical office, returned to the school he had established in Cologne, and for the rest of his life devoted himself to teaching.

Albert, a prolific author, wrote on a wide variety of topics. Because of his encyclopedic knowledge of philosophy, theology, and the natural sciences, his contemporaries revered him as someone unrivaled in scientific learning and Christian wisdom. Known as the *Doctor universalis* and the *Doctor expertus*, he sought a Christian synthesis of Platonic and Aristotelian thought, laying important groundwork for the future achievements, most notably those of his student and fellow Dominican friar, Thomas Aquinas.

In theology, Albert is most known for his commentaries on sacred scripture and on Pseudo-Dionysius, as well as many works of systematic theology such as *Commentary on the Sentences* and *Summa theologiae*. His treatises and prayers on the Eucharist reflect both his profound philosophical and theological knowledge and his deep devotion to Jesus' sacred body and precious blood.[1]

Albert's Spirituality

Albert's prolific and wide-ranging literary output demonstrates his skill as a philosopher, theologian, and spiritual writer. His collected works fill twenty-one large folios, including commentaries on scripture, Aristotle, Pseudo-Dionysius, and Peter Lombard. He also wrote a *Summa*

---

1. The information in this section comes from *CH*, 2:328–30; *IPMT*; *HCS*, 2:327–30.

de creaturis and a *Summa theologica*, as well as a number of ascetical works and treatises on the natural sciences. Although he himself held with many elements of Augustinianism, he gave the Christian philosophy and theology of his day a marked Aristotelian emphasis. Thomas Aquinas brought this cause to its logical conclusion.[2]

Emphasizing the difference between reason (philosophy) and faith (theology), Albert wrote extensively about the nature and teleology of all existing things. While Aquinas' theological synthesis would eclipse Albert's assimilation of Aristotelian thought, his commentary on the Neoplatonism of Pseudo-Dionysius had a great impact on his immediate disciples as well as on later figures such as Meister Eckhart, John Tauler, Henry Suso, and John Ruysbroeck. His Eucharistic writings, moreover, influenced many schools of spirituality in the later medieval period and beyond.[3]

Albert made important contributions to scriptural exegesis, moral philosophy, dogmatic theology, and mystical theology. When interpreting scripture, he moved away from the spiritual senses and emphasized the literal meaning of the text. He also laid the groundwork for thorough and systematic textual analysis and championed the notion of the progressive development of revelation. In moral philosophy, he based his presentation of a life rooted in virtue on both Aristotle and Augustine. He also was sensitive to the importance of scientific training and personal wisdom in making important decisions. In dogmatic theology, he simplified the scholastic methodology of his day by omitting extraneous arguments and listing only the essentials of a particular issue, often leaving readers to draw their own conclusions. His many works on Mary and the Eucharist are marked by a deep personal piety that complements his probing and ever-curious scholastic intellect. Albert shines most

---

2. See *CH*, 2:330.
3. See *IPMT*, 263

brightly in his works on mystical theology, especially in his commentaries on Pseudo-Dionysius.[4] These works alone secure his place as a leading spiritual writer of his day, and perhaps of all time. In the Bull of Albert's canonization, Pope Pius XI describes the revered scholastic doctor:

> Albert's numerous theological works, and above all, his commentaries on the sacred Scriptures, bear the marks not only of an enlightened mind and a deep knowledge of Catholic training, but they are stamped with the spirit of piety and arouse in souls the desire to cleave to Christ. We readily discern therein a holy man discoursing of holy things.... His mystical writings show that he was favored by the Holy Spirit with the gift of infused contemplation.[5]

Albert on the Eucharist

Towards the end of his career Albert wrote three books concerning the Eucharist: treatises on the Mass (*De mysterio missae*), on the Body of the Lord (*De corpore Domini*), and on the Eucharist as a sacrament (*De Eucharistico Sacramento*). All three are significant in liturgical history since they explain the nature of the Mass, the meaning of the terms and symbols used in it, and the inner dispositions necessary for those participating in it. His sermons on the Eucharist were extremely popular, and his many prayers for Eucharistic adoration were widely disseminated.[6]

Albert speaks about the Eucharist with particular clarity in his *Commentary of the Gospel of Luke*, especially his reflection on the words of institution in chapter 22, verse 19:

---

4. See M. Albert Hughes, "Albert the Great," *Spirituality Today Supplement 39* (1987), chap. 7, pp. 3–5 at: http://www.spiritualitytoday.org/spir2day/ag07.html [Accessed: February 12, 2013].
5. Cited in Ibid., chap. 7, p. 4.
6. Anon., "Albertus Magnus," *The Shrine of Wisdom* (no. 67, 1936) at: http://www.btinternet.com/~southcote/SoW67.htm [Accessed: February 12, 2013]. For Albert the Great's works, see http://suburbanbanshee.wordpress.com/st-albert-the-greats-complete-works-volumes-available- online/ [Accessed February, 12, 2013].

Albert the Great: Infinite Delight

"Do this in memory of me."[7] Commenting on this verse, he points out that Jesus commanded his disciples to celebrate the Eucharist "in memory of his going to death for us."[8] He writes that Jesus "could not have laid down a commandment more profitable or delightful, one more healthful, or attractive, one more like to life eternal."[9] This commandment, he says, draws us toward it, brings us joy, and makes us whole. "The sacrament," moreover, "profits us by forgiving our sins, and is of utmost use to us by the outpouring of grace in our life."[10] Christ commands us to celebrate the Eucharist so that we might benefit from his sacrificial offering to the Father and thus share in his sanctity: "Christ's holiness lies in his sacrificial action, that is, he offered himself in the sacrament: to his Father to redeem us; to us for our use."[11]

In a series of brief acclamations concerning the Eucharist, Albert maintains that nothing could be more delightful, more healthful, or more attractive. Delight: "What could ever be more delightful than that in which God offers us infinite delight?"[12] Health: "Nothing more healthful could ever have been commanded. This sacrament is the fruit of the tree of life: when any man receives it with devotion of heartfelt faith, then he shall never taste death forever."[13] Attraction: "Nothing more attractive could have been commanded. This sacrament is operative to produce both love and union with Christ. The greatest showing of love is to give oneself as food."[14] The Eucharist, for Albert, is a commandment of love that allows us to become one with Christ and to share in his holiness. By dying on the cross,

---

7. Albert the Great, *Commentary on Luke's Gospel*, 22.19 in *The Divine Office*, vol. 3 (Collins, 1974), 397ff. Excerpted in *RPA*, 97–98.
8. Ibid., 97.
9. Ibid.
10. Ibid.
11. Ibid., 98.
12. Ibid.
13. Ibid.
14. Ibid.

Jesus demonstrated the extent of his willingness to save us. By becoming our food he extends this love to each of us specifically. Through the Eucharist, "It is as if Christ had said: 'I have loved them so greatly, and they me, that I desire to be eaten by them: they have desired to receive me within them, to be embodied in me as my members. In no deeper way, or one more consonant to nature, can they be in me and I in them.'"[15]

Albert reveals his devotion to the Eucharist in the many prayers he wrote in its honor. One in particular connects his love of the Eucharist with his devotion to the precious blood of Jesus: "O Precious Blood of Jesus, flower of creation, fruit of virginity, ineffable instrument of the Holy Spirit...I rejoice at the thought that You came from the drop of virginal blood on which eternal Love impressed its movement."[16] He maintains that the sacrament flows not only from the mystery of the Incarnation, but also from Christ's passion and death on the cross:

> I adore You, Blood of the new, eternal Testament, flowing from the veins of Jesus in Gethsemane, from the flesh torn by scourges in the Praetorium, from His pierced hands and feet and from His opened side on Golgotha. I adore You in the Sacraments, in the Eucharist, where I know You are substantially present.[17]

Albert considers the Eucharist to be the sacrament of the Precious Body and Blood of Christ that came into the world in the mystery of the Incarnation, was shed in Christ's redemptive self-offering on Calvary, resides with us in the Blessed Sacrament, and as a healing and restorative food brings us eternal life. It is also the instrument of conversion and the source of humanity's regeneration. The precious

---

15. Ibid.
16. Albert the Great, "Meditation on the Precious Blood of Jesus," http://www.theworkofgod.org/Prayers/eucharist_prayers.asp?key=17 [Accessed: February 13, 2013].
17. Ibid.

blood of Jesus falls upon his people "drop by drop into the hearts that have wandered from [God] to soften their hearts."[18]

Observations

This brief summary of Albert's views on the Eucharist reveals his intellectual acumen and thirst for holiness. The following remarks explore these elements of his Eucharistic thought and place them in their proper context.

Albert wrote extensively on the Eucharist, concerning the sacrament's sacrificial nature, Christ's substantial presence in the consecrated elements, the sacrament as a sacred meal providing important spiritual sustenance for the soul, and the deep piety and devotion one should have when approaching the sacrament. He covers these topics using a variety of literary genres (commentaries, treatises, sermons, prayers), all rooted in traditional sources (Scripture and the Church fathers). At the same time, he employs the innovative tools of scholastic methodology to deepen his understanding of the sacrament (the use of dialectics in theological reasoning; the Aristotelian categories of nature, substance, accidents). These details show that his teaching on the Eucharist is both traditional and innovative, highlighting the main currents of the Church's teaching and presenting it in a heartfelt and intellectually sound manner.

Albert presents the Eucharist as a commandment of the New Covenant, in contrast with the precepts of the Old Covenant. In the New Covenant, Jesus commands by way of attraction, giving delight and offering wholeness. The visible sign of God's new work is his Son, sent into the world to redeem his wayward people. By his sacrificial death, on our behalf Jesus offers love to the Father. When we receive this sacrament worthily, we participate in the bond of love between

---
18. Ibid.

Jesus and his Father; we become God's adopted sons and daughters. The Eucharist is a new way by which God relates to his people. God relates to us not as a divine lawgiver, but as he does to his Son. The Eucharist is a visible sign that we are God's children, who relate to him as a loving Father.

Albert points out that the Eucharist forgives our sins. Although it does not replace the sacrament of reconciliation, proper reception of the sacrament connects us with Christ's sacrificial action on Calvary, its healing effect extending to every dimension of the human person. For Albert, the human dimension that most needs healing is the spiritual. As spiritual food, the Eucharist renews the weakened powers of the spirit, making it whole and once again alive to God's Spirit. It does so by transfusing us with the Blood of Christ and incorporating us as members of his Body. The Eucharist's medicinal properties flow from its being a sacramental enactment of the redeeming sacrifice of Calvary. When we receive the Eucharist, we come in intimate contact with Christ, the New Adam, the firstborn of the new creation. By partaking worthily of his body and blood, we move away from sin and fervently follow Christ along the way of holiness.

By calling the Eucharist "the fruit of the tree of life," Albert contrasts it to the fruit of the knowledge of good and evil that Adam and Eve ate in the Garden of Eden (Gn 2:17; 3:6). Christ, the New Adam, gives us the Eucharist to cancel the consequences of the Old Adam's disobedience. Sin and death, which entered the world by our ancestors' eating the fruit of the tree of knowledge of good and evil, will be overcome by our eating the fruit of the tree of life. This parallel between the Old and New Testaments suggests the Eucharist's effect in our lives. Albert attests, "The greatest showing of love is to give oneself as food." Through the Eucharist, Jesus manifests his great love for us by offering himself as the "fruit of the tree of life." By becoming our very food and drink, he gives himself to us in the deepest and most intimate way. By giving us his own body to eat and his own blood to drink, his very life becomes ours.

Albert says that we receive the Eucharist to make us one with Christ. Christ established the concrete, visible sign of this sacrament to sustain our relationship with him. Through it, our sins are forgiven, our redemption accomplished, and our share in Christ's intimate relationship with the Father affirmed. The Eucharist makes us one with Jesus, members of his body, the Church. Receiving his body and blood makes us one with Christ's humanity, the Father's adopted sons and daughters. The Eucharist allows our sinful humanity to reach God. Nothing else unites us to Christ so deeply. The analogy of consuming suggests such unity, but even that falls short of the Eucharistic reality. As food becomes a part of our very flesh and blood, so we become one with Jesus' body and blood whenever we partake of this holy sacrament. Even Albert finds that his reflection on the Eucharist cannot capture its great mystery.

Through the Eucharist, Jesus' precious blood falls "drop by drop" to soften hardened hearts and effect their conversion. Albert makes this point using the imagery of a journey. The sacrament is for those who have wandered from God, those who have lost their way and do not know which way to turn. It draws these lost souls back to the right path by preparing their hearts to receive God's Word. Once they have found their way, they become pilgrims on a journey to meet their Lord. The Eucharist, as a result, becomes their food for the journey, bread and wine to sustain them until they reach their destination. Albert reminds us that the Eucharist is for those still making their way toward their heavenly home, even those who have lost their way. He invites us to consider how the Eucharist draws wandering hearts back to God, offering them food for the journey.

Conclusion

Albert the Great was one of the great Christian thinkers of his day and arguably of all time. A prolific author, he had unrivaled knowledge of the natural sciences, philosophy, and theology prevalent in his day. His contemporaries gave him the title *Magnus* ("the Great"), affirming his reputation for learning and his place in tradition as an undisputed authority.

Albert was the first theologian to synthesize Christian thought using the insights of Plato and Aristotle. He would be eclipsed by Thomas Aquinas, his student at Cologne and fellow Dominican friar, but his substantial contribution was necessary for later developments. His reputation as a man of wisdom and mystical intuition, moreover, made him stand out among his contemporaries, even up until the present era.

Albert wrote a great deal on the Eucharist, in many literary genres. He stood firmly in the Catholic tradition, yet used the tools available in his day to probe the meaning of the sacrament and base it firmly in philosophy and theology. Most importantly, his profound learning never diminished his deep love and devotion for the sacrament. Albert considered the Eucharist to be the sacrament "par excellence." It embodies not only the essence of the Lord's message, but the very Body and Blood of the Lord himself. He understood that laying down one's life for one's friends is the highest expression of love. The Eucharist demonstrates not only that Jesus had laid down his life for us by dying on the cross, but also becomes our very food and drink. Albert, the *Doctor universalis*, saw the Eucharist as the universal sacrament of salvation, a visible sign instituted by Christ to lead wandering souls back to God.

Reflection Questions

- If it is true, as Albert says, that nothing is more delightful, more healthful, or more attractive than the Eucharist, why do many view it as a burden and obligation? How can you convey the great joy of celebrating the sacrament?

- Albert claims that we receive the Eucharist to make us one with Christ. How do you know you have been united with Christ? What are the signs of this unity? A clear conscience? A longing for conversion? A deep desire to grow in virtue and the life of holiness?

- Albert teaches that, through the Eucharist, Jesus' precious blood falls "drop by drop" to soften those with hardened hearts and effect their conversion. How has the Eucharist softened your heart? Made you more aware of your sinfulness and need for conversion? Helped you find your way back to God?

Voice Eight

Bonaventure: Rapturous Love

> This sacrament contains the true body and immaculate flesh of Christ, in such a way that it penetrates our being, unites us to one another, and transforms us into Him through that burning love by which He gave Himself to us [in the incarnation], offered Himself up for us [in the passion], and now gives Himself back to us, to remain with us until the end of the world.
>
> *Bonaventure*

Our next voice on the Eucharist represents the flowering of the Franciscan tradition and, with his Dominican counterpart Thomas Aquinas, is often cited as one of the greatest theologians of his generation and of all time. Known for his broad grasp of scholastic theology, he is especially remembered for his insights into the mystical life. In many ways he represents a convergence of the patristic and scholastic traditions. In line with these synthesizing tendencies, he is careful to draw proper distinctions about the sacrificial nature of the Mass and the real presence, while at the same time highlighting the deep influence worthy reception of the sacrament has on our spiritual life.

Theologian and Mystic

The renown of Bonaventure of Bagnoregio (1217–1274) as a scholastic thinker and mystical theologian earned him the title, *Doctor Seraphicus* ("The Seraphic Doctor"). He entered the Franciscans in 1243, achieved the title "master of theology" from the University of Paris in 1254, and was Regent Master at the Franciscan school there until 1257, when he was elected Minister General of the Franciscans.

As head of his order, Bonaventure dealt with tensions related to interpretations of the vow of poverty and oversaw a period of the great growth and expansion, so much so that he is also known as the "Second Founder" of the Franciscan Order. In 1273 he was designated cardinal bishop of Albano. This mystic, gifted speculative theologian, and son of the Church died in 1274 while attending the second Council of Lyons. Pope Sixtus IV canonized him in 1482, and Pope Sixtus V declared him a doctor of the Church in 1587.

A prolific writer, many of Bonaventure's works are counted among the classics of Christian literature. He is most remembered for his lives of St. Francis (1261) and such theological and mystical treatises as *The Reduction of the Arts to Theology* (*De reductione artium ad theologiam* (1254–55), *Breviloquium* (a theological summa, 1254–57), and *The Journey of the Mind to God* (*Itinerarium mentis in Deum*, 1259–60). His views on the Eucharist, which reveal a unique blend of scholastic precision and mystical insight, lie at the heart of his spiritual and theological vision.[1]

Bonaventure's Spirituality

Bonaventure's vocation as a theologian was deeply influenced by his Franciscan calling.[2] He saw no discrepancy between Francis' humble embrace of poverty and the theologian's call to probe the scriptures and the book of

---

1. For the major dates and chronology of St. Bonaventure, see J. Guy Bougerol, *Introduction to the Works of St. Bonaventure*, trans. José de Vinck (Paterson, NJ: St. Anthony Guild Press, 1964), xiv, 171–77. For a brief summary of his life and works, see Ewert Cousins, "Introduction" in Bonaventure: *The Soul's Journey into God, The Tree of Life, The Life of St. Francis, The Classics of Western Spirituality* (New York/Ramsey/Toronto: Paulist Press, 1978), 2–16.
2. See Bougerol, *Introduction to the Works of St. Bonaventure*, 3–11.

creation for their hidden riches. His theology, centered on Christ, was intimately related to his spirituality. Describing Bonaventure's theological outlook, J. Guy Bougerol states:

> Christ is indeed the center of everything: the middle One of the divine Persons; the exemplary Cause of the whole creation; and, by His redeeming incarnation, the Mediator of salvation and life, the Light who brings to man understanding and the certainty of truth. He is also the Goal toward whom tend all the efforts of ascesis and all the desires of the soul in its quest for God through contemplation.[3]

Bonaventure believed that contemplating the mysteries of the faith would lead to intimate communion with Christ and enable the believer to view all things in the sacrament of creation as simple "words" or "signs" from God.

At heart an Augustinian, Bonaventure maintained a Neoplatonic philosophical outlook. He believed that Christ, the Divine Word, was the exemplary form of creation and that, even in a fallen world, vestiges of the divine could be seen beneath the appearances of things. In this fallen world, God's image could still be detected in human nature and, once renewed by God's transforming grace, even the divine likeness. For Bonaventure, faith is humanity's guiding light, a conviction that he applied even to the use of reason. Although he respected the teachings of Aristotle and quoted him often, he scrutinized the philosopher's opinions to discern which conformed to the tenets of the Christian orthodoxy. He also suspected those contemporaries who valued the conclusions of human reason equally or more than the revealed truths of the faith. Christ was the rule by which he measured everything. To quote Bougerol again: "His [Bonaventure's] master was Christ, and no one else: he taught the doctrine of Christ through faith and the Holy Scriptures."[4]

---
3. Ibid., 9.
4. Ibid., 27. For a brief summary of Bonaventure's theological system, see Cousins,

Bonaventure shaped his ideas on the sacraments through his Augustinian outlook, which resonated with his teachings on the Trinity, creation, the fall, the incarnation, and the outpouring grace of the Holy Spirit in the Church. He called the sacraments "sensible signs divinely instituted as remedies through which 'beneath the cloak of material species God's power operates in a hidden manner.'"[5] Such outward signs, he held, were necessary because the sensible world, which helped bring about the downfall of the soul, had a necessary role in its being raised. Christ instituted the sacraments to apply the fruits of his redemptive self-offering to individuals. Bonaventure was clear about the sacraments' origin, function, and purpose: "Their origin is Christ the Lord; their function is to produce a prompting, teaching, and humbling effect; and their fruit is the healing and salvation of men."[6] The sacraments exist, for Bonaventure, to help believers in their struggle against evil: "Baptism is for those entering the battle, Confirmation for those fighting. Holy Eucharist for those recuperating, Penance for those rising anew, Extreme Unction for those about to leave, Orders for those bringing in new recruits, and Matrimony for those providing these recruits."[7] Each sacrament has a specific task in the economy of salvation.[8] Each, including the Eucharist, confers a specific curative grace that serves as a healing balm for the soul.

Bonaventure on the Eucharist

Bonaventure examined the Eucharist many times in his writings, but perhaps nowhere more thoroughly than in Part VI of his "Summa of Theology," the *Breviloquium*. In this

---

"Introduction," 24–27.
5. Bonaventure, *The Breviloquium*, 6.1.2 in *The Works of Bonaventure*, trans. José de Vinck, vol. 2 (Paterson, NJ: St. Anthony Guild Press, 1963), 223.
6. Ibid., 6.1.6 (225).
7. Ibid., 6.3.4 (232).
8. Ibid., 6.3.2 (231).

work, which he wrote while teaching at the University of Paris (1254–57), Bonaventure offers a systematic rendering of the truths of the Christian faith.

In Part VI, Bonaventure examines the sacraments in detail, focusing on their origin, diversity, division, institution, administration, renewal, and integrity. In this section of his "Summa" he calls Christ the "supreme Physician" and likens the sacraments to "sacred medicaments."[9] Using Aristotelian categories, he identifies their efficient cause (institution by God), material cause (representation through sensible signs), formal cause (sanctification through grace), and final cause (the healing of men through a proper medicine).[10]

Bonaventure says that the Eucharist restores the soul from venial sin and leads to charity.[11] As with Baptism and Orders, Jesus established it, brought it to perfection, and received it in person: "He fully instituted these three, and was also their first Recipient."[12] He also maintains that, along with Penance and Extreme Unction, the proper administration of the sacrament requires priestly orders and "may be repeated without offense when new occasions arise."[13]

Discussing the sacrament's integrity, he states its two species, bread and wine, become Jesus' true body and blood when consecrated by a priest: "When these words are said by the priest with the intention of consecrating, the substance of the elements is transubstantiated into the body and the blood of Christ. While the species remain unchanged in their sensible form, both contain the whole Christ, not as confining Him in space, but sacramentally."[14] Whoever receives this sacrament worthily is "more fully incorporated into the mystical body of Christ, being also refreshed and

---

9. Ibid., 6.1.5 (225).
10. Ibid., 6.1.6 (225).
11. Ibid., 6.3.3 (231); 6.3.4 (232).
12. Ibid., 6.4.1 (233).
13. Ibid., 6.5.1 (237); 6.6.5 (244).
14. Ibid., 6.9.1 (252).

cleansed in himself."[15] Those who receive the sacrament unworthily, however, eat and drink judgment on themselves.[16] Bonaventure maintains that the Eucharist nourishes us once we have been born in Baptism and strengthened in Confirmation. In it, Christ provides a sacrificial offering, a sacramental union, and sustenance for our pilgrim way. He connects the Eucharist with Jesus' passion and death, emphasizes the intimate communion it brings about between God and man, and commends the nourishing and curative properties of Christ' sacramental body and blood.[17]

Bonaventure maintains, moreover, that the Eucharistic species are actually transformed ("transubstantiated") into Jesus' glorified body and blood.[18] Since this body cannot be divided into parts or separated from God, in each of the consecrated elements it is complete and undifferentiated: "There is but one utterly simple sacrament containing the whole Christ."[19] Faith alone enables us to recognize Christ in the sacrament, and charity alone gives us the desire to love him. Those lacking these virtuous dispositions or who approach it with irreverent or careless hearts receive the sacrament unworthily. They would be better to wait until they are ready to receive the sacrament in a devout and attentive manner.[20]

Bonaventure also insists upon proper celebration of the sacrament. It should be

> ...surrounded with great solemnity, of place as well as time, of words and prayers as well as of vestments, in the celebration of Masses; so that both the celebrating priests and the communicants may realize the gift of grace through which

---

15. Ibid.
16. Ibid.
17. Ibid., 6.9.2 (252–53).
18. Ibid., 6.9.1 (252).
19. Ibid., 6.9.5 (255).
20. Ibid., 6.9.6 (256).

they are cleansed, enlightened, perfected, restored, vivified, and most ardently transformed into Christ by rapturous love.[21]

A dignified celebration of the sacrament reflects the interior dispositions of both celebrant and communicants, as well as the seriousness with which they practice their faith and receive the fruits of Christ's sacrifice.

Observations

These key elements of Bonaventure's teaching on the Eucharist invite a number of comments.

Bonaventure's teaching on the Eucharist flows from his Christocentric view of the universe. Christ is the exemplar of creation and the means of its redemptive re-creation. The transformation of the bread and wine into the glorified body and blood of Christ represents the first fruits of the kingdom and the means by which humanity is cured of its primal spiritual wounds and elevated to share in an intimate relationship with the divine. The Eucharist has special powers to cure the lesser, venial sins of daily life. It enables us to regain our balance after faltering in our walk with the Lord and nourishes us for the journey still ahead. Through the Eucharist, God's grace cleanses the soul so that the divine image and likeness may shine through it more clearly. It is the sacrament instituted by Christ for those "recuperating" from sin yet still vulnerable to its powerful sway.

Bonaventure's teaching on the Eucharist also flows from his understanding of the Church as Christ's mystical body. Those who worthily partake of this sacrament are more deeply incorporated as members of his body. They grow in holiness, becoming more closely conformed to Christ in their attitudes, thoughts, and actions. Through the action of Christ's Spirit, they are bound to Christ as the head of the Church and continue his mission on earth through their

---

21. Ibid., 6.9.7 (256).

love shared among themselves and with others. Through the Eucharist, believers are fortified in their faith, empowered in their struggle to overcome sin, and strengthened in their capacity to love. Through them Christ acts in the world; they are the leaven by which his Spirit transforms the world into a new creation. Through the Eucharist, Christ enables others to deepen their relationship with him and, through him, to the source of the divine Godhead.

Bonaventure's teaching on the Eucharist, which flows from his general teaching on the sacraments, forms a plan whereby the fruits of redemption are concretely applied for humanity's sanctification. While obviously related, each of the seven sacraments plays a specific role in this process of sanctification. With the other sacraments of initiation, Baptism and Confirmation, the Eucharist marks a person's full membership in Christ body, the Church. Unlike Baptism and Confirmation, however, it does not impart a specific character to the soul and may be repeated. In this respect, it resembles the healing sacraments of Penance and Extreme Unction. To be sure, Christ, the "supreme Physician," uses the Eucharist as a "sacred medicament" to incorporate us into his mystical body, to heal our tendency toward lesser sins, and free us from undue attachments so we can follow Christ more freely.

In emphasizing the sacrificial, unitive, and nourishing qualities of the Eucharist, Bonaventure touches upon the major themes of Christian orthodoxy regarding the sacrament. He draws out the intimate sacramental bond between the Eucharist and Christ's passion and death, highlighting the ever-deeper communion between Christ and the members of his body, pointing to the messianic banquet of which the bread and wine are visible, sacred signs. His discussion positions him as a loyal son who seeks to understand more deeply and better express what has been handed on to him by the scriptures and the Church's living tradition. His education as a scholastic theologian, moreover, enabled him to express a balanced intellectual assessment of the mystical dimensions of the Church's sacramental teaching.

While Bonaventure's emphasis on exemplarism reveals his Augustinian leanings, he also uses insights from other thinkers and systems of thought to express his teaching on the sacraments more clearly. Using Aristotle to explain the efficient, material, formal, and final causes of the Eucharist demonstrates his regard for the peripatetic philosopher and his desire to rely on his wisdom even if others may have over-emphasized his insights. Bonaventure, in fact, often conveys his thought through a creative blend of Augustinianism and Aristotelianism. This "eclectic" tendency shows that instead of wedding himself to any one thinker or system of thought, he explains the mysteries of the faith using the best available insights. Reason can help one better understand the faith, but never to change its material content. The mysteries of faith must be received as supernatural truths. They cannot contradict reason, exist as parallel truths, or be reduced to rational principles.

Bonaventure's reverence for the Eucharist manifests itself in his careful teaching and in his insistence upon its proper administration and celebration. As a scholastic theologian skilled in making distinctions, he distinguishes the Eucharist from the other sacraments and emphasizes the special graces it imparts. This "theology of the Eucharist," however, is magnified by his care and respect for the sacrament. He insists that the sacrament be properly administered in accordance with the rites set forth by the Church and with appropriate reverence and solemnity. As a "visible sign of a hidden reality," the Eucharist offers a glimpse into the beyond. Celebrating it with reverence and respect allows the light of Christ that shines through the sacrament to illumine and transform our hearts.

Finally, Bonaventure warns those that those who receive the sacrament unworthily eat and drink judgment upon themselves. A lack of respect for the sacrament points to a lack of faith in the divine mysteries and to a lack of love for the Person who instituted them. Without the interior dispositions of faith and love, we cannot receive the fruits of the sacraments, particularly its healing and transforming effects. A lack of reverence for the sacrament compounds participants' sinful state because they make a mockery of the sacred. As a result, those who receive the sacrament unworthily do not draw closer but actually move away from God by their own actions. Depending on the disposition of participants as they receive it, the Eucharist brings life or death. The judgment they eat and drink is their own.

Conclusion

Bonaventure, one of the great scholastic theologians of his day, is particularly noted for his contributions to the Christian mystical tradition. His renown as a theologian remains strong, and his writing has weathered the winds of change. Often cited for his ability to combine theological speculation with adherence to orthodox Christian thought, he is admired for his comprehensive vision of the faith, imbued with childlike simplicity and passionate love for truth.

In his life and thought, Bonaventure juxtaposed opposing forces in what is often described as a "coincidence of opposites."[22] At the end of his life, this simple Franciscan friar found himself numbered among the princes of the Church. He was a mystic at heart, yet involved himself in scholastic disputations and in resolving controversies that threatened the cohesion and life of his religious order. He was a man of faith who fought to give reason its proper place in the search for truth, a man of reason who understood reason's limitations in probing the nature of the divine.

---

22. See, for example, Ewert H. Cousins, *Bonaventure and the Coincidence of Opposites* (Chicago: Franciscan Herald Press, 1978).

Bonaventure's teaching on the Eucharist reflects his theological outlook, his mystical depth, and his deep loyalty to the Church. It also reveals his Christocentric world view, his belief in the unity of truth, and his affirmation of the revealed truths of the faith. In this sacrament, God who is infinite becomes small. Humanity regains its resemblance to the divine likeness. Bread and wine, the work of human hands, are transformed into the body and blood of our Risen Lord and Savior.

Reflection Questions

- Bonaventure claims that the Eucharist restores the soul from venial sin and leads it to charity. When have you experienced these healing effects of the Eucharist in your own life? How does receiving the sacrament make it easier for you to overcome evil and extend your love to others?
- Explain what Bonaventure means when he says that faith alone enables us to recognize Christ in the sacrament and that charity alone gives us the desire to love him. How would you describe the state of your faith? What can you do to increase it? How deep is your love? What can you do to deepen your love for Christ? What can you do to love him even more?
- Bonaventure says that those who receive the sacrament unworthily will eat and drink judgment upon themselves. What does it mean to receive the Eucharist unworthily? How can you overcome the "habit" that leads you to receive the Eucharist without reflecting on whether you are doing so worthily?

Voice Nine

Thomas Aquinas: Transubstantial Change

The presence of Christ's true body and blood in this sacrament cannot be detected by sense, nor understanding, but by faith alone, which rests upon Divine authority. Hence, on Luke 22:19, "This is My body, which is given for you," Cyril says "Doubt not whether this be true; but take rather the Savior's words with faith; for since He is Truth, He lies not."

Thomas Aquinas

Our next voice on the Eucharist has had a lasting effect on nearly every area of Catholic thought. A creative and innovative thinker, he developed a compendium of theology based on Scripture, the patristic tradition (especially the insights of St. Augustine), and Aristotelian philosophy. A student of Albert the Great and a contemporary of St. Bonaventure, he emphasized the complementary nature of faith and reason and how they can be used together to build a theological structure whose grandeur has been compared to a great gothic cathedral. His teaching on the Eucharist occupies a central place in his theological synthesis.

A Dominican Master

Thomas Aquinas (1224/25–1274) was a Dominican friar and scholastic theologian. Born into a family of lower nobility at the castle of Roccasecca in the northwest of the Kingdom of Sicily, when he was only five years old his family presented him as an oblate to the Benedictine monastery of Monte Cassino. At the University of Naples (1239–44), he studied Aristotle and met the newly formed Dominican order. His family strongly opposed his decision, at the age of twenty, to join the Dominicans. For about a year he was held against his will in the hope he might change his mind.

After Thomas's determination to remain with the Dominicans became clear, his family released him and his superiors sent him to Paris for novitiate and to continue his university program (1245–48). Later, he studied at Cologne under Albert the Great (1248–52) and then completed a degree in theology at Paris (1252–56). He was ordained in 1251, became a master of theology in 1256, and was regent master in theology at Paris from 1256 to 1259 and again from 1269 to 1272. He also lectured in Naples (1259–61; 1272–73), Orvieto (1261–65), Rome (1265–67), and Viterbo (1267–68). On December 6, 1273, at Naples, he suffered a mysterious breakdown that left him unable to continue his heavy workload of writing. He died at Fossanova on March 7, 1274 as he was making his way to the Second Council of Lyons. Although Bishop Stephen Tempier of Paris implicitly and later explicitly condemned some of his positions (in 1270 and in 1277), he was exonerated and in 1323 was canonized.

Aquinas is most remembered for using Aristotelian philosophy in his great synthesis of Christian thought, represented in works like the *Scriptum super libros Sententiarum* (1252–56), the *Summa contra gentiles* (1259–64) and the *Summa theologiae* (1266–73). His teaching on the Eucharist fits well into this synthesis and reflects his spiritual and theological outlook.[1]

---

1. For a chronology of Aquinas' life and a listing of his works, see James A. Weisheipl, *Friar Thomas D'Aquino: His Life, Thought and Works* (Garden City, NY: Doubleday, 1974), 351–405.

Aquinas' Spirituality

Aquinas was a progressive, forward-minded spiritual thinker who remained loyal to the Church. His circular understanding of the relationship between faith and reason allowed him to steer a middle course between conservative Augustinians, who gave precedence to faith, and the Latin Averroists, who considered them parallel, almost double truths. He believed that reason, weakened but not totally corrupted by humanity's fall from grace, had the capacity to illumine the truths of faith. Because reason is enfeebled, however, it needs divine revelation to know the truths necessary for salvation. Reason could shed light on these divine truths, but not contradict them.

As a scholastic theologian, Aquinas sought to use reason to clarify the objective content of the faith. He was a master at applying dialectics, the skill of syllogistic reasoning, to problematic and difficult areas in the body of Christian knowledge. His theological method, which he applied to the entire deposit of faith and incorporated into his many works—scripture commentaries, philosophical and theological treatises, comprehensive theological syntheses—was to identify a tension within the tradition and then make reasoned distinctions that resolve the conflict while remaining faithful to the tradition, at times even moving it forward. As a result, he became one of the most noted Biblical commentators of his time and transformed the theological landscape of his day by applying Aristotelian method and theory to the entire corpus of Christian knowledge.

Thomas's sources included the scriptures, the Fathers of the Church (especially St. Augustine and [*Pseudo*-]Dionysius the Areopagite), Aristotle, and an array of other Christian and pagan sources. His literary corpus includes over 100 works, under categories such as theological syntheses, academic disputations, expositions of Holy Scripture, expositions of Aristotle, other theological and philosophical expositions, polemical writings, treatises on special subjects, expert opinions, letters, liturgical pieces, and sermons. His classic work, the *Summa theologiae*, is a comprehensive compendium of theology based on a Neoplatonic organizational structure, authoritative Christian sources, and the dialectal insights of Aristotelian philosophy. From the latter, he borrowed useful philosophical tools like the simple syllogism, the potency/act distinction, the definition of substance and accidents, and a hylomorphic (i.e., matter/form) perspective on visible reality. The resulting innovative and comprehensive synthesis of the mysteries of the Christian faith gained momentum in Catholic ecclesiastical circles, eventually achieving acclaim and authoritative (some would say "classic") status.

Thomas envisioned the *Summa* as an introduction to theology for beginners. In keeping with this intention he simplified the "article," the basic building block of scholastic methodology, by limiting the opening objections and counter objections to a minimum and by resolving the tension created by inconsistencies in the theological tradition through appropriate distinctions in a straightforward response. By simplifying the scholastic method in this way, he covered all of sacred doctrine in a relatively limited space.

Aquinas divided his *Summa* into three major parts and structured it according to the Neoplatonic idea that all things flowed from the source of all reality (*exitus*) and eventually returned to it (*reditus*). In this schema, the First Part deals with the *exitus*, covering a dogmatic treatment of God, creation, and the fall. The Second and Third Parts focus on the *reditus*, encompassing Thomas's moral theology in the Second and Christology, Mariology, and sacramental theology in the Third. These cover everything necessary for fallen humanity to return to God.

Thomas subdivides his Second Part into general and special sections. The first section of the Second Part covers moral topics like humanity's final end, the nature of the human act, a general treatment of virtue, the types of law, and a treatise on grace. The second section of the Second Part covers the theological and moral virtues, their corresponding vices, action and contemplation, and the states of life. The Second Part differs from the Third in that it deals with the abstract requisites for humanity's return to God, while the Third focuses on the requisites that flow from God's intervention in human history as a result of the Incarnation.[2]

Aquinas on the Eucharist

Although Thomas often discusses the Eucharist, his most mature and comprehensive exposition of the topic comes in questions 73–83 of the Third Part of the *Summa theologiae*. Thomas composed these questions during his regency at the University of Naples from 1272–73, a year or two before his death. With the questions on Penance, they number among the last that he treated before his collapse made him give up writing altogether.[3]

Thomas's treatment of the Eucharist appears after his questions on the sacraments in general (*ST*, III, qq. 60–65) and those on the sacraments of Baptism and Confirmation (*ST* III, qq. 66–72), but before those on Penance (ST, III, qq. 84–90). From a schematic standpoint, he divides his questions on the Eucharist according to a twofold movement: from the perspective of the Sacramental Presence (qq. 73–78) to the Sacramental Effects (q. 79), and then from that of the Minister and the Proper Celebration of the Sacrament (qq. 82–83) to that of the Recipient of the Sacrament (qq.

---

2. For a presentation of Aquinas' sources, method, and theological outlook see M.D. Chenu, *Toward Understanding St. Thomas*, trans. A.M. Landry and D. Hughes (Chicago: Regnery, 1964), esp. 11–99, 156–99.
3. For the Third Part of the *Summa theologiae*, see Weisheipl, *Friar Thomas D'Aquino*, 298–320.

80–81). The eleven questions he devotes to the Eucharist comprise 84 articles.[4]

In these questions, Thomas affirms that the Eucharist is a single sacrament with one specific purpose — to provide spiritual food. He describes its sacramentality in terms of *sacramentum tantum* ("sign only"), *res et sacramentum* ("reality and sign"), and *res tantum* ("reality only"). Although this terminology applies to all the sacraments, it is particularly helpful for understanding the Eucharist. Before the consecration, the bread and wine are only signs of a reality yet to come (*sacramentum tantum*). Once the consecration takes place, these signs exist along with the real sacramental presence of Jesus' body and blood (*res et sacramentum*). Once they are consumed, the devout recipient is given grace and spiritual nourishment (*res tantum*). In this process the substance of the bread and wine are actually changed ("transubstantiated") into the body and blood of the Risen Lord. Aquinas considers the matter of the sacrament to be the elements of bread and wine, and the form to be the words of institution pronounced by a validly ordained priest whose intentions correspond to those of the Church. With respect to the Eucharist's effects on the recipient, he holds that the sacrament conveys grace, leads to eternal life, forgives venial (but not mortal) sins, preserves a person from future sins, and by virtue of its sacrificial character can benefit others in addition to those who receive it.[5]

Concerning the minister of the sacrament, Aquinas affirms that only a priest, operating in the person of Christ, has the power to consecrate bread and wine. By virtue of his ordination, he does so even when not in the state of grace. This applies also to validly ordained heretics, schismatics,

---

4. See William Barden, "Introduction," in St. Thomas, *Summa theologiae*, Blackfriars, vol. 58 (London/New York: Eyre & Spottiswoode/McGraw-Hill, 1963), xxi.
5. See Thomas Aquinas, *Summa theologiae*, III, qq. 73–79. See also William Barden, "Appendix I: The Sacramentality of the Eucharist," in St. Thomas, *Summa theologiae*, Blackfriars, 58:197–200; Walter Farrell, *A Companion to the Summa*, vol. 4 (New York: Sheed and Ward, 1942), 295–318.

the excommunicated, and even priests who have returned to the lay state—although all who do so commit a sin. Whenever a priest consecrates, moreover, he must receive the sacrament in its integrity, i.e., both body and blood. Thomas identifies the celebration of the Eucharist as a sacrifice of Christ, which generally should be celebrated with sacred vessels in a church according to the proper ritual. Because it represents the whole mystery of salvation, it should be performed with greater solemnity than are the other sacraments.[6]

Concerning those who receive the sacrament, Aquinas states that the Eucharist can be received sacramentally, spiritually, or sacramentally *and* spiritually. Those who receive sacramentally while in the state of mortal sin are guilty of a serious sacrilege. A priest should not refuse the sacrament to those he knows not to be in a state of grace, but should warn them to receive only after they have repented and been reconciled to the Church. Moreover, priests should not refuse even public sinners, especially at the hour of their death. Those receiving the sacrament should abstain from food and drink according to Church norms. They should receive it not only because the Church requires it, but also because of the Lord's command. Those who are properly disposed may receive the Eucharist daily. If they previously have exhibited devotion to it, those who may have lost their sense of reason may receive at the hour of death if there is no danger that they might vomit or spit it out. Although by virtue of their consecrating office priests should always receive both the body and the blood of the Lord, Church custom permits others to receive only one species.[7]

---

6. Thomas Aquinas, *Summa theologiae*, III, qq. 82–83. See also Charles Keenan, "Baptism, Confirmation and the Holy Eucharist," in St. Thomas Aquinas, *Summa theologica*, trans. English Dominican Province, vol. 3 (New York: Benziger Brothers, 1948), 3449–54; Farrell, *A Companion to the Summa*, 4:319–32, 334–42.
7. Aquinas, *Summa theologiae*, III, qq. 80–81; Keenan, "Baptism, Confirmation, and the Holy Eucharist," 3453; Farrell, *A Companion to the Summa*, 4:330–334.

Observations

This general summary of Aquinas' teaching on the Eucharist focuses more on his conclusions than on his actual reasoning. The comprehensive scope of his teaching makes it difficult to include the fine points of his arguments in a brief essay. Nevertheless, the following remarks emphasize some of the implications of his thought.

Thomas, a sacramental realist, firmly believes that the Eucharistic elements are changed into the body and blood of the Risen Lord by means of a transubstantiating action. He also believes that through the consecrated elements Jesus sanctifies those who receive the Eucharist worthily. He explains the dual process of transubstantiation and sanctification via the principle of instrumental causality. The Holy Trinity uses Jesus' sacred humanity to sanctify sinful humanity. Through the ministry of the priest, Jesus becomes present to the believing community so that simple bread and wine can be sacramentally transubstantiated into his body and blood. In other words, God uses Jesus' sacred humanity and the ministerial priesthood, as instruments to mediate his sanctifying power and be personally present to his people.[8]

Although Thomas speaks about the "sign only" (sacramentum tantum), *the "reality and sign"* (res et sacramentum), *and the "reality only"* (res tantum), *it is important to remember that Christ is continually present throughout the entire sacramental action.* Using the priest as his instrument, the Risen Lord changes the bread and wine into his body and blood and confers grace upon recipients, an action that remains constant throughout the process. The Risen Lord impresses a character upon the "signs" so that they may contain his sacramental presence. Because he is the

---

8. See Barden, "Appendix I," 58:197–200.

primary person acting in the sacramental process, all other elements—the bread and wine, the words of institution, the consecrating priest, the believing community—are secondary.[9]

Aquinas was not the first to use the term "transubstantiation" to describe the transformation of the Eucharistic elements into the body and blood of Christ. It had been used as early as 1130 and was cited at the Fourth Lateran Council in 1215. Aquinas is responsible, however, for providing a sound philosophical justification for the term. Using Aristotle's distinction between "substance" (a thing's underlying reality) and "accidents" (a things external observable qualities), he argues that the "substances" of the bread and wine are changed into the "substance" of Jesus' glorified body, while their "accidents" remain the same. The substances of the Eucharistic elements are not destroyed to make way for the substance of the Risen Lord, nor do they remain behind and simply coexist with it. On the contrary, they themselves are changed ("transubstantiated") into the substance of the Risen Christ. This explanation remains a mainstay of Catholic teaching. Transubstantiation is a sign of the resurrected, glorified existence that those who remain in Christ will one day fully enjoy.[10]

Although Aquinas' explanation makes sense within the context of the Aristotelian premises upon which it is based, many Enlightenment and post-Enlightenment philosophies have raised doubts about the validity of these traditional categories. Any philosophy is only as good as the premises upon which it is based. Because later philosophies reject the foundations of Aristotelian hylomorphism that renders the visible world in terms of substance and accident, it follows

---

9. See William Barden, "Appendix II: The Presences of Christ in the Eucharist," in St. Thomas, *Summa theologiae*, Blackfriars, 58:201–6.
10. See William Barden, "Appendix III: The Metaphysics of the Eucharist," in St. Thomas, *Summa theologiae*, Blackfriars, 58:207–14.

that they also will not accept applications based on these categories to explore theological concerns. Although they criticize Aristotelianism, such philosophies have not developed another satisfactory explanation of the change that takes place in the Eucharist. The Church, in turn, maintains that "transubstantiation," while open to further discussion, is the best the human mind has so far been able to devise.[11]

Finally, although Thomas does concentrate on matters pertaining to the real sacramental presence, he also discusses the other modes of Jesus' presence during the Eucharistic celebration. During the Eucharistic ritual, Jesus is present through the action of the priest. He is also present to his Father and intercedes with him on our behalf. In doing so, Jesus mediates the Father's loving mercy to the believing community and presents their heartfelt worship to the Father, making it an acceptable sacrifice of praise and thanksgiving. Although Thomas does emphasize Christ's real ontological presence in the Eucharist, he explores his other important presences (moral, physical, psychological), or the sacrificial dimensions of the celebration, or how the Eucharistic may be considered a real foreshadowing of the heavenly banquet. All of these presences are intimately related, since in the one sacred Eucharistic action there is only one Christ who manifests himself in many ways.[12]

Conclusion

The "Angelic Doctor," Thomas Aquinas, one of the great scholastic thinkers of his time, remains a towering figure of Catholic theological thought. Although some of his theological positions were condemned after his death, his progressive ideas were later vindicated and the fathers of the Council of Trent (1545–63) invoked his theology to make a challenging and comprehensive response to the

---
11. See Günter Koch, "Real Presence," in *HCT*, 566–69.
12. See Barden, "Appendix II," 205.

revolutionary ideas of the Protestant Reformation. Since then, Thomas's thought has remained a resilient mainstay of Catholic teaching.

Thomas invoked the insights of Aristotle to shed light on the mysteries of the Christian faith. Many consider his theological synthesis to be the summit of medieval scholasticism; it has continued to be a reference point for generations of Catholic thinkers. His teaching on the Eucharist, an important element of this synthesis, presents a carefully reasoned exposition of the doctrine of transubstantiation, a theory which uses the distinction between substance and accident to find a middle ground between "crude materialism" and "pure symbolism."[13] Although Thomas was not the first to use the term "transubstantiation," he provided the strong philosophical underpinnings that helped make it the preferred explanation in Catholic theology. His teaching also addresses the sacrificial dimensions of the Mass and the other ways in which Jesus is present in the sacrament. It serves as a theological marker that helps to define the Catholic position. Anyone who wishes to improve upon that position and move the tradition forward must take Aquinas' thought seriously.

---

13. See Raymond Maloney, "Eucharist," in *NDT*, 348–49.

Reflection Questions

- Thomas taught that the Eucharistic elements are changed into the body and blood of the Risen Lord. Do you believe that the bread and wine are actually transformed into the substance of Christ's body and blood? What effect does this sacramental realism have on your daily actions?
- Thomas taught that only a priest has the power to consecrate bread and wine into the person of Christ and, by virtue of his ordination, does so even if not in the state of grace. Why is it important that a Mass is valid even if the priest is not in the state of grace?
- Thomas pointed out that a person can receive Holy Communion sacramentally, spiritually, or sacramentally *and* spiritually. What are the differences between these possibilities? Which do you consider the best way to receive the sacrament? Why?

Voice Ten

Meister Eckhart: Returning to the Divine Ground

> We shall be changed into him and wholly united, so that what is his becomes ours, and all that is ours becomes his, our heart and his heart, our body and his one Body. Our senses and our will, our intention, our powers and our members shall be so brought into him that we sense him and become aware of him in every power of our bodies and souls.
>
> *Meister Eckhart*

Our next voice on the Eucharist considered life to have but one purpose: union with the Divine Ground. His view toward the sacrament relates closely to his belief that all of reality will eventually return to its divine source through the birth of the Word in the soul. The Eucharist, he believed, was a primary way of gaining access to God's hidden, innermost being, which he called the "God beyond God." Through it, God "breaks through" to the soul so that the soul may "break through" to God.

Speculative Mystic

Meister Eckhart (c. 1260–1327/28), an intellectual giant of his day, is the father of speculative German mysticism. Born to a noble Thuringian family in Hochheim, he joined the Dominican friars around 1275. His early formation and novitiate took place at the Dominican monastery at Erfurt, then he studied at the *studium generale* in Cologne and later at the University of Paris, where in 1302 he earned the title of "Master of Sacred Theology."

Eckhart taught at Paris, Strasbourg, and Cologne, became provincial of Saxony in 1304, vicar general of the province in Bohemia in 1307, and for many years served as chaplain to several monasteries of Dominican nuns in the Rhineland. A number of Eckhart's teachings were questioned, and after his death in 1329 even condemned by the Church. Nevertheless, during his lifetime he defended himself vigorously, yet offered to retract anything in his writings found to be erroneous. Those condemned teachings include statements such as these: "All creatures are one pure nothing"; "We are totally transformed into God and are converted into Him"; and "Whoever blasphemes God praises God.

Eckhart's works include *Commentary on the Sentences*, *Parisian Questions*, and *Counsels on Discernment*, as well as many surviving sermons. His effect on the development of speculative mysticism has continued even until today. His teaching on the Eucharist represents a microcosm of his thought.[1]

Eckhart's Spirituality

A balanced assessment of Eckhart's spiritual outlook requires examination of both his academic works (written in Latin) and his popular sermons (written in German). As a theologian, he generally follows Thomas Aquinas, but was also very much influenced by Christian Neoplatonism. Believing that reason can penetrate God's incomprehensible nature, Eckhart seeks to describe in philosophical terms the depths of the Christian mystical experience. His twofold interpretation of the scriptures — an evident sense and a

---

1. The historical data in this chapter comes from Meister Eckhart: *The Essential Sermons, Commentaries, Treatises, and Defense*, trans. and introduction by Edmund Colledge and Bernard McGinn, CWS (Mahwah, NJ: Paulist Press, 1981), 5–23; *CH*, 2: 425–27; *IPMT*, 299–300.

hidden, mystical one—suggests a resemblance between the truths revealed by Scripture and those uncovered by rational inquiry.[2]

Eckhart believes the Incarnation represents a point midway between the emanations within the Godhead (*bullitio*) and the act of creation (*ebullitio*). He focuses on the themes of detachment, the soul's being shaped by the divine, its subsequent nobility, and the purity of the Divine Ground. He thinks that all of reality flows from the Divine Ground through the inner emanations of the Divine Persons and is subsequently reflected in creation. Reality, in turn, will return to the Divine Ground through the birth of the Word in the soul and its subsequent penetration or "breaking through" into the "God beyond God." Unlike Aquinas, Eckhart insists upon the utterly simple homogeneous ground of the Godhead, who exists beyond all plurality and distinctions. The relations of the Trinity, he thinks, do not enter into the substance of the Divine Ground, but stand somewhat apart from God's hidden, innermost being.[3]

Eckhart's views on creation and the fall also reflect his strong Neoplatonism. He distinguishes between the emanations of the Divine Persons and the created universe, but also affirms their close interconnection. He bases this assertion on the role given to the Word (or Logos) in creation. He believes that all things have an eternal virtual existence in the Word eternally spoken by the Father. Although all created things have an ephemeral, temporal existence, in the Divine Mind they have existed from all eternity and therefore have a deeper reality than their created nature suggests. Eckhart describes the deeper reality of created things as the "divine spark" that originates in the Logos and yearns to return to it. In his vision of reality, the need for redemption arises from the lack of order and harmony in the universe, which

---

2. See *Meister Eckhart*, 24–29.
3. Ibid., 30–39.

is intimately tied up with the divinity's creative outpouring into plurality.

Following Augustine, Eckhart understands evil as a lack or defect in the existing order of things. Stemming from plurality itself, this lack of order is bound up with the creative action of God, who permits it for the ultimate good of the universe. Although Eckhart accepts the existence of the powers of darkness, his explanation of the fall does not dwell on it. He understands that the lack of order comes from a creative diffusion into plurality, which the ultimate return of all things to the Divine Ground will overcome.[4]

Eckhart depicts creation and redemption in the light of the divine *exitus* and *reditus*, the creative outpouring of all things from the Godhead and their subsequent return. He speaks of this circular movement in terms of two graces: one representing the act of creation and the movement of all things away from God; the other, the return of all things to their divine source. A careful reading reveals a profound appreciation for how through the Incarnation, the Church, and the sacramental mysteries God has initiated the redemptive return of all things to the Divine Ground. His notion of the three births of the Eternal Word—eternally begotten from the Father, born of the Virgin Mary, and born within the soul—reflects the depth of his speculative mysticism, particularly how God "breaks through" to the soul so that the soul may "break through" to God. God brings about this divine return of humankind through the Eucharist.[5]

Eckhart on the Eucharist

Eckhart offers his most extensive treatment of the Eucharist in *Counsels on Discernment*. Written in German, this work contains a series of spiritual lessons given in the 1290's to young Dominican friars during dinner conversations with Eckhart. Scholars consider this vernacular trea-

---

4. Ibid., 39–45.
5. Ibid., 45–57.

tise to be authentic, perhaps the author's earliest surviving work. Because he was addressing a young audience, perhaps he was conscious of his need to offer them practical teaching rather than abstract speculation. Of the twenty-three chapters, the twentieth focuses on the Eucharist.[6]

Entitled, "Of the Body of the Lord: how one should often receive it, and with what manner and devotion,"[7] *Counsel 20* opens with Eckhart's assertion that one should be motivated to receive the Body of Christ not by certain feelings or sentiments but by the proper will and intention. He then highlights three conditions for receiving the Eucharist worthily: a clear conscience, turning one's will to God, and desiring that one's love for the blessed sacrament and for the Lord steadily increase.[8] Eckhart urges frequent reception of Holy Communion: "The oftener, the better, and the dearer to God. For it is our Lord's delight to dwell in man and with him."[9] Doing so, he maintains, will not diminish one's love for the Lord, but greatly increase it.

Those who dare not receive the sacrament because they feel empty and cold, he says, have even more reason to turn to the Lord, who will kindle them and make them holy. To those who find nothing but poverty within themselves, he suggests that Christ alone is the treasure that will satisfy them. To those who have committed too many sins and feel that they cannot be forgiven, he replies that Jesus has already atoned for all their sins. Finally, to those who say that they would like to utter praises but cannot, he replies that Jesus himself is the only thanks and praise that the Father will accept.[10]

By receiving the Eucharist worthily and often, Eckhart insists, one's sins can be forgiven. Those who receive

---

6. See *Meister Eckhart*, 67, 247.
7. Meister Eckhart, *Counsels on Discernment in Meister Eckhart*, 270.
8. Ibid., 270–71.
9. Ibid., 271.
10. Ibid., 271–72.

frequently become one with Jesus and his Body. Those who receive worthily, he says, become so closely joined to God that not even the angels can tell the difference between them: "There never was a union so close; for the soul is far more closely united with God than are the body and soul that form one man. This union is far closer than if one were to pour a drop of water into a cask of wine; there, we still have water and wine, but here we have a changing into one that there is no creature who can find the distinction."[11]

Eckhart responds to further questions. To those who wonder how intimacy with God can come about without feeling, he replies that intimacy is rooted in faith and that the less one feels, the more praiseworthy is one's faith. To those who wonder how they can have faith in greater things when they feel deficient and distracted, he replies that Jesus too, like them, had superior and inferior powers by which he could operate simultaneously on different levels. As the Lord enjoyed blessedness amid intense physical and spiritual suffering, so can they withstand the hardships and difficulties of life; they need to keep their superior powers directed toward God. Eckhart affirms that those who receive the Eucharist worthily receive extraordinary graces and so should receive it often. To emphasize the importance of frequent communion, he states: "If there were two men alike in their whole lives, and one of them had received the Body of our Lord once more often than the other, through that he could appear like a shining sun in comparison with the other, and could receive a singular union with God."[12] Eckhart also emphasizes the importance of spiritual communion, which a person can do "a thousand times and more in a day, whether he be sick or well."[13] Spiritual communion should be approached "as if it were the sacrament itself, according to the dictates of good order and with

---

11. Ibid., 272.
12. Ibid., 273.
13. Ibid.

great longing."[14] Eckhart concludes that even without such longing, people should try to incite it, get ready for it, and act as it leads them to in order to gain holiness in both this world and the next.[15]

Observations

This summary of Eckhart's views on the Eucharist invites a number of observations concerning the consequences of his thought and the context in which they should be placed.

Eckhart's teaching on the Eucharist is tied to his speculative mysticism and the notion of the pouring out (exitus) and return (reditus) of all things from the Divine Ground. Through the person of Jesus Christ, the Divine Ground has poured itself out into humanity and through the Eucharist into the visible world. Those who receive the Body of the Lord in the Eucharist connect with this divine outpouring and participate in a gradual divinizing return to the source of all things. In this participatory return, the ontological distinction between creatures and their Creator is maintained, yet the subjective categories of mystical experience are merged.

Eckhart's emphasis on proper will and intention when receiving the Eucharist reflects a strong Thomistic influence. Thomas understands the human act as a hylomorphic (matter/form) combination of reason and will. As a result, human action involves a deliberative movement between the rational and volitional powers of the soul. Feelings are fundamentally educable and open to reason's gaze. They can contribute to decision-making, but should not be the *sole* guide for human action.

---

14. Ibid.
15. Ibid., 273–74.

Eckhart's three conditions for worthy reception of the Eucharist also reflect his strong Thomistic background. A clear conscience, a will oriented toward God, and a desire to grow in love reflect the core values of Thomas's understanding of growth in holiness. Eckhart shares these values with his young Dominican confreres, identifying them as prerequisites for Holy Communion. Each of these conditions is necessary for proper reception of the sacrament. Disregarding them shows disrespect for the Body of the Lord and risks sacrilege.

Eckhart emphasizes frequent communion because he believes in the transforming power of the sacrament and its role in the return (reditus) *of all things to the Divine Ground.* Worthy reception of the Eucharist has so great an effect on the soul that frequent reception cannot be overemphasized. Frequent communion demonstrates the desire to draw ever nearer to God. It makes our relationship with the Lord grow and moves us on our pilgrim journey home.

The question and answer format of Counsels on Discernment may reflect actual conversation during his evening meal with young Dominican friars. It could also be a literary device that captures the imagination and helps readers see that Jesus in the Eucharist warms the heart, strengthens the body, forgives sins, and satisfies every longing. For Eckhart, the Body of Christ answers every spiritual question and offers extraordinary graces to those who receive it.

Eckhart's distinction between a person's superior and inferior powers explains how it is possible to experience a profound, intimate union with the divine while remaining active in the world, even when burdened by troubles and circumstances. The different levels of experience allow a person access to both the material and the spiritual worlds while maintaining overall well-being. We have potential for the eternal amid the temporal, and vice versa.

Eckhart's description of the union between the soul and God after receiving the Eucharist might be considered unorthodox. Likening the union between human beings and God to the relationship between body and soul or to a drop of water in a cask of wine tend to blur the distinction between Creator and creature. Some consider them to be expressions of pantheism. Such statements did get Eckhart into trouble with Church authorities, but trying to express the inexpressible can cause philosophical and theological language to be mixed with psychological and rhetorical discourse. This mixture can make his thought seem theologically obscure and difficult to understand.[16]

Eckhart uses nuanced language to describe the union between Jesus and those who receive him sacramentally. He speaks of being wholly united to Christ so that all things are shared in common: "All that is ours becomes his, our heart and his one heart, our body and his one Body. Our senses and our will, our intention, our powers and our members shall be so brought into him that we sense him and become aware of him in every power of our bodies and souls."[17] Such a statement might be considered orthodox, or heretical; it can probably be interpreted either way. Perhaps Eckhart's lack of clarity here is purposeful. His ambiguity could be a way of challenging his young Dominican audience to examine their Eucharistic beliefs more closely and explore the depths of their own experience.

Eckhart sometimes employs exaggerated rhetoric to make a point. One example is his comparison between the two men of similar backgrounds who differ like night and day simply because during his lifetime one has received the Eucharist one more time than the other. Eckhart is making the point here that a single Communion brings the recipient

---
16. See *IPMT*, 301.
17. Ibid., 271.

extraordinary graces, and that frequent reception would bring even more. Although his comparison may seem forced, exaggeration often attracts attention and can be a useful teaching device.

Finally, Eckhart emphasizes the value of spiritual communion in response to those who complain about their limited access to sacramental communion. To receive the benefits of the Eucharist, a person need only express in a respectful way his or her longing to be in communion with God. Because a person can receive it often, at any time or place, spiritual communion makes all of the graces of sacramental communion available. Although it cannot replace sacramental communion, it provides a useful complement that deepens a person's spiritual life.

Conclusion

Meister Eckhart, one of the great mystical theologians of his day, has made a deep and lasting impression on the Catholic imagination. He was loyal to the Church and submitted everything that he had taught and preached to its judgment. Although he defended his positions with tenacity and profound intellectual acumen, he was humble enough to acknowledge Church authority and the limitations of his own theological and mystical insights.

Eckhart's theological outlook was influenced by his Thomistic background and by his strong Christian Neoplatonic leanings. He expressed his mystical experience in philosophical and theological language, blended with psychological or rhetorical terminology. His understanding of reality was founded on the notion of the hidden God beyond the Trinity and the related *exitus/reditus* notion that all of reality pours forth from a Divine Ground and will one day return to it. Although he sometimes seems to blur the distinction between the natural and the supernatural, and between creatures and their Creator, many of these tendencies appear in the German works, which Eckhart did not prepare as carefully as his Latin texts. Many of his vernacular sermons and counsels were reports (*reportationes*) transcribed by his listeners that he may not have had the opportunity to correct.[18] For this reason, it is important to judge Eckhart's teaching in the context of his entire literary corpus, keeping in mind his intention to always remain faithful to the orthodox Christian faith.

Eckhart's views on the Eucharist flow from his theological outlook, particularly his *exitus/reditus* understanding of reality. During the celebration of the Mass, Jesus pours himself into the Eucharistic elements and then initiates in those who receive him a process of return to the Divine Ground from which all things come, calling attention to the sacrament's transforming power. Eckhart presents the Eucharist as an important means for fostering an intimate, mystical union with Christ. Through such a union, the believer returns with Christ to the Divine Ground of all reality that exists in itself, beyond all relations and distinctions, in pure and utter simplicity. This close connection between the Body of the Lord and the mystical life deserves a widespread, attentive, and sympathetic hearing.

---

18. See *Meister Eckhart*, 66.

Reflection Questions

- Eckhart says that to receive the Eucharist worthily recipients must have a clear conscience, turn their will to God, and desire a deeper love for the Blessed Sacrament. Which of these requirements do you find the hardest? How are they related?
- Eckhart suggests the value of frequent reception of the Eucharist. How often do you receive Communion? What positive benefits come from receiving the Eucharist frequently? What are the negative aspects of such a practice?
- Explain what Eckhart means in saying that through the Eucharist God "breaks through" to the soul so that the soul may "break through" to God. When have you had such an experience? Did you find it to be an experience of the emotions, the will, or the intellect? Which of the levels of our human makeup does the Eucharist seem to affect most?

Voice Eleven

Catherine of Siena: A Radiating Sun

[The Lord says], "I have said that this body of his is a sun. Therefore you could not be given the body without being given the blood as well; nor either the body or the blood without the soul of this Word; nor the soul or body without the divinity of me, God eternal. For the one cannot be separated from the other—just as the divine nature can nevermore be separated from the human nature, not by death or by any other thing past or present or future. So it is the whole divine being that you receive in that most gracious sacrament under the whiteness of bread."

Catherine of Siena

Our next voice on the Eucharist brought hope to a world torn by disease, political turmoil, and religious strife. Born during the time of the Black Plague, when a third of Europe's population perished, she reassured the suffering that God loved them and demonstrated what love can accomplish in the human heart. The Eucharist was central to her life and key to the peace of mind and heart needed by the desperate people of her day.

A Reforming Mystic

Catherine of Siena (1347–80), Doctor of the Church, patroness of Italy, mystic, and member of the Third Order of St. Dominic, was a tireless Church reformer who was influential in bringing the pope back from his long exile in Avignon. Her reputation as a reformer was tied to her sanctity and deep love for the Church.

Catherine was the twenty-third child of a wealthy Sienese dyer named Giacomo di Benincasa. As early as five or six years of age, she began to have contemplative visions and experiences of mystical ecstasy. As she matured, she led an austere life and took vows of virginity despite her parents' plans for her betrothal. As an adult, she lived for years in a secluded cell in her family home, continuing to experience visions that eventually led to a mystical marriage with God. In later years, she committed her visions to writing in order to record the depth and intensity of her saintly life.

Among the visions recorded in her *Dialogue* (c. 1378) appears a presentation of the Eucharist that celebrates the sacrament and expresses deep sadness over its abuse by those who administer it. For Catherine, the Eucharist lay at the heart of the Church. To rise from the mire of sin and corruption into which it had fallen, the Church needed to regain dignity and reverence for the sacrament. The freshness of her teaching on the Eucharist still resonates in the hearts of all who thirst for holiness.[1]

Catherine's Spirituality

Faith was central to Catherine's spiritual outlook. It permeated her soul, allowing her to see with rare clarity. It gave direction to her strong will and feisty temperament, leading her to place her entire life at the service of the Church. It led her to deep contemplative prayer and compelled her to act on her experience. It enabled her to balance contemplation with action and bring a message of love to a Church badly in need of reform. She believed that the light of faith given

---

1. See *CH*, 2: 374–75; Alois Maria Haas, "Schools of Late Medieval Mysticism," in *CS*, 2:166–73.

at baptism showed believers the way to eternal life. It is the pupil of the spiritual eye that discerns and follows the way of truth. Without it, souls would be blinded behind a dark, impenetrable veil. Catherine sought to rekindle this light within those she served by conforming herself completely to Christ through constant humble prayer: "For by such prayer the soul is united with God, following in the footsteps of Christ crucified, and through desire and affection and the union of love he makes of her another himself."[2]

Catherine's *Dialogue* reveals a person deeply in love with God and in close touch with the movements of the Spirit. This radical openness to God enabled her to convey divine love in intimate conversations on topics of great concern to the well-being of Christ's body, the Church. Some sources relate that Catherine dictated these dialogues during her mystical ecstasies; the text suggests also that it was carefully edited. Some surmise that Catherine herself had a hand in its revision and that she likely finished the manuscript sometime before she was called to Rome in November of 1378.

Catherine's *Dialogue* covers topics such as the way of perfection, the need for mercy, the crossing (i.e., "bridge") to truth, the gift of tears, the Church as Christ's mystical body, Divine Providence, and obedience to God's Word. This masterful presentation of her intimate conversations with God is considered a classic work of Western Christian mysticism. Her teaching on the Eucharist, in the section "The Mystic Body of Holy Church," presents the sacrament's centrality in the Christian life.[3]

---

2. See *Catherine of Siena: The Dialogue*, trans. and ed. Suzanne Noffke, *CWS*, Prologue (New York/Mahwah, NJ: Paulist Press, 1980), 25 (chap. 1).
3. See ibid., 205–76 (chaps. 110–134). The other relevant biographical and literary information in this section comes from Ray C. Petry, ed., *Late Medieval Mysticism* (Philadelphia: The Westminster Press, 1957), 263–69; Suzanne Noffke, "Introduction," in *Catherine of Siena: The Dialogue*, 1–22; Max Saint, "Italian Spiritual Writers: Catherine of Siena," in *SS*, 311–12.

Catherine on the Eucharist

In this dialogue, the Lord speaks to Catherine about the ministers of the Church. He wants Catherine to see the dignity he has bestowed on them as well as the wretchedness of those who abuse their calling. He tells Catherine that he has blessed his priests, who administer the body and blood of his Son to the members of his body, with a dignity that transcends all others created in his image and likeness, even beyond those re-created by grace through the blood of his only Son. He likens the Eucharist to "the sun I have given them to administer, for I have given them the light of learning, the heat of divine charity, and the color that is fused with the heat and the light, the body and blood of my Son."[4]

The Eucharist, the Lord tells Catherine, sheds light on everything around it. It is united to the Father, inseparable from him: "This Sun never leaves its orbit, never divides. It gives light to all the world, to everyone who wants to be warmed by it."[5] This light is the Divine Wisdom and its heat the fire of the Holy Spirit. These Christological and Trinitarian dimensions lie at the heart of Catherine's understanding of the Eucharist. In the consecrated species Jesus, who is human and the divine, is intimately related to the Father and the Spirit. Because the light of the Eucharist contains the color of humanity, when we receive it we are permeated by the light of the Godhead and "kneaded into one dough"[6] by the light of the Father and the heat and fire of the Holy Spirit. All who partake of the body and blood of Christ worthily receive this light so that they might have life in abundance.

In the dialogue, the Lord extends the metaphor of the sun, saying that the Eucharist is a sacrament of unity that cannot be broken or diminished: "Just as the sun cannot be divided, so neither can my wholeness as God and as human

---

4. *Catherine of Siena: The Dialogue*, 206 (chap. 110).
5. Ibid.
6. Ibid.

in this white host."[7] He also uses the image of a broken mirror: "It is just as when a mirror is broken, and yet the image one sees reflected in it remains unbroken. So when this host is divided, I am not divided but remain completely in each piece, wholly God, wholly human."[8] He also likens the Eucharist to a burning lamp that can kindle many other lamps or candles without losing its strength. When we receive the Eucharist, our candles are lit with the light of Christ while not diminishing the infinite light of his divinity. This light permeates our lives and deepens our participation in Christ's love.[9]

The Lord also reveals to Catherine some awful abuses of the sacrament. Those who receive the sacrament while guilty of a deadly sin receive no grace from it whatsoever. Such a person "is like a candle that has been doused with water and only hisses when it is brought near the fire. The flame no more than touches it but it goes out and nothing remains but smoke."[10] The Lord told Catherine of the great dignity of the priesthood so that she could mourn all the more the failure of those who have abused their sacred charge: "If they themselves had considered their dignity, they would not have fallen into the darkness of deadly sin nor muddied the face of their souls."[11] He uses the metaphor of a chalice to emphasize this point: "Just as these ministers want the chalice in which they offer this sacrifice to be clean, so I demand that they themselves be clean in heart and soul and mind. And I want them to keep their bodies, as instruments of the soul, in perfect purity."[12] The self-centeredness, impurity, pride, and greed that lie at the root of their sinfulness affect not only them but all the members of Christ's mystical body. God reveals the great dignity of the

---

7. Ibid., 207 (chap. 110).
8. Ibid.
9. Ibid.
10. Ibid., 208 (chap. 110).
11. Ibid., 212 (chap. 113).
12. Ibid., 213 (chap. 113).

sacrament and priesthood to Catherine so that she can weep over the sinful abuses present at all levels of the Church's hierarchy and resolve to work for its reform.[13]

Observations

These are only the main contours of the teaching given to Catherine concerning the Eucharist and its ministers. The following remarks explore these insights further and highlight their relevance for today.

We should pay attention to the way this teaching is presented. Catherine's insights into the Eucharist come in the form of a dialogue with the Lord. This conversation takes place while she is in deep mystical prayer. The message is meant for her, but also for all members of Christ's mystical body, especially those who administer the sacraments. In her day, a woman like Catherine in medieval society had little or no authority herself, so in these conversations it is the Lord speaking through her. Her visions are a gift to the entire Church and the means by which God will rouse the hearts of the faithful, especially those in positions to effect reform. In this light, her mystical voice centered on deep respect for and devotion to the celebration of the Eucharist, resonates in its call to reform the Church.

Catherine does not make a systematic presentation of the Eucharist, but uses a wealth of images (e.g. a sun, a mirror, a candle, etc.) to convey the Lord's message. This poetic way of presenting the Eucharist touches many important elements of the faith. Her vision is orthodox in the truest and deepest sense of the word. Its imagery and metaphor presents the sacrament's great beauty and its mysterious character, which cannot be conveyed by the limited tools of rational thought. Catherine's language, moreover, is suited not only to the mystical experience she attempts to describe,

---

13. Ibid., 244 (chap. 126).

but also to the nature of the sacrament itself. The words God places on her lips reveal the sacrament's mystical purpose and nature. To receive the Eucharist worthily is a concrete sign of the divine light that burns brightly in the soul. That light will ultimately lead us to a face-to-face encounter with God as deep and intense as Catherine's.

The images and metaphors in Catherine's vision link the dignity of priesthood with the sacredness of the sacrament. The Eucharist is a wonderful gift from God, which only those chosen to live the priestly life are worthy to administer. This dignity derives not from a person's temperament or degree of holiness, but from a special character imprinted on the soul at ordination. Even if a priest's soul is marred by pride and self-centeredness, this character can never be erased. As a result, even the most sinful priests still celebrate a valid sacrament, although they themselves only compound their sins by also committing sacrilege. Catherine's vision reaffirms Augustine of Hippo's argument against the Donatists that a sacrament's validity is independent of the holiness of its minister. She conveys this message, however, not with harsh polemic or bitter accusations, but by allowing the light of the Eucharist to reveal the true identity of these unworthy ministers.

Although a priest's holiness does not increase the validity of the sacrament, it is still important for manifesting the reverence and respect it deserves. One of the most striking images in her visions likens the holiness of the priest to using a clean chalice at Mass. No one would think of putting the wine, soon to be turned into the precious blood of Christ, in a dirty vessel. In a similar way, the priest himself, whose hands will hold the chalice and whose lips will pronounce the words of consecration, should be in the state of grace when he celebrates the sacrament. To be in the state of grace means that he has opened his heart to the Lord and asked forgiveness for his sins. By turning one's heart "inside out" to the Lord in this way (and seeking sacramental reconciliation when necessary), the priest emphasizes the dignity and sacredness of the sacrament. He does so not on his own behalf, but on behalf of all God's people.

Similarly, there is a direct relationship between the holiness of a priest and his reverence and respect for the celebration of the Eucharist. Holiness and spirituality must become a part of a priest's daily practice. The way he celebrates the sacrament—arguably the most important action of his day—will reflect his own spiritual life. If he shows little concern for the dignity and sacredness of the sacrament, he probably has little appreciation of the dignity of his own priestly office. That is not to say that there is only one way to demonstrate one's deep love for the sacrament. On the contrary, the richness and depth of this divine mystery allow for many authentic expressions of Eucharistic devotion. It is necessary, however, that the priest take care in the responsibility he exercises on behalf of the Church and that he understand his role at Mass as an *alter Christus* ("another Christ") to the faithful.

The same can be said for the faithful themselves; their orientation and attraction toward the sacrament indicates their own love for God and thirst for holiness. They too must show respect for the sacrament by readying themselves properly for the great gift they are about to receive. By doing so, the grace of the sacrament can transform them inwardly and overflow into their interior life and outward actions. Those without interest or active participation in the sacrament, or who are lackadaisical, demonstrate how they view their relationship with the Lord. One of the most important duties of the priest in serving the faithful is to heighten their awareness of the gift God has given them in the Eucharist and to foster in them a sense of reverence and devotion that will deepen their relationship with the Lord and love for the Church.

Finally, Catherine's vision reminds us that the Eucharist lies at the heart of the Church's life and mission. The priesthood, or the Church, or the world itself for that matter, cannot be reformed except by the power of God manifested in this sacrament. The Eucharist, which lies at the heart of the Church, will be effective only if its members open their hearts and receive it with deep faith, sorrow for their sins, and a spirit of humble service. Catherine manifested all of these qualities in her life. As a result, God accomplished many great things through her. Her vision reminds us that we too are called to love the Lord in the service of the Church and of all humanity. It tells us that we must keep our eyes on the Lord and our ears open to what he is telling us. It highlights our own call to sanctity and affirms that first and foremost we hear the call to reform deep within our hearts.

Conclusion

God blessed Catherine of Siena with deep mystical insights into the Catholic faith. Her reputation for holiness and the charismatic authority she acquired in her visions and intimate conversations with the Lord made her a leading voice of reform in a Church that had compromised its adherence to the gospel message and so needed to change. Her teaching on the Eucharist was central to her message of reform.

In her conversations with the Lord, Catherine saw a connection between eating and drinking the body and blood of Christ and a person's hunger and thirst for holiness. This insight was especially true for ministers of the sacrament. By their ordination, priests are blessed with a special dignity, by which they can bring the body and blood of the Lord to the faithful. Although their personal holiness does not determine the validity of the sacrament they celebrate, it is reflected in the reverence and respect they show toward it. There is, in other words, an intimate relation between the Eucharist and a priest's holiness. It forms him in holiness, challenges him to offer himself entirely to God, and makes him an instrument of conversion in the lives of the faithful.

Catherine's teaching on the Eucharist has relevance today for a Church wounded by scandal and moral corruption. It reminds us that renewal of the Church depends on priests who love the Lord deeply and who approach his table with awe and recognition of their own constant need for God. As the sacrament of love, the Eucharist allows priests to demonstrate their love for God and his Church. The more they identify with the sacrament of Christ's mystical body, the more will the Church remain true to its calling to live the gospel and to spread its message throughout the earth.

Reflection Questions

- Catherine likens the Eucharist to the Sun, which sheds light on everything beneath it. How does this metaphor help you understand the Eucharist? How does it convey the Eucharist's centrality in the life of the Church and her faithful? What other images might you use?

- Explain the connection Catherine sees between eating and drinking the body and blood of Christ and our hunger and thirst for holiness. Why are these actions important? How would your life change if you tried to focus it on the Eucharist? How does the Eucharist satisfy your hunger and thirst for holiness?

- Catherine says the Eucharist is a sacrament of unity that cannot be broken or diminished. With whom does the Eucharist unite us? How does it do so? What does it tell us about the larger Christian community that the Eucharist is a source of unity but also a point of contention?

Voice Twelve

Julian of Norwich: God's Maternal Love

> He [Jesus] might die no more, but that does not stop him from working, for he needs to feed us... it is an obligation of his dear, motherly love. The human mother will suckle her child with her own milk, but our beloved Mother, Jesus, feeds us with himself, and with the most tender courtesy, does it by means of the Blessed Sacrament, the precious food of all true life.
>
> *Julian of Norwich*

Our next voice on the Eucharist challenges some of our traditional images of God and enables us to see the limitations of language and imagination to express fully the mystery of Divine Love. Although she rarely (if ever) left her cell, her mystic visions led her to the threshold of the divine, where she experienced God's love in a deeply personal way. She understood the Eucharist as an expression of Jesus' maternal love for us and nourishment with the life-giving food of eternal life. The image of Jesus' divine motherhood runs deep in her mystical visions and has influenced Christian spirituality and mysticism.

A Mother's Love

Julian of Norwich (d.c. 1416), an English anchorite, was one of the great mystics of medieval Europe. There are two versions of her book *Showings* (also known as *Revelations of Divine Love*), one long and one short. She wrote it twenty years after a mystical experience that included fifteen "showings" that profoundly altered her understanding of God. This vision centered on the experience of God as Mother, a startling, even provocative, image that permeated her spiritual outlook and led her to explore the depths of Divine Love. Her teaching on the Eucharist, which includes strong maternal imagery, still touches believers today.

Little is known about Julian's life. She lived as an enclosed solitary, with an assistant who looked after her needs, in a cell attached to St. Julian's Church in Norwich. While she is named in some last wills and testaments from that time, the most important historical witness concerning her is Margery Kempe, whose *Book of Margery Kempe* (1438)—often considered the first autobiography written in English—notes that she once sought spiritual guidance from Julian. Scholars feel confident that Julian never confided her revelations to Margery; had that happened, Julian's spiritually inquisitive and historically-minded visitor certainly would have mentioned it.

Although Julian claims to have been illiterate at the time of her revelations, scholars believe that this was a literary fiction driven by her modesty and humble opinion of herself. She probably had a rudimentary education, and over time she developed and mastered her literary skills. It seems that she knew of the Latin Vulgate and was familiar with spiritual works of the Western spiritual tradition such as *The Cloud of Unknowing*, Walter Hilton's *Scale of Perfection*, William of St. Thierry's *Golden Epistle*, and the letters of Catherine of Siena. Scholars surmise that at an early age Julian entered a religious order (probably the Benedictines), where she learned her letters before becoming an anchorite.

Little else is known about Julian. She writes that she received her revelations on May 13, 1373 at the age of thirty. Manuscript evidence demonstrates that she was still alive as late as 1413 and a bequest in a will suggests that she was still living some three years beyond that date. Other than this, we know little else about her.[1]

Julian's Spirituality

For twenty years Julian pondered her fifteen revelations before writing down what has come to be known as her shorter version. More than fifteen years later, a deeper explanation of her "showings" provided an interpretive key for all her religious experience: The center of all reality is love. This insight allowed her to interpret the purpose of human life and the mystery of Redemption. Even sin and evil did not trouble her, for she believed that the love of the Trinity manifested in Christ's redeeming love made all things well: "I may make all things well, and I can make all things well, and I shall make all things well; and you yourself will see yourself that every kind of thing will be well."[2]

Julian's spirituality, which has a strong Pauline flavor, is steeped in themes like the mysteries of sin, grace, and redemption in Christ. She approached these mysteries with a deep sense of humanity's solidarity in the crucified Lord. Although rooted in the Church's rich spiritual tradition, her outlook is still creative and deeply personal. The longer version of *Showings*, for example, describes the mystery of God's love through the allegorical parable of a loving lord who sends his dutiful servant on a mission. Despite his good intentions, this servant falls into a ditch, suffers grave injury, and cannot fulfill his lord's intentions. In turn, the loving lord never ceases to look upon his servant "very meekly and mildly, with great pity and compassion."[3] At

---

1. The information for this section comes from Edmund Colledge and James Walsh, "Introduction," in *Julian of Norwich: Showings*, trans. and eds. Edmund Colledge and James Walsh, *CWS* (New York/Mahwah, NJ: Paulist Press, 1978), 17–119; Bernard McGinn, "The English Mystics," in *CS*, 2: 202–5; Clifton Wolters, "The English Mystics," in *SS*, 335–37.
2. See *Julian of Norwich: Showings*, Long text, chap 31 (pp. 229–31); McGinn, "The English Mystics," 203.
3. See *Julian of Norwich: Showings*, Long text, chap 51 (p. 268).

various points in her explanation, Julian shifts perspective of the parable by associating the dutiful servant first with humanity's fall in Adam and then with God, who "fell with Adam, into the valley of the womb of the maiden"[4] in order to redeem us. This parable conveys the limits of our capacity to understand the mystery of divine love.[5]

As a mystic, Julian sometimes juxtaposes contrary beliefs to convey a sense of the divine mystery. For example, she says that God will make all things well, but does not claim that all will be saved. She affirms the horror and shamefulness of sin, yet also affirms that sin is unavoidable but every soul that never fully assents to it has a "godly will."[6] She conveys some of her most creative insights in a threefold explanation of divine love: charity uncreated, created, and given. The first pertains to the Trinity, which we know about only through revelation. The second has to do with the soul's participation in this divine love, made possible by the crucified Jesus. The third is the life of virtue, which we live in return for the love we have received. She also uses the powerful image of divine motherhood to connect the uncreated charity of Christ with our soul's created participation in divine love. Although the theme of God's motherhood has a long, venerable tradition and is not unique to Julian, she develops the metaphor more than anyone before her and carries it further. It is not a surprise, therefore, that the image of "Jesus as mother" is central to her teaching on the Eucharist.[7]

---

4. Ibid., chap 51 (pp. 274–75).
5. Much of the information in this section comes from McGinn, "The English Mystics," 203.
6. See *Julian of Norwich: Showings*, Long text, chap 37 (p. 242). See also McGinn, "The English Mystics," 204.
7. McGinn, "The English Mystics," 204.

Julian on the Eucharist

Julian's teaching on the Eucharist appears most strikingly in chapter 60 of the long version of her book, which explains the parable of the loving lord and his dutiful servant (chaps. 51–63). Through the image of divine motherhood, Julian demonstrates how God establishes a bond between his uncreated charity and the soul's participation in it. The foundation was laid in the womb of his mother: "It was in this lowly place that God most high, the supreme wisdom of all, adorned and arrayed himself with our poor flesh, ready to function and serve as the Mother of all things."[8]

Jesus' Divine Motherhood, she asserts, is made possible by God's power working in the womb of Mary, the woman specially chosen by God to be the mother of his Son.

The mystery of the Incarnation permeates Julian's teaching on the Divine Motherhood, especially the Motherhood of Christ: "A mother's is the most intimate, willing, and dependable of all services, because it is the truest of all. None has been able to fulfill it properly but Christ, and he alone can."[9]

Because of this mystery, she asserts that God relates to us in a new and different way; motherhood, she believes, best describes this new relationship. Jesus, Julian says, is "our true mother."[10] Just as a mother carries her child in love and labors in pain until she gives birth, so does Christ carry us lovingly within himself and undergo intense suffering and even the pains of death so that we might be reborn unto eternal life.[11]

Julian says that Jesus' motherly love for us does not end with his suffering and death. He also nourishes us as a mother nurses a child at her breast: "The human mother

---

8. See *RPA*, 112. See also *Julian of Norwich: Showings*, Long text, chap. 60 (p. 297).
9. *RPA*, 112. See also *Julian of Norwich: Showings*, Long text, chap. 60 (p. 297).
10. RPA, 113. See also *Julian of Norwich: Showings*, Long text, chap. 60 (p. 299).
11. See *RPA*, 112. See also *Julian of Norwich: Showings*, Long text, chap. 60 (p. 297–98).

will suckle her child with her own milk, but our beloved Mother, Jesus, feeds us with himself, and with the most tender courtesy, does it by means of the Blessed Sacrament, the precious food of all true life."[12] Moreover, Jesus feeds us not only through the Eucharist, but also through the grace of every sacrament: "He keeps us going through his mercy and grace by all the sacraments. This is what is meant when he said, 'It is I whom Holy Church preaches and teaches.'"[13] Jesus' motherhood manifests itself also in preaching, teaching, and the sacramental ministry of his Body, the Church.

Jesus, Julian goes on to say, does even more than what a mother typically does for her child:

> The human mother may put her child tenderly to her breast, but our tender Mother Jesus simply leads us into his blessed breast through his open side, and there gives us a glimpse of the Godhead and heavenly joy—the inner certainty of eternal bliss.[14]

Because of Jesus' passion and death, we are nurtured and fed not merely upon his breast but from within it. We enter his body, mingle with his blood, and feed within upon his "blessed breast." For this reason, Julian believes that it is proper that the word "Mother" be used to refer to Jesus as well as to his own mother, Mary, who has now become our own.[15]

Observations

This presentation, which sketches the main contours of Julian's teaching on the Eucharist, does not exhaust her views on the subject. The following remarks will highlight their originality and note their relevance for today.

---

12. *RPA*, 113. See also *Julian of Norwich: Showings*, Long text, chap. 60 (p. 298).
13. Ibid.
14. Ibid.
15. *RPA*, 113. See also *Julian of Norwich: Showings*, Long text, chaps. 57, 60 (pp. 292, 299).

Julian's teaching on the Eucharist must be seen in the larger context of her views concerning the motherhood of God. Although she is certainly not the first Christian author to speak of God in these terms, she takes this image to its logical conclusion, placing it at the center of her thought. Although she would agree that God can be described in many ways (e.g., Father, Mother, Brother, Savior),[16] she believes that the image of God as Mother best conveys the depths of divine love and compassion for humanity. For Julian, God as Mother has Trinitarian, Christological, and especially Eucharistic dimensions. The Divine Motherhood provides the model or exemplar of all other forms of motherhood, even the human.

Julian's teaching on the Eucharist must also be seen as part of her understanding of divine love. It is important to note that she has found a way to bind together her threefold understanding charity — uncreated, created, and given. For her, the Eucharist is one of the main ways in which God's uncreated love is mediated to the soul. By receiving the Blessed Sacrament, the soul gains access within the confines of its limited creaturely status to God's love for all humankind. Only by participating in this love can a person reach out and share it with others. The Eucharist mediates God's love to the soul and then to others. It turns her threefold understanding of divine charity into a participatory unity with profound Trinitarian dimensions.

Julian's teaching on the Eucharist must also be seen in the light of her views on the Incarnation. For her, this divine mystery is above all an expression of God's love for humanity. She uses the parable of the divine lord and the dutiful servant to express the nature and degree of this love. Jesus enters the womb of the virgin and takes on human flesh in order to lift our wounded humanity out of the ditch into we

---

16. See *Julian of Norwich: Showings*, Long text, chap. 58 (p. 293).

have fallen. He does so out of loving compassion, giving up his life to elevate us and make us whole. Julian considers the Eucharist to be the means by which Christ's compassionate love comes to each person in an intimate and personal way. God not only takes on human flesh, but also becomes food and nourishment for us. As such, the sacrament is a testament of God's love and shows the extent to which God will go to restore our broken humanity.

Julian's teaching on the Eucharist also has profound ecclesiological implications. She understands that the Jesus nourishes us through his body and blood as well as through the preaching, teaching, and other sacramental actions of the Church. The Church continues his salvific mission through time. Through its ministry of Word and sacrament, it pours out Jesus' compassionate love, opening us to his healing, life-giving grace. The Church not only safeguards the truths of the faith, but also mystically extends Jesus' life in the world he came to save. Christ encourages us, teaches us, and nourishes us through the Church. If Jesus is our Mother, then the Church is the expression of that motherly love.

Julian's teaching on the Eucharist must also be viewed in the light of her underlying trust in God's Providence. She sees the sacrament as a concrete sign of God's love for humanity, an expression of the message that, in the end, all manner of things will be well. Partaking in the Eucharist affirms our belief in God's ongoing care for the world. All will be well because God has visited our world and taken us into himself by feeding us with his own body and blood. Such a self-giving God will not turn away from those who sincerely search and call out for help. Through the Eucharist, God pledges to accompany us in our journey through life and to be present especially in our hour of need. Although we are free to reject God's freely-offered help, God never ceases trying to elicit our reciprocal response to that free and enduring love.

Julian's teaching on the Eucharist is also closely tied to the deep mystical sensitivities of her life as an anchorite. It should not surprise us that the Eucharist is so important to someone who chose to live an enclosed, solitary life in close physical proximity to the Blessed Sacrament. This physical closeness symbolizes Julian's deep spiritual affinity to Jesus' presence in the sacrament. Just as he occupies the solitary space of the tabernacle where he waits for others to visit him when they come to Church, so did Julian set herself apart to receive visitors seeking solace and spiritual guidance. In doing so, she created a space in her own heart where the Lord could dwell and reveal himself to her. She spent most of her time pondering the insights she received and writing them down when she felt ready to do so. Although few are called to live as Julian did, every heart can be opened so that God might dwell within and give peace and light.

Finally, Julian's teaching on the Eucharist has a strong Marian dimension. In Mary's womb Jesus took on human nature and laid the foundation of our redemption. For this reason, Julian believes that Jesus' motherly character is derived from God, our mother in all things, as well as from his own human mother. The mystery of the Incarnation implies that Jesus' Motherhood has both divine and human dimensions: one from God; the other from the Virgin Mary. These come together in the sacrament of the altar, by which Jesus takes us into himself and nourishes us with the divinized humanity of his body and blood. Jesus, who was with Mary as he took shape within her womb, was also with her as he hung from a cross and his side was pierced with a lance. As she watched her son give up his spirit, her own heart was pierced with a sword of sorrow. From these wounded hearts

Jesus and Mary nourish their children with motherly care and devotion.

Conclusion

The mysticism of Julian of Norwich, a great English figure of the Late Middle Ages, is still renowned today. Her life as an anchorite allowed her to probe the depths of her soul and ponder the divine revelations with which she had been blessed. Both versions of *Showings* convey her experience of God through images and metaphors that capture the imagination and move the human heart.

Central to Julian's teaching on the Eucharist is her presentation of Jesus as a compassionate mother. Although not the first to use this vivid and striking image, she alone places it at the heart of her understanding of God's compassionate love and redemptive plan for humanity. Through the Eucharist, Jesus takes us into his wounded side and feeds us from within with his own body and blood. In doing so, he nourishes us as no mother can do.

Julian's teaching recalls the ways in which we experience God's love. It highlights the limitations of language and demonstrates how powerful and even shocking images can arouse our senses so we can interpret our experience of God in new and different ways. She challenges us to think of God in a different light and to see how the divine mystery transcends all human attempts to describe or capture it. Although Julian's mystical voice is but one of many in the Christian tradition, it is strong and worth listening to. Those who ponder it will see Jesus and the sacrament of his body and blood in a new way.

Reflection Questions

- Julian compares Christ's suffering and death to a mother's labor pains during childbirth. What is the connection between Christ on the cross and the womb of divine love? How do these images help you understand why Christ suffered and died for us?
- Julian says that Jesus feeds us with the Eucharist as well as with the other sacraments. How is Jesus' motherhood manifested in the preaching, teaching, and sacramental ministry of the Church? How are these various actions related? How is giving nourishment a maternal action? How is it something every person can do?
- Julian believes that the word "Mother" can be used to refer to Jesus as well as to his own mother, Mary. How does her teaching on Jesus' Motherhood affect your understanding of Mary's Motherhood? Which has priority? Does Jesus' Motherhood take anything away from Mary's? Does it add anything to it?

Voice Thirteen

Thomas à Kempis: Intimacy with Christ

O my God, protector of my soul, healer of human weakness, and giver of all inward comfort, you have given—and you continue to give—many good things in the Sacrament. Through it, you comfort your beloved people in every trial, and you lift them from the depths of dejection to the hope of your protection. You continually refresh and enlighten them with some new grace. Though they may at first have felt uneasy and unloving before Holy Communion, afterward they always find themselves changed for the better, having restored themselves with this heavenly food and drink.

Thomas à Kempis

Our next voice on the Eucharist wrote a book that, after the Bible, is the most widely read in all of Christian literature. Ever since it was published in the early fifteenth century, *The Imitation of Christ*[1] has attracted a wide audience. Most scholars agree that it was written by Thomas à Kempis (1379–1471), a canon regular at the monastery of Mt. St. Agnes in present-day Holland. His

---

1. For a translation and commentary, see Thomas à Kempis, *The Imitation of Christ*, trans. William C. Creasy, commentary, Dennis J. Billy (Notre Dame, IN: Christian Classics, 2005). Parts of this article are adapted from the introductory material.

teaching, piety, and devotion to the Eucharist can teach us how to deepen our relationship with Christ.

Devotio Moderna

Thomas was born in Kempen and educated in the local grammar school. At the age of thirteen, he joined his older brother John to continue his education with the Brothers of the Common Life at their monastery school at Deventer, in the diocese of Utrecht. The Brothers were a loosely organized group of priests and laity who lived in community, led popular missions, and wrote great numbers of books and tracts of popular devotion.[2] They were an expression of the late medieval movement of piety and devotion known as the *Devotio moderna*, inspired by the evangelical preaching of Master Gerard Groote (1340–84) and influenced by the spirituality of the Rhineland mystic, John Ruysbroeck (1293–1381).

As proponents of the *Devotio moderna*, the Brothers of the Common Life focused on "living in Christ, reading Scripture, progressing in moral sanctity, and developing interiority."[3] Suspicious of the subtle distinctions and overintellectualized atmosphere of late medieval scholasticism, their schools emphasized a well-rounded, humanist education that placed Christian piety at the center of their students' lives, not on the periphery. Noted for their emphasis on the practical dimensions of living out a Christian calling, the influence of these schools on the spiritual and intellectual life of northern Europe has lasted for centuries.[4]

In 1399, Thomas entered Mt. St. Agnes, a contemplative branch of the order that followed the rule of St. Augustine and where his older brother John had recently been installed as prior. There, Thomas led a quiet religious life. He was

---

2. *CH*, 2: 454.
3. John Van Engen, "Introduction," in *Devotio Moderna: Basic Writings*, trans. John Van Engen, CWS (New York/Mahwah, NJ: Paulist, 1988), 27.
4. Ibid.

professed in 1406, ordained to the priesthood in 1413, and elected sub-prior in 1425. As the monastery's chronicler he spent much of his time copying the scriptures and liturgical books. He wrote a number of biographies and books of pious devotion including *The Imitation*, probably completed shortly before and after his priestly ordination.[5]

Kempis' Spirituality

This powerful book of meditations has been described as "a philosophy of Light and of Life."[6] Its simple yet attractive Latin style avoids the speculation characteristic of the intellectual climate of the day. It focuses instead on what is needed to lead a holy life in a world beset by trials and constant temptations.

The book seeks to mend the rift between learning and devotion in late-medieval Catholicism and that for centuries has continued to haunt Western theology. The result is an appreciation of learning in the service of Christian virtue and a rejection of the rarefied intellectual debates promulgated in the universities of the time. Its criticism of academic life should be understood as a reaction to a sterile intellectual environment. Instead, it proposes learning as a vehicle for growth in the virtues and deepening one's relationship with Christ. Although Kempis demonstrates his breadth of learning on nearly every page of this "Summa of Spirituality" (*summa spiritualitatis*),[7] such knowledge in the service of the gospel to deepen readers' faith.

Himself a religious, his primary audience were other members of his community. Therefore, the work exhibits many characteristics of late medieval religious piety and devotion. *The Imitation* is divided into four books: "Counsels

---

5. Most of the bibliographical data in this section comes from Leo Sherley-Price, "Introduction," in Thomas à Kempis, *The Imitation of Christ* (Harmondsworth, England/ New York: Penguin, 1952; reprint 1980), 20–23.
6. Brother Azarias, *The Culture of the Spiritual Sense* (New York: Steigel & Co., 1884). Cited in Sherley-Price, "Introduction," 13.
7. Otto Gründler, "Devotio Moderna," in *CS*, 2:183.

on the Spiritual Life" (Book One), "Counsels on the Inner Life" (Book Two), "Inner Consolation" (Book Three), and "The Blessed Sacrament" (Book Four). In them, Thomas develops the practical implications of the purgative, illuminative, and unitive ways. One author describes Kempis' intentions in this way: "This life consists in the practice of the Christian virtues; the practice of the Christian virtues leads up to union with Christ; and union with Christ is consummated in the Holy Eucharist."[8]

Thomas à Kempis on the Eucharist

In the fourth book of *The Imitation*, "The Book of the Sacrament," Kempis develops his teaching on the Eucharist. Its eighteen short chapters cover a range of themes that emphasize the importance of the Eucharist for spiritual life. He encourages reverence in receiving Christ, respect for the dignity of the priesthood, frequent communion, and fervent love for the Lord.

Kempis considers the Eucharist to be the culmination of a believer's spiritual journey. It subsumes the purgative, illuminative, and unitive stages of the spiritual life into itself and points to a final consummation when time itself will pass into eternity and we will all stand before the judgment seat of God. The eschatological dimension that permeates *The Imitation* is most vivid in his emphasis upon keeping our eyes on the one thing that matters: our intimate relationship with the Lord.

Kempis also explores the unfathomable nature of the Eucharist. Because human reason can achieve only a partial understanding of the divine mysteries, we must not allow idle curiosity to lead us into the incomprehensible. Understanding the Eucharist should be coupled with reverence for the sacrament, humility concerning our own intellectual

---

8. Azarias, *The Culture of the Spiritual Sense* (New York: Steigel & Co., 1884). Cited in Sherley-Price, "Introduction," 13.

capacities, and respect for the teachings of the Fathers. If we cannot achieve comprehensive understanding of human knowledge, we certainly cannot do so for divine knowledge. It is better that we walk the way of the Lord with simplicity of heart and respect for his commandments. In the light of faith, the Lord will reveal his wisdom and show us what is necessary for salvation.

Such themes are important, but the book's emphasis on private devotion and strong affective piety (a major current of late medieval spirituality) needs to be adapted to post-Vatican II sensitivities, in which devotion to the Blessed Sacrament is considered an extension of communal liturgical celebrations. To appreciate them, we should view the author's insights on the Eucharist in their historical perspective. By doing so, contemporary readers can appreciate his presentation of Eucharistic devotion as an integration of the purgative, illuminative, and unitive ways.

Observations

Today's readers of The Imitation's teaching on the Eucharist should keep in mind ten points that are as true today as they were for Kempis' audience over 600 years ago.

We have an open invitation to live in intimate communion with the Lord. This invitation is extended most clearly in the Eucharist, when we receive the body and blood of Jesus in Holy Communion. It is important, however, that we prepare ourselves. Most of us do not have to travel far to enter into Our Lord and Savior's presence. Jesus makes himself present in the form of bread and wine; we should receive him with proper reverence and respect.

We should not take this sacrament for granted. In the past, many stayed away because they feared receiving the Eucharist unworthily; today many seem to receive it without examining the state of their souls. We reverence the Lord by preparing ourselves to receive his body and blood. Even a short prayer before Mass begins or as we approach in the communion line can help us ready ourselves for the gift we are about to receive.

When we invite guests to our home, we make sure to make it clean and orderly before they arrive. We must do the same for Jesus when he comes into our hearts. Although we cannot make ourselves worthy of so great a gift, we must do our best to offer him what we can. Even though we are poor and undeserving, we must offer him our best hospitality. It is important to cleanse our hearts and open them to the gentle breeze of the Spirit. After we receive the body and blood of Our Lord, we should keep our hearts open through heartfelt prayers and fervent petitions.

We should approach the altar with reverence and humility. We should be sorry for our sins and other daily lapses. In the depths of our hearts, we should confess our sins to the Lord. There are so many things we should regret, from a lack of forgiveness to distraction in prayer to not carrying out our resolutions. Before we receive Holy Communion, we should examine our hearts and ask God's forgiveness for our sins and failings. In this way the sacrament we are about to receive can bring about a gradual conversion in our lives.

The Eucharist is the remedy for every spiritual illness. When we receive it with devotion, our bad habits are gradually healed, our unruly passions calmed, our temptations lessened, our virtues quickened. The graces we receive confirm us in faith, strengthen us in hope, and deepen our love for God and neighbor. Those who eat and drink the body and blood of Christ are slowly transformed into new persons. Having acknowledged our weaknesses and limitations, we are filled with gratitude for all the good things that come from the Lord.

We are nurtured by the Eucharist and by doctrine, especially as it comes to us through Sacred Scripture. Upon these two tables are set the treasure of the Church's living tradition. Nourished by the Eucharist and by the living Word, we are incorporated into the Body of Christ. Holy Communion imparts the wisdom of Christ's living body, which enables us to hear the Lord's voice in the events of daily life and to rejoice with the saints for God's many gifts. Listening to God's Word and consuming his body and blood are the most important acts we can perform. Priests should take their ministry at the two tables seriously. With God's help, they can lead others into an even deeper appreciation of the Lord's banquet.

If we wish to be Christ's disciples we must offer ourselves to God with all our hearts. Jesus held nothing back from the Father when he offered himself on the cross for our sins. To be like him, we must follow his example. He desires nothing else from us. Everything we do must be involved in this offering of self to Christ. The Eucharist draws us into communion with Christ's own total offering of self. It gives us the grace to do what we cannot accomplish alone. Through it, we can transcend our weaknesses and love as Christ loves.

To live in such an intimate union, we need to open our hearts and converse with Jesus. Such a conversation can take place, however, only if we acknowledge our weaknesses and in humility and truth place them before the Lord. If we pretend to be what we are not, the Lord will not enter into conversation with us. If we come to him with pure and humble hearts, he will come to us, acknowledge us as his friends, and dwell within us.

We should never be afraid to bring our needs to the Lord. Even though he already knows what we will say, nothing can replace our own words and petitions. Bringing our needs to the Lord and asking for the graces we need to grow in virtue and holiness demonstrates our trust in God. If we do not believe our prayers will be heard and answered, why should we bring our needs to the Lord? We do so because we have confidence that he hears our prayers and will provide for us as a father does for his children. We may not get exactly what we ask for, but we always get what we need for our spiritual growth.

Finally, we should tell the Lord of our deep desire for holiness. Like Mary, who proclaimed the greatness of the Lord in her humble *fiat*, and like John the Baptist, who leapt for joy in his mother's womb at the coming of the Lord, we too should sing the praises of Jesus, our Lord and Savior. We do this best by participating in the Eucharistic celebration with fervent love and devotion. The Eucharist is the sacrament of Christian holiness. As we approach the altar, we have good reason to leap for joy and sing God's praises. If we offer our hearts to the Lord in this sacrament, he promises to draw them deep into his own and gradually transform them.

Conclusion

The Imitation of Christ is considered a classic of Western spirituality not because it is still widely read or because it has the same literary freshness as when it was first composed or because its spiritual message has the same relevance and immediacy today that it did over six centuries ago. It is a classic because it still can deepen readers' desire for an intimate friendship with Christ.

Each generation needs to interpret the great spiritual classics for itself. *The Imitation of Christ* is no exception. Although its spirituality is tied to the historical and religious climate from which it sprang, its message continues to attract those who manage to peer beneath its late-medieval veneer. For those who do so, Thomas à Kempis connects them with the great themes of the gospel through his meditations and leads them through the stages of spiritual growth to a face-to-face encounter with Jesus Christ himself.

These meditations offer guidelines for anyone's spiritual journey. They outline the purgative, illuminative, and unitive ways and integrate them into a dynamic process of conversion that leads away from self-centeredness to total dedication to God. As the source and summit of Christian life, the Eucharist brings about this gradual transformation and movement toward sanctity.

Reflection Questions

- Kempis considers the Eucharist to be the culmination of a believer's spiritual journey. Where are you on this journey? What progress have you made? Where have you fallen short? What has helped you in this journey? What has been the role of the Eucharist in your journey?

- Kempis reminds us of the unfathomable nature of the Eucharist. What does this statement imply about the nature of God? Why can the human mind never exhaust the mystery of the sacrament? How do feel, knowing that you will never be able to grasp its full meaning?

- Kempis says we should ready our hearts before receiving Holy Communion. How do you ready yourself to commune with Jesus? What do you ask of the Holy Spirit? What practices have you found most useful for preparing your heart to receive Jesus?

Voice Fourteen

Ignatius of Loyola: Informing Daily Life

> One of the most admirable effects of Holy Communion is to preserve the soul from sin, and to help those who fall through weakness to rise again. It is much more profitable, then, to approach this divine Sacrament with love, respect, and confidence, than to remain away through an excess of fear and scrupulosity.
>
> *Ignatius of Loyola*

Our next voice on the Eucharist had an enormous impact of the church of his day and still does now. This towering figure of early modern Catholicism, founder of the Society of Jesus, wrote a classic work on spiritual direction. A man of deep passion and love for the life and mission of Jesus, he sought to give glory to God in all things and to enable others to do the same. Through his *Spiritual Exercises* he created a language by which people could discern their calling and be faithful disciples of Jesus in their everyday lives. His teaching on the Eucharist reflects a contemplative yearning to receive Christ and to let this relationship overflow into his day-to-day actions.

A Life of Conversion

Born in 1491 to the noble northern Spanish Loyola family, Ignatius (1491–1556) was raised and educated to be a soldier. At the age of thirty, however, his military career ended when he suffered a serious leg wound during the Battle of Pamplona. While convalescing at the Loyola family castle, reading the lives of the saints brought about in him a deep spiritual conversion. As a result he decided to disown all worldly pursuits and dedicate his life to doing glorious and holy deeds for God.

This desire deepened during an eleven-month retreat at Manresa, where his spiritual depth and insight deepened and the meaning of his vocation matured. During this time, he was blessed with mystical insights that shaped his spirituality. After a pilgrimage to the Holy Land, including Jerusalem, Bethlehem, and Jericho, he returned to Spain understanding that his apostolic pursuits needed a firm academic background. From 1524–1535 he studied at Alaclá, Salamanca, and Paris.

In Paris he shared his ideals and spiritual vision with others. On the feast of the Assumption, August 15, 1535, he and six of his friends vowed themselves to poverty in Christ, the spiritual welfare of others, and loyalty to the pope. From this small group of devoted followers emerged the Society of Jesus. On June 24, 1537, they received Holy Orders in Venice, where they were waiting for passage to the Holy Land. Because the impending war with the Turks made travel impossible, the group eventually made its way to Rome to put themselves at the service of the pope.

During the next nineteen years in Rome, Ignatius devoted himself to establishing, organizing, and governing the new Society. During what may have been the most fruitful period in his life, he received many deep mystical experiences and with even greater clarity saw his call to do all things for the greater glory of God. During this period he also generated his most productive literary output: the *Constitutions of Society of Jesus*, the *Spiritual Exercises*, his *Spiritual Diary*, an *Autobiography*, and well over 6,000 letters. Ignatius died in Rome on July 31, 1556, leaving behind a rich spiritual legacy and a religious order deeply committed to spread the gospel in hearts and minds of the faithful throughout the world. He is a great saint of early modern Catholicism and one of the greatest spiritual writers of all time.[1]

Ignatian Spirituality

Ignatius' spirituality is marked by a passionate desire to discern and carry out God's will. After his conversion, he tried very hard to understand what God wanted from him. Through prayer and intense self-reflection, he came to see God's hand in all events and circumstances, leading him to dedicate his life to helping others understand and follow their own personal callings. Over many years he developed his *Spiritual Exercises*, which reached their final shape between 1539–41. They offer a set of meditations rooted in personal experience, as well as guidelines designed to help others discern God's will. These exercises aimed to help people come to know, love, and serve the Lord with all their minds and hearts. In doing so, they would be giving glory to God and building up his kingdom both within their hearts and around them.

Ignatius' spiritual outlook was contemplation-in-action. He saw spiritual experience not as an end in itself but as a call to give glory to God through service to humanity. For him, contemplation and action were two sides of the same coin. Jesus lived this way while he walked the earth, and now bids his followers to do the same. The members of the Society of Jesus were called to meditate upon the life of Jesus and then follow in his footsteps. Like Jesus, they were to cultivate a contemplative attitude toward life and carry it with them in their apostolic endeavors. Ignatius refused to limit the Society to a single missionary task, be it education, the foreign missions, preaching retreats and missions, or parish work. He did not define the specifics so

---

1. The information in this section comes from George E. Ganss, ed., *Ignatius of Loyola: Spiritual Exercises and Selected Works, CWS* (New York/Mahwah, NJ: Paulist Press, 1991), 9–63.

that the process of discernment might unfold over time. He believed the Society's specific tasks would flow from their life of prayer and their insistence on following God's will. The vow of obedience to the pope also reflects the Society's deep pastoral concern, since he would be in a special position to know the Church's specific needs on a universal level. Ignatius understood the relationship between obedience and listening for God's will. He asked the members of the Society to empty themselves of self-will to be open to the will of God as they discern it in their own lives and as it is expressed by their religious superiors. In this way, he unleashed a tremendous spiritual force within the Church with strong repercussions that still resound today.

Ignatius desired to unite his will as well as his entire being to Christ and his Mystical Body, the Church. He sought to do all things *ad maiorem Dei gloriam* ("for the greater glory of God"). His yearning for this union is probably best expressed in a famous prayer from his *Spiritual Exercises*: "Take, Lord, and receive all my liberty, my memory, my understanding, and my entire will, all that I have and possess. Thou hast given all to me. To Thee, O Lord, I return it. Dispose of it wholly according to Thy will. Give me Thy love and Thy grace, for this is sufficient for me."[2] Ignatius considered the Eucharist to be the most immediate and practical way to affirm this desire and walk in communion with Christ.[3]

Ignatius on the Eucharist

Throughout his writings, Ignatius examines the Eucharist. His approach to the sacrament reflects the main themes of Jesuit spirituality, including method, trust in divine inspiration, meditation on the human life of Christ, the

---

2. Ignatius of Loyola, *Spiritual Exercises*, 234 in Ganss, ed., *Ignatius of Loyola*, 177
3. For a general synthesis of Ignatian spirituality and its influence on the early Jesuits, see John O'Malley, "Early Jesuit Spirituality: Spain and Italy," in *Christian Spirituality: Post-Reformation and Modern*, eds. Louis Dupré and Don E. Saliers (New York: Crossroad, 1989), 3–27.

ministry of the Word, world-affirmation, the importance of action, purity of intentions, spiritual combat, turning over one's will and affections to God, and total service to God and the Church.[4]

The Eucharist allows a person to enter into an intimate communion with Christ. It is a sacred moment, a special opportunity to place ourselves in God's hands and to renew our total offering of self to God's plan. It is important, therefore, to prepare properly before approaching the sacrament, to give full attention to its celebration, and afterwards to thank God for the graces received.

Ignatius emphasized the importance of frequent, even daily communion[5] as the means for entering an ever deeper and more intimate union with God. The Eucharist enables a person to continue being converted to God so as to walk more securely along the way to holiness.

Ignatius highlights his deep devotion to the sacrament in an entry from his *Spiritual Diary* dated February 23, 1545.[6] It begins with a reference to his meditation before Mass:

> While they were making the altar ready, Jesus presented Himself to my mind, and invited me to follow Him; for I am quite convinced that He is the head and guide of the Society, and that it is especially on this account that it ought to practice poverty and renunciation in the highest degree, though there are also other motives which I have considered in coming to a decision.[7]

As he vests, these insights move from his mind to his heart:

> While I thought of all this, and was vesting for Mass, my emotions increased. I saw in them a confirmation of the resolve I had taken; I had no other consolations. The Holy

---

4. See *MTCF*, 169–71.
5. See, for example, Ignatius' letter to Teresa Rejadell on frequent communion in Ganss, ed., *Ignatius of Loyola*, 339–41.
6. *RPA*, 115–16; Ganss, ed., Ignatius of Loyola, 248–49.
7. *RPA*, 115–16. See also Ganss, ed., *Ignatius of Loyola*, 248.

Trinity itself seemed to confirm my decision, as the Son communicated Himself thus to me, for I recalled to mind the time when the Father deigned to place me with His Son. When I was vested, the name of Jesus impressed itself upon me more and more.[8]

The experience extends into his celebration of the sacrament:

When I had begun the Holy Sacrifice, I received many graces and pious emotions and gentle tears, which lasted long. As the Mass continued, many inspirations confirmed what I had resolved; and when I raised the Sacred Host, I felt as it were an inward suggestion, and a powerful impulse never to abandon Our Lord, in spite of all obstacles; and this was accompanied by a new delight, and fresh impressions.[9]

His experience of Jesus at the Eucharist then overflows into the rest of his day: "This...lasted the whole time, even after Mass, and throughout the day. Whenever I thought of Jesus this pious feeling and fixed purpose returned to my mind."[10]

Ignatius attempted to burn his diary, which contains some of his most private thoughts and feelings, but it survived. It demonstrates how the Eucharist was central in his day, providing him with a focus for meditation that influenced his thoughts, feelings, and actions.[11]

Observations

This presentation offers only a glimpse into Ignatius' love for the Eucharist. The following remarks will explore his contemplative approach to the sacrament more closely and discuss its meaning and relevance today.

---

8. *RPA*, 116; Ganss, ed., Ignatius of Loyola, 248–49.
9. Ibid.
10. Ibid.
11. *Ibid.* 229.

Ignatius prepares carefully for celebrating the Eucharist. He would meditate on the life of Christ and reflect upon its meaning for his own. While reflecting on the Gospel, he quietly waits for some insight or inspiration concerning the issues facing him. He meditates in this way even as the altar is being prepared and as he vests. We too should spend some time in quiet prayer and reflection before we go to Mass so as to enter into the celebration of the sacrament. Doing so will help us recollect before God and appreciate what is about to take place. It will also let us rest in silence and listen to the Lord speaking deep within our hearts.

Ignatius' meditative prayer carries over into the celebration of the Eucharist itself, so much so that he seems to be praying at different levels at the same time. As he celebrates the Eucharist, the graces and inspirations he is receiving move him to tears. As he celebrates the sacrament, an important decision he had reached concerning the Society of Jesus was confirmed for him. As we approach the Eucharist, we too should recognize our levels of consciousness; God may move us deeply on one level even as we are performing attentively on another. If, like Ignatius, we open our hearts and allow the Spirit to move freely, God can also touch us deeply and affirm our decisions. Just as the Eucharist could connect with Ignatius' life, it can connect with ours.

Ignatius found that his experience at Eucharist overflowed into his daily life. His awareness of Christ's presence did not come to him in a single moment, but remained with him over a period of time. The Eucharist, therefore, informed his daily activities and influenced his conduct. It nurtured a contemplative attitude by which he could see God's presence in the circumstances of his life. As it did for Ignatius, the Eucharist can overflow into our daily lives only if we prepare our hearts and minds to receive it properly and allow it to inform our lives. A period of thanksgiving after receiving the Eucharist will help foster the attitudes for this to happen.

The Eucharist allowed Ignatius to renew each day by offering his memory, will, understanding, and affections to God. It provided him a sacred time and place in which God's body and blood could nourish his very being. Strengthened by this intimate communion with Jesus, he had the strength to focus on and carry out his mission. Ignatius could not be a contemplative-in-action without this deep Eucharistic dimension of his spirituality. His love for the sacrament should likewise inspire us. We too can place it at the center of our lives so as to live in close, personal communion with Jesus. The Eucharist then can overflow into our daily lives so that we, like Ignatius, become contemplatives-in-action by living the gospel on "a deep level of consciousness."[12]

Finally, the Ignatian ideal of doing everything for the greater glory of God originates in the Eucharist and flows from it. Ignatius realized that on his own he could do little (if anything) for God. He recognized that he must convert always and that without God's help his thoughts, words, and actions would be self-serving and full of pride. The Eucharist provides a visible, concrete way by which human beings are offered not only God's help, but also his very self. He could dream of doing everything for God, because he knew what God was doing for him through the sacrament. Because of the Eucharist, we too can dedicate everything in our lives to the glory of God. Like Ignatius, however, we can do so, only by humbly recognizing that we cannot do so by ourselves.

---

12. The phrase, which describes authentic Christian mysticism, comes from William Johnston, *Mystical Theology: The Science of Love* (London: HarperCollins, 1995), 9.

Conclusion

Ignatius of Loyola bequeathed to the Church and to the religious order he founded a spiritual legacy that had worldwide impact in his own day, and continues to do so today. His desire to do all things for the greater glory of God drove him to help men and women understand God's will for them, placing all things in God's providential care. His *Spiritual Exercises* are a rich resource for all—whatever their call in life—who seek to discern the way of holiness and walk in the company of Jesus.

Ignatius' insights into the spiritual life are rooted in his own cultural context; nevertheless, they can also serve believers living in different historical circumstances. Although not every aspect of his spiritual outlook applies the present age, it still has a distinctive presence in the lives of today's believers, particularly his teaching on the Eucharist.

Devotion to this sacrament was central to Ignatius' life. He prepared for it, celebrated it, and reflected upon it with attentive care. The highlight of his day, it overflowed throughout his life. He loved the Eucharist, the epitome of what it meant to give honor and glory to God. Ignatius' meditative and reflective approach to the Eucharist helped him discern God's will for himself and for the order he founded.

Today's believers can take this same approach. All who seek a contemplative attitude toward life and live the gospel on "a deep level of consciousness" should reflect upon Ignatius' passionate love for the sacrament and likewise place it in their own hearts. Only then will they understand what it means to live in close communion with Christ *ad maiorem Dei gloriam*.

Reflection Questions

- Ignatius cultivated the practice of meditating upon the life of Christ and reflecting upon its meaning for his own. Which scenes from Christ's life touch you the most? What have you discovered about Christ through them? What have you discovered about yourself?
- Ignatius' experience at Eucharist flowed over into his daily life. How can you carry the Lord with you when you leave Mass? How might the fruits of Holy Communion affect your daily actions?
- Ignatius' deep Eucharistic spirituality enabled him to be a contemplative-in- action. How might you develop a deep Eucharistic spirituality? What would such a spirituality mean for you? How would it affect your life? How would it change you?

Voice Fifteen

Teresa of Avila: Daily Bread

As His Majesty has already given His Son to us, by sending Him, of His will alone, into the world, so now, of that same will, He pleased not to abandon us, but to remain here with us for the greater glory of His friends and the discomfiture of His enemies. He prays for nothing more than this "today" since He has given us this most holy Bread. He has given it to us forever, as I have said, as the sustenance and manna of humanity. We can have it whenever we please and we shall not die of hunger save through our own fault, for in whatever way the soul desires to partake of food, it will find joy and comfort in this Most Holy Sacrament.

Teresa of Avila

Our next voice on the Eucharist, one of the great Christian mystics of all time, was a contemplative nun, religious reformer, monastic founder, spiritual writer, and poet. She lived in Spain during the period of early modern Catholicism, when Western Europe struggled amid reform and bitter religious rivalry. Her teaching on the Eucharist reveals her loyalty to the Catholic Church and roots her mysticism in a thoroughgoing sacramental realism.[1]

---

1. For a chronology of Teresa's life, see Victoria Lincoln, *Teresa: A Woman* (Albany, NY: State University of New York Press, 1984), xxv–xxix. For a relatively recent biography, see Cathleen Medwick, *Teresa of Avila: The Progress of a Soul* (New

A Religious Reformer

Teresa of Avila (1515–1582) was born Teresa Sánchez de Cepeda y Ahumadanear on her family's farm near Avila in central Spain on March 28, 1515. Her father, Alonso de Cepeda, was the son of a wealthy Jewish merchant from Toledo who had converted to Christianity. She entered the Carmelite Monastery of the Incarnation in Avila in 1535 and the following year professed her vows. In 1554, at the age of 39, two experiences that touched her deeply changed her outlook about her spiritual journey. In one, she felt Christ's healing and redeeming power while praying before a statue of the suffering Christ. The other was a deep sense of the Lord calling her as she read St. Augustine's account of his conversion in *Confessions*. A deep peace and sense of the Lord's abiding presence in her life helped her let go of her fears and worldly attachments and give herself entirely to the Lord's service.

Teresa's reputation as a reformer begins with these experiences of personal conversion, by which she brought her life into conformity with God's will. In September, 1560, dissatisfaction with life at the Monastery of the Incarnation led a small group of nuns to gather in her cell to share their dream of reforming their order. Despite opposition from other sisters in the monastery, the Carmelite order, and among the local townspeople, this reform gradually took root. With the support of Peter of Alcántara, Teresa gained permission from Rome and on August 24, 1562, in Avila, established a reformed monastery of Carmelites dedicated to St. Joseph. Her close friend and associate, St. John of the Cross (1542–1591), helped her bring the reform to the male branch of the order. He too, like Teresa, faced opposition at nearly every turn.

Teresa spent the rest of her life crisscrossing Spain to promote her reform. She established 14 reformed Carmelite

---

York: Doubleday, 1999).

monasteries and left behind a large body of works: *The Book of Her Life* (1562–65), *The Way of Perfection* (1562–69), *Meditations on the Song of Songs* (1567), *The Book of Foundations* (1573), and *Interior Castle* (1577). She died at Alba deTormes on October 4, 1582, was beatified in 1614, proclaimed patroness of Spain in 1617, canonized in 1622, and declared a doctor of the Church in 1970.[2]

Teresa's Spirituality

Intense suffering and periods of dryness as well as deep mystical experience made Teresa of Avila feel called to a life of conversion. Her teaching on prayer, which reflects these themes, is contained in works such as *Life*, *The Way of Perfection*, and *Interior Castle*. Because they were written at different times for diverse audiences and for distinctive purposes, it is difficult to form an overall synthesis of her spiritual doctrine.[3]

Over time, moreover, Teresa matured spiritually. Her insights into mystical prayer deepened as, drawing closer to God, she experienced the lasting inner peace of spiritual marriage. Readers, therefore, must expect certain inconsistencies between her earlier and later writings because of this growth. Nevertheless, her teaching on prayer, although not uniform at every point, has a remarkable coherence. She makes the classical distinctions between *oratio* (vocal prayer), *meditatio* (meditation or mental prayer), and *contemplatio* (contemplation), using them to develop a treatise

---

2. The historical information in this section comes from: Marcelle Auclair, *Teresa of Avila, The Vivid Dramatic Life Story of a Great Woman: Organizer, Foundress, Mystic, Saint*, trans. Kathleen Pond (New York: Pantheon Books, 1953), 439–45; NCE, s.v. "Teresa of Avila, St.," by O. Steggink; Kieran Kavanaugh, "Introduction," in Teresa of Avila, *The Interior Castle*, CWS, trans. Kieran Kavanaugh and Otilio Rodriguez (New York, Ramsey, Toronto: Paulist Press, 1979), 1–6.
3. For a brief description of Teresa's life and writings, see Dennis J. Billy, *Teresa of Avila, Interior Castle: The Classic Text with a Spiritual Commentary* (Notre Dame, IN: Christian Classics, 2007), 10–12.

on prayer rooted in experience and explained through metaphor.[4]

Nowhere does Teresa lay out the grades of prayer in a systematic and fully integrated way. All in all she identifies nine types: (1) Vocal prayer uses words to express our hearts and minds to God. (2) Meditation or mental prayer is "nothing but friendly intercourse, and frequent solitary converse, with him who we know loves us."[5] (3) Affective prayer brings meditation from the level of the head to that of the heart. (4) Acquired recollection is a simple, loving gaze upon a concrete representation of the divine (e.g., an icon, the tabernacle, the consecrated host). (5) Infused contemplation marks the beginning of mystical prayer in the life of the believer. (6) The prayer of quiet takes the person praying into an even deeper experience of God. (7) The prayer of union brings the person praying to an experience of the divine that is deeper yet. (8) Spiritual betrothal occurs when the divine light captivates the soul's external senses. (9) Spiritual marriage brings about the total absorption of the soul into God.[6]

These nine grades of prayer correspond to the beginning or "purgative" (grades one to four), the progressive or "illuminative" (grades five and six), and perfect or "unitive" ways (grades seven through nine). These "ways" or "stages" of the spiritual journey, however, do not always occur one after another. Usually they are mingled in a person's life and difficult to isolate. Detachment from worldly things, for example, although typically associated with the purgative

---

4. For a discussion of these categories, see Romano Guardini, *Prayer in Practice*, trans. Leopold of Loewenstein-Wertheim (New York: Pantheon, 1957), 120–57. For the last two categories, Guardini prefers the terms "inward" and "mystic" prayer.
5. Teresa of Avila, *Life*, chap. 8 in *The Complete Works*, trans. Kieran Kavanaugh and Otilio Rodriguez, vol. 1(Washington, D.C.: ICS Publications, 1976), 67.
6. Although Teresa does not specifically use the term "affective prayer," she certainly refers to this grade of prayer in chapters 13 and 14 of her *Life*. See *Teresa of Avila: The Collected Works*, trans. Kieran Kavanaugh and Otilio Rodriguez, vol. 1(Washington, D.C.: ICS Publications, 1976), 89–101. For more on the various stages of prayer, see Billy, *Teresa of Avila, Interior Castle*, 12–17.

way, is also necessary for growing in self-knowledge and acquiring wisdom, which are normally associated with the illuminative way. Each, in turn, is necessary for the intimate communion with God associated with the unitive way. For this reason and others, each of these stages may be dominant in a person's life at any particular moment and suggest the direction in which he or she is moving, i.e., toward or away from union with God. Determining this usually indicates a person's spiritual state.[7]

Teresa on the Eucharist

Teresa writes about the Eucharist at various places in her writings, most notably in *The Way of Perfection*, a commentary on the Lord's Prayer written for the nuns of St. Joseph's convent, where Teresa began her Carmelite reform movement.[8]

She writes about the Eucharist in chapters 33–35, commenting on the words, "Give us this day our daily bread."[9] She begins by saying that Jesus understood that doing God's will is difficult and so prays to the Father on our behalf. This prayer demonstrates his humility and deep love for us. It also reveals his desire to carry out the Father's will even more perfectly by giving himself to us not merely by dying on the cross, but also by becoming our very food and nourishment. Jesus himself is "our daily bread."[10] He identifies himself with our situation and offers himself to supply all our needs. By eating Jesus' body and blood, we enter into intimate communion with him and are given the strength to

---

7. The three stages or degrees of charity are nothing more than divisions that characterize in a general way the infinite variety of aspects in the Christian life. The path of the supernatural life is a winding path, and its stages offer a variety of transitions and levels that will differ with each individual. We must never think that the three basic stages are self-contained compartments, and that those who are at a given time in one stage will never participate in the activities of another stage." See Aumann, *Spiritual Theology*, 115–16.
8. Teresa of Avila, *The Way of Perfection* in *The Complete Works*, 2:37–204.
9. Ibid., 2:165–76.
10. Ibid., 2:166.

overcome temptations and to offer our lives to the Father as a living sacrifice.[11]

Teresa emphasizes Jesus' great humility in seeking how to do the Father's will with greater perfection. In the Eucharist, Jesus found a way to give us himself daily, even though it would mean each day being crushed and insulted by his enemies. For Teresa, the sacrament signifies that Jesus still offers himself to the Father on our behalf. By taking on human nature, he became one with us, making no distinction between himself and us. By becoming our very food and nourishment, he strengthens our bond with him as members of his body and enables us to join him each day in giving glory to his Father.[12]

His humility and deep love show that Jesus does not wish to abandon us, but to remain with us forever. In her commentary on the Lord's Prayer, Teresa writes that "daily" means "forever."[13] She applies this to the sacrament, saying that Jesus "has given us this most sacred bread forever."[14] Therefore, she suggests not to worry about material needs: "Have no fear that you will be in want of bread if you are not wanting in what you have said about the surrender of yourselves to God's will."[15]

We should be concerned only with serving our Lord, letting him supply our daily needs. The Eucharist, she adds, is a "great medicine" for both spiritual and bodily ills. Because of this sacrament, we too are living in the time of Christ and have easy access to his vital healing power.[16]

Teresa teaches with remarkable sacramental realism:

> Receiving Communion is not like picturing with the imagination, as when we reflect upon the Lord on the cross or

---

11. Ibid.
12. Ibid., 2:166–68.
13. Ibid., 2:168.
14. Ibid., 2:169.
15. Ibid., 2:170.
16. Ibid., 2:171.

in other episodes of the Passion, when we picture within ourselves how things happened to Him in the past. In Communion the event is happening now, and it is entirely true. There is no reason to go looking for Him in some other place farther away.[17]

She notes, moreover, that as long as the accidents of bread and wine remain Jesus remains in the Blessed Sacrament . When we receive it, Jesus is truly present within us. We therefore may have even greater access to him than when he walked the earth:

> Now, then, if when He went about in the world the mere touch of His robes cured the sick, why doubt, if we have faith, that miracles will be worked while He is within us and that He will give what we ask of Him, since He is in our house?[18]

When Jesus receives a hospitable welcome, Teresa says, he pays well for his lodging. That is why after receiving Communion, during the hour or so when he remains substantially present to us, we should converse with him in a deeply intimate way. Even though he comes to us in the form of bread and wine and speaks to us only in silence, the Lord is truly and personally present after we receive Communion. At such times, we should close our bodily eyes and open those of the soul and look deep within our hearts. Jesus will show himself only to those who relate to him as true friends from the depths of their hearts. Teresa therefore emphasizes conversing with him on familiar terms after receiving Communion. When we cannot receive him in the sacrament, she encourages us to make a spiritual communion so that the Lord will see how much we love him.[19]

---

17. Ibid., 2:172.
18. Ibid.
19. Ibid., 2:172–76.

Observations

The above presentation provides only the main contours of Teresa's teaching on the Eucharist and in no way exhausts the quality of its depth and insights. The following remarks seek to probe her teaching still further and highlight its relevance for today.

To begin, Teresa's teaching on the Eucharist emphasizes the humility of Christ's kenotic self-emptying. The Word of God took on human flesh in the Incarnation and gave himself completely to us through his passion and death on the cross; now he becomes our food, our nourishment. He does not have to do this, but does so to carry out the Father's will more fully. Through the Eucharist, Christ can extend the mystery of his redemptive suffering through time and become "daily bread" for the human heart. His humility provides a remedy for temptation and the effects of sin in our lives.

The insults and maltreatment Jesus receives in the Blessed Sacrament is a continuation of his passion and death. By becoming our Eucharistic bread, Jesus allows himself to be broken and crushed day after day. He also must put up with the insults of unbelievers and even maltreatment by some who believe in him. Teresa helps us connect Jesus' kenotic self-emptying in the Eucharistic bread and his suffering and death. When we partake of the sacrament, we share in Jesus' kenotic self-emptying and offer ourselves in loving service to others.

Teresa emphasizes Jesus' solidarity with all of humanity. By taking on our nature, Jesus has become fully human, like us in all things but sin. For this reason, he is able to lead us in prayer saying "*Our* Father" and asking for "*our* daily bread."[20] He intercedes as one of us, as someone who makes

---
20. Ibid., 2: 167–68.

no distinction between himself and the rest of humanity. As a result, his power of intercession takes on new dimensions, since what he asks of the Father on our behalf, the Father hears as a personal request of his Son. The Eucharist is a concrete sign of Jesus' intimate union with humanity. By becoming our food and drink, he assures us that he is one of us and that our concerns are his.

Teresa presents the Eucharist as a way that Jesus has found to remain with us each day. He does not abandon us, but remains ever present in the sacred bread and wine that are his body and blood. This heavenly manna helps us to keep our minds on heavenly things. It lets us put the difficulties of life in perspective and focus on the essential. It teaches us to set our wills on the things to come and recognize the transitory nature of this world. It helps us not to be anxious about our material needs and gives us the strength to bear every trial and persecution. By becoming our daily bread, Jesus has found a way to nourish our souls and shape them after his own heart.

Because Jesus himself experienced the heights of contemplative prayer, receiving Christ's body and blood fosters in us an appreciation for the life of prayer. His silence in the Blessed Sacrament makes us appreciate the silence within our own hearts and teaches us to quiet ourselves in order to listen for the movement of his Spirit within us. His presence hidden beneath the accidents of bread and wine makes us look beneath the appearances of things and to view the world with a deeper sense of its spiritual nature.

Because the Eucharist has power to heal, we should bring our physical and spiritual ills to the Lord. Since Jesus is substantially present in the Blessed Sacrament, it offers us the same physical and spiritual healings that he performed when he walked the earth. Examples from Teresa's own experience point out the sacrament's power to heal and remind us that with God all things are possible. The Eucharist is a medicine that can cure our ills and make us whole. The heavenly food the Lord gives us will meet our every need.

Because the Lord is present in the Eucharist, Teresa urges a prayerful attitude after receiving the sacrament. Since Christ is truly present in the bread and wine, we should open our hearts to him after Communion. Since Christ is substantially present within us as long as the accidents of the bread and wine remain intact, we should recognize the honor God has bestowed on us by entering the tabernacle of our hearts and dwelling within us. Recipients should quiet themselves after Communion so their hearts can be more in tune with Lord's presence and open to the promptings of the Spirit.

Teresa's sacramental realism enables her to distinguish between Jesus' real presence within us after receiving Communion and using prayerful imagination to picture him in our minds. Because Jesus is truly present, we do not need images as aids to prayer, nor need we wonder what it was like when he walked the earth. His presence in the sacrament guarantees our real and immediate access to him and encourages us to bring to him our needs. Even though he disguises himself under the appearance of bread and wine, our instincts of faith let us place our hope in him.

The Eucharist makes us true, intimate friends of Jesus. Jesus' ultimate gift of himself in the Blessed Sacrament encourages us to receive him and to converse with him about what really matters. By opening our hearts in this way and revealing our innermost thoughts and desires, we invite him into our heart to share its burdens in a way we never thought possible. Jesus gives us his undivided loving attention in the Eucharist, inviting us to do the same by spending time before him and sharing with him as one close friend to another. In this way, the Eucharist helps us to nourish our relationship with Christ and turn it into a deep, lasting friendship.

Finally, because of our mutual friendship with Jesus, we should make a spiritual communion when we cannot receive him sacramentally. The bond of friendship is so important that we long for physical closeness to Jesus even when circumstances make it difficult or impossible to receive him. Because we can talk to Jesus anytime or anywhere, we can ask him to enter our hearts spiritually and strengthen our bond of friendship with him. By doing so, we enter into a deeper communion with him and prepare our hearts for our next reception of Holy Communion or visit with him before the tabernacle.

Conclusion

We cannot assimilate all of Teresa's teaching on the Eucharist, let alone explain it. But we can establish a dialogue with her words that will let us enter her world and understand at least partially what the Eucharist meant to her. Doing so will let us understand Teresa's teaching and apply it to our own journey to God.

For Teresa the Eucharist is a gift from Jesus that continues his act of kenotic self-emptying through time and—with those who believe in him, trust him, and receive him—forges an intimate bond of divine and human friendship. The Eucharist is a visible sign of God's hidden love, a sign that, when received, enters and takes root deep in our souls. The Blessed Sacrament makes us blessed. It leads us to holiness rooted in God's love for humanity and to the bond of friendship he desires to establish with us.

Reflection Questions

- In the Eucharist, Teresa says, Jesus found a way of giving himself to us daily. How does the Eucharist express Jesus' humility? How does it express his love for humanity? How does receiving the Eucharist help you become more like Jesus?

- Teresa says that "daily" means "forever." What does receiving Jesus as our daily bread teach us about the nature of his love for us? How can the Eucharist transform your relationship with others?

- Teresa says that Jesus' presence in the Blessed Sacrament gives us greater access to him than when he walked the earth. How could you strengthen your contact with Jesus? When you are troubled how can Jesus in the Blessed Sacrament help you?

Voice Sixteen

John of the Cross: Living Fountain

The eternal source hides in the Living Bread
That we with life eternal may be fed
Though it be night.

Here to all creatures it is crying, hark!
That they should drink their fill though in the dark,
For it is night.

This living fount which is to me so dear
Within the bread of life I see it clear
Though it be night.

John of the Cross

Our next voice on the Eucharist is a poet, mystic, spiritual writer, theologian, and religious founder. A doctor of the Church and a member of the male branch of the Discalced Carmelite order (which he founded with Teresa of Avila), he dedicated his life to mapping the inner pathways of the soul's mystical search for God. His legacy that includes the *Spiritual Canticle* (1578), *The Dark Night of the Soul* (1578–79), *The Ascent of Mount Carmel* (1581–85), and *The Living Flame of Love* (1585–86). His spiritual vision revolves around the conviction that the soul must empty itself through a series of active and passive nights (or purgations) before God can fill it, bringing it to the heights of mysticism. His teaching on the Eucharist reflects this conviction and shows how he understands the path to holiness.

Carmelite Reformer

John of the Cross (1542–1591) was born John de Yepes y Alvarez at Fontiveros near Avila in the central plateau of old Castile. He received his early education at the College of the Children of Doctrine run by Augustinian nuns. Eventually he was taken under the tutelage of Don Alonso Alvarez of Toledo, who secured him a position at a smallpox hospital at Medina del Campo. In 1555 he enrolled at the newly founded Jesuit college, where he began to study for the priesthood.

In 1563 John entered the novitiate of the Carmelite Order in the local College of St. Anne and at his religious profession received the name John of St. Matthias. In 1564, he was sent to the Carmelite College of St. Andrew at Salamanca to finish his studies in scholastic theology and philosophy. In 1576 he was appointed "master of students," lectured to the seminarians of the Carmelite college, and was ordained a priest.

At one point, John's longing for solitude tempted him to leave the Carmelites and join the Carthusians, an order of hermits known for their intense austerity and discipline. Persuaded by Teresa of Avila not to follow through on this desire, he eventually became her confessor and spiritual director at the monastery of the Incarnation in Avila. He joined her in leading a reform at Incarnation and at other monasteries of the Carmelite order.

In 1577, he was abducted and incarcerated in Toledo by members of the Mitigated Carmelite Observance, who had outlawed this reform movement as dangerous and subversive. Refusing to recant, he was left in the darkness of his tiny cell, from which he plotted a daring escape a year later. During his imprisonment John wrote his *Spiritual Canticle*, the first of many poems and treatises on the spiritual life that have become classics in Western mystical literature. At this time he also reaffirmed his commitment to the Carmelite reform, to which he dedicated the rest of his life.[1]

John's Spirituality

John's writings convey his appreciation of divine transcendence and his sense of awe at God's infinite majesty. God, he writes, is a "living flame of love"; its brightness blinds the soul. Because the soul perceives the Divine Light as Darkness, it needs grace to adapt its spiritual eyes to God's incomprehensible and inaccessible brightness. John insists that we purify ourselves of all earthly influences and desires before we can enter the Lord's presence.[2]

At the same time, his spiritual outlook is realistic. He understands our capacity for self-deception and exposes the illusions that can captivate us and easily lead us astray. He also realizes human weakness, and our penchant for grasping apparent goods rather than seeking what truly benefits us. Therefore, he seeks to strip readers of their masks and pretensions so that they can see themselves truly.[3]

John's spiritual outlook is also ascetical. For him, the Christian life involves arduous training and preparation. The mystical life is a gratuitous gift from God, but these extraordinary graces are often found among those dedicated to lives of prayer, penitence, and fasting. Like all those who journey, Christians must start at the beginning and must

---

1. For an outline of the life of John of the Cross and a general introduction to his writings, see *The Complete Works of Saint John of the Cross*, trans. and ed. E. Allison Peers, 3 vols. (Wheathampstead—Hertfordshire: Anthony Clarke, 1978), xvii–lxiii. My quotations from this translation have, at times, been slightly changed in order to produce a more fluid English style. See also *The Collected Works of St. John of the Cross*, trans. Kieran Kavanaugh and Otilo Rodriguez (Garden City, NY: Doubleday, 1964), 16–37; St. John of the Cross, *The Dark Night of the Soul*, trans. Kurt F. Reinhardt, (New York: Frederick Ungar Publishing Co., 1957), xv–xxv.
2. See E. Allison Peers, *Spirit of Flame: A Study of St. John of the Cross* (Wilton, CT: Morehouse-Barlow Co., 1946), 199–201.
3. Ibid., 201–3.

live through the purgative dimension of the threefold way of purgation, illumination, and union.[4]

John's outlook is also mystical. Although at the end of life all will see God face-to-face, some experience beatitude (even if imperfect) in the here-and-now. By examining first the end of human existence, he instills the hope that one day we will experience God in his essence, if not in the present, in the life to come. Himself blessed with deep mystical experience, John carefully maps the unchartered regions of the soul to help others through his experience.[5]

John emphasizes the transcendent nature of the divine while appreciating God's immanence. He unmasks human foibles while revering humanity's noble origins. He expounds the difficulties pilgrims face while reveling in humanity's mystic destiny. His spiritual outlook is obscure and enigmatic, yet purposeful, direct, and refreshing. His teaching on the Eucharist is the same.

John on the Eucharist

At a number of places in his writings John refers to the Eucharist. He warns beginners in the spiritual life to avoid approaching the sacrament solely out of a desire for sensory or pleasurable delights. Those unaware of their great unworthiness may receive the sacrament when not properly prepared or even in the state of serious sin. They should submit themselves to the directions of their confessors and spiritual directors, lest they presume to act on their own opinions. Those who thus approach the sacrament unworthily receive little, if any fruit from it.[6]

Such recipients, he goes on, treat God poorly:

> [T]hey have not realized that the least of the benefits which come from this Most Holy Sacrament is that which concerns

---
4. Ibid., 203–4.
5. Ibid., 204–7.
6. John of the Cross, *Dark Night of the Soul*, 1.6.5 in *The Complete Works*, 1.345–46.

John of the Cross: Living Fountain

the senses; and that the invisible part of the grace that it bestows is much greater; for, in order that they may look at it with the eyes of faith, God often withholds from them these other consolations and sweetnesses of sense.[7]

John insists that the Eucharist be approached with the eyes of faith and that God not be considered as familiar or easily accessible, thus available to the physical senses. Not approaching the Eucharist through faith reduces God's mystery to tangible reality and causes recipients to not acknowledge the invisible reality to which the sacrament points and discloses.

Elsewhere, John describes the darkness of faith that those making progress in the spiritual life may experience:

> I gaze on Thee, to assuage my pain, / Beneath the sacramental veils, / Yet even here my spirit fails / Because Thy Self I cannot gain.[8]

Despite this darkness, the Eucharist gives a knowledge of God that satisfies the heart and brings joy to the soul:

> Call'd to this living fount, we creatures still
> Darkly may feed hereon and take our fill,
> Although 'tis night.[9]

Faith enables us to appreciate the Eucharist for what it is and to see despite the darkness:

> This living fount which is so dear to me
> Is in the bread of life, which now I see,
> Although 'tis night.[10]

---

7. Ibid.
8. John of the Cross, *Poems* (*Verses of the soul that craves to see God*), 5.5 in *The Complete Works*, 2.428.
9. John of the Cross, *Poems* (*Song of the soul that rejoices to know God by faith*), 8.10 in *The Complete Works*, 2.432.
10. Ibid., 8.11; 2.432.

John knows that some will reject his teaching. Just as many refused to believe Jesus when he said that he would feed them with his own flesh and blood, worldly people not interested in the things of the spirit cannot see the great mystery that the Eucharist discloses in the darkness and obscurity of faith.[11]

Even those who reject John's teaching, however, should acknowledge the Eucharist's power to move the human heart. The New Testament provides evidence of this. After some of his disciples left on account of this difficult teaching, Jesus turned to his apostles and asked them if they too would leave. Peter responded on their behalf, "Lord, where shall we go, for you have the words of eternal life?"[12]

Observations

The above presentation provides only a brief summary of John of the Cross's teaching on the Eucharist and in no way exhausts its quality and depth of insight. The following remarks seek to probe his teaching still further and highlight its relevance for today.

John exhorts us to not take the Eucharist for granted, but to treat it with reverence and respect. Each time we celebrate the sacrament, a great miracle takes place in our midst: a God of infinite majesty humbles himself for our sake by turning bread and wine into his own body and blood. Although we cannot physically see this miracle, our faith tells us that in the Eucharist God enters our world in an intimate, personal, and substantial way. Therefore, we should realize the greatness of the gift God has given us in the sacrament and our unworthiness to receive it. We can do nothing to deserve the Eucharist. The sacrament is a total, utter gift, and we should approach it with deep gratitude for all that God has done for us.

---

11. John of the Cross, *Living Flame of Love*, 1.5 in *The Complete Works*, 3.19
12. Ibid., 1.6 in *The Complete Works*, 3.19. See also Jn 6:69.

Beneath the external appearances of bread and wine, moreover, lies the mystery of the Eucharist. It draws us to ever deeper levels of experience, even to the inner regions of the soul where God can be found in the dark light of faith. Apparent goods like momentary pleasures and passing delights easily come and go but provide no true spiritual nourishment. The Eucharist takes us to our True Good by offering us intimacy with the God who created us, redeemed us, and now sanctifies us. Such intimacy, however, comes at a price. To possess God we must let go of all external and internal attachments through a process of purgation known as the Dark Night. The Eucharist is a living flame of love that burns the soul and purges it of all that is not of God.

The Eucharist offers something at each stage of the spiritual journey: the purgative, illuminative, and unitive. The purgative stage of the spiritual life, marked by asceticism and detachment, gradually instills the capacity to lead a life of virtue characteristic of the illuminative. These, in turn, ready us for the gifts of the Spirit, which give us a connatural knowledge of God and enable us to respond moment by moment to the Spirit's inspirations. John focuses most of his attention, however, on the mystical, face-to-face experience of God that comes in the unitive stage. He does so because of his reflection on his own mystical experience and his desire to let readers glimpse the summit of the spiritual life so that they will be able to recognize God's gifts when they are bestowed.

The Eucharist is linked with the sacrament of reconciliation. Communion should not be received if confessors or spiritual directors do not approve, since they can sense our strengths, weaknesses and sinfulness before God and can understand our spiritual makeup in ways that we cannot. It would be imprudent for us to disregard their counsel and follow our own opinion on such matters. Such acts of spiritual immaturity demonstrate disrespect for the sacrament. The important link between the Eucharist and the sacrament of reconciliation needs to be reaffirmed and strengthened. John's teaching reminds us of the importance of disclosing our inner lives to our confessors and spiritual directors, of pondering their advice, and of taking it to heart.

John recognizes that the Eucharist can be a stumbling block for faith. More than once, many of Jesus' followers abandoned him when he told them how his own flesh would become Living Bread for life eternal. Those who reject Jesus' teaching reject Jesus himself and lose a great source of hope and nourishment. Although challenging, belief in the Eucharist is a grace given by God. John is confident that the sacrament has the power to convert those who open their hearts and minds to the possibility that God's ways are not human ways and that with God all things are possible. Reason cannot plumb the mystery of the Eucharist or map its causes and effects. Those who reject it may have too narrow an understanding of reality or too limited a sense of the rational. John's mystical teaching on the sacrament demonstrates the limits of reason concerning the supernatural; the mystery of the Eucharist must be viewed through the darkened mirror of faith.

Life's goal is to partake in the divine nature. This requires, however, a series of purgations that will cleanse us of our false attachments and sinful impurities. John realizes that the Eucharist puts us in direct contact with this divine nature, but is equally aware that we are ill-prepared to benefit fully from this contact. Many Eucharistic recipients do not appreciate the gift that they have consumed; many lose heart because they feel no tangible effects from receiving the sacrament; still others have their internal, spiritual senses blinded by the intensity of the divine light and experience its brilliance as a dark obscurity. Only those who have undergone the suffering of the dark night of the senses and of the soul can partake fully of the divine nature.

John also realizes that a perfect sharing in the divine nature can only take place in heaven. In the present life we can hope at most for a faint taste of it. Even imperfect beatitude is enough to fill us with a sense of God's personal and intimate love. Its divine light bathes our minds, wills, internal senses of memory and imagination, even our external senses, moving us out of and beyond ourselves into an authentic, yet fleeting experience of the divine. The Eucharist holds out the promise of both imperfect and perfect beatitude. It brings the fullness of the divine life into our midst and at each stage of our journey leads us into God. John's teaching on the Eucharist lies at the center of his mystical theology. It is the essential means God uses to lead us by his grace into ever deeper experiences of his love.

John expresses his deep reverence and regard for the mystery of the Eucharist through his poetry, in which he juxtaposes images to suggest the indescribable nature of the mystical experience. He speaks, for example, of the "living fount" that he sees so clearly in the midst of night "within the bread of life."[13]

Although trained in scholasticism and capable of making clear theological distinctions, he uses poetry to convey his deepest spiritual insights into the meaning and nature of the Eucharist. He writes of how "the eternal fount is hidden in living bread"[14] and comes to light only in the dark night of faith. In John's mystical poetry, the Eucharist is an enigmatic reality that simultaneously discloses and obscures.

---

13. John of the Cross, *Poems (Song of the soul that rejoices to know God by faith)*, 8.11 in *The Complete Works*, 2.432.
14. Ibid., 8.9; 2.432.

The soul must become passive before God in order to be open to the gifts of divine light, yet John rejects a false quietism that requires the soul to annihilate any movements of the will that originate in the self. The Eucharist transforms both the lower and higher powers of the soul so that they can act with energy and freedom. God does not destroy our self-will, but transforms it so that it will act in harmony with the inspirations of the Spirit and the movement of divine grace. John considers the Eucharist to be the major means that God uses to achieve that purpose. For this to happen, however, we must cooperate with grace and work for our salvation. Although receptivity is required to reach the heights of spiritual ecstasy, John's mysticism requires an active passivity that seeks not to limit the powers of the soul, but to open them up to the movements of divine grace.

John's teaching on the Eucharist must be viewed in the context of his entire theological and spiritual vision—and vice versa. Many of John's mystical writings simply presuppose the sacramental life of the Church as the foundation for a life of faith and a deepening relationship with God. John's reverence for and devotion to the Eucharist derives from his Catholic roots and his conviction that in Catholic faith is contained the fullness of God's revelation. For this reason, his mystical vision is bound up with his faith and the sacramental beliefs and practices upon which it is based. In his vision, his fundamental beliefs about God's providential plan for humanity are linked with the great healing and transforming power of the sacraments. John's mystical vision, in other words, flows from the doctrinal and moral teachings of the Catholic faith and continues its sacramental practices, especially those relating to the Holy Eucharist.

Conclusion

John of the Cross was one of the great mystics of early modern Catholicism. His challenging prose and poetry are noted for their vivid imagery of the spiritual life and their capacity to inspire us to deepen our relationship with God through a dedicated life of prayer.[15] They depict the mystical life as the fruit of a harrowing journey through a process of purgation steeped in suffering that leads to profound spiritual delight.

John teaches that the soul in search of God is gradually cleaned of its sinful impurities and learns to let go of its attraction to apparent goods and inordinate attachments. In time, it begins to focus its energies more and more on its relationship with God and makes progress in the virtuous life and the life of prayer. In the later stages of its journey to God, the soul becomes more receptive to divine grace and the promptings of the Holy Spirit. The transition from purgation to illumination and then to union requires a cleansing or purgation that he refers to as the "Dark Night of the Senses" and the "Dark Night of the Soul."

John considers the Eucharist to be an accompaniment at every stage of our spiritual journey. Although our spiritual depth and maturity may not be enough to reap the full benefits of the sacrament and at times may even be blinded by the sacrament's intense, penetrating light, our simple faith and God's grace working in our lives make it a source of strength and consolation. The Eucharist, for John, is the "Living Bread" that nourishes us and leads us into the mystery of God's inner life. If we do not take it for granted but approach it with reverence, faith, and devotion, our darkness will be turned into light and we will be led, in this life or the next, to the heights of spiritual ecstasy.

---

15. For the principal figures of speech used by John of the Cross, see *The Complete Works*, 3.449–51.

Reflection Questions

- John says that the Eucharist discloses a great mystery in the darkness and obscurity of faith. What does he mean? What can you do to treat the sacrament more reverently? How can you keep before you the mystery that the Eucharist is seeking to reveal, even as you receive it frequently?

- The Eucharist draws us to ever deeper levels of experience and leads us to explore the inner regions of the soul. What aspects of your inner life might the sacrament help you to understand? When has it enabled you to delve beneath the level of appearances and plumb the depths of your heart?

- For John, the goal of life is to partake in the divine nature. How has the Eucharist helped you in this regard? How has it cleansed you? How has it enlightened you? How has it brought you into intimate contact with the Lord? To what extent has it led you, even now, to have a faint share in the divine nature?

Voice Seventeen

Francis de Sales: Health of the Soul

> So far I have not mentioned the most important and sacred of all devotions, namely the sacrifice and sacrament of the Mass. The Mass lies at the very heart of the Christian religion and devotion, a most wonderful mystery, containing within itself the fountainhead of love, and is the chief means used by God in pouring out upon us his graces and favors.
>
> *Francis de Sales*

Our next voice on the Eucharist helped implement the reforms of the Council of Trent. Bishop of Geneva during the Protestant Reformation, a time of great turmoil in the Church, his reputation for sanctity earned him renown as a spiritual master. This prolific author concentrated on living the devout life in everyday circumstances. He considered the Eucharist to be indispensable for the sanctification of the faithful.

Master of the Devout Life

Francis de Sales (1567–1622) was born into one of the great aristocratic families of Savoy. He studied at the college of Clermont in Paris and later at the University of Padua, where he received a doctorate in law in 1592. A deepening religious conversion that began during his student days in Paris led him to decide to forgo a promising career in the courts and magistracy of Savoy and to remain celibate. Led instead by his heart's desire, he dedicated himself to the Blessed Mother, took a vow of chastity, and entered ecclesiastical life. He was ordained in 1593 and became Provost of the Chapter of Geneva. In 1602 he was consecrated bishop of Geneva and with Jane Frances de Chantal helped found the women's Order of the Visitation of Holy Mary (Visitandines) in 1610.

Francis was known as a master of the devout life and was recognized for his great apostolic zeal, manifested in preaching, hearing confessions, caring for the sick, and writing profound spiritual treatises. He was canonized by Pope Alexander VII in 1665 and declared a Doctor of the Church by the Pope Pius IX in 1877. His teaching on the Eucharist reflects his love for God and desire to serve the Church and all its members.[1]

Francis' Spirituality

A pillar of Francis' spirituality was his conviction that everyone in the Church is called to holiness. This belief was manifested in his apostolic works as bishop of Geneva: religious instructions for all the laity in his diocese (both young and old), sensible spiritual and pastoral guidelines for priests, and reform of the religious communities under his care, particularly the Order of the Visitation. This community was established for young women and widows who felt called to religious life but not to the rigors of the more established orders. Francis' conviction about the universal call to holiness is also reflected in his own simple lifestyle of plain food, simple dress, and frugal living. It was pointless, he believed, to ask others to strive for holiness if he did not do so himself. His desire to bring others to Christ that

---

1. See *DM*, s.v. "Francesco di Sales," by A. Pedrini; *WDCS*, s.v. "Francis de Sales, St.," by Gordon S. Wakefield.

began with himself spread to the priests, religious, and laity of his diocese—and beyond.[2]

Francis' prophetic insight about the universal call to holiness was embraced by the Church in the teachings of the Second Vatican Council. He envisioned the spiritual life as a struggle with our lower nature, to be dealt with by uniting our will with God's through love and through ascetical practices. Both are necessary in the quest for holiness. He emphasized the role of love in the spiritual journey and considered penance an expression of our desire to be of one heart and mind with God. The entire goal of human existence, he believed, was to live in union with God through faithfulness to his will.[3]

In his writings, including the well-known *Introduction to the Devout Life* (1606) and *Treatise on the Love of God* (1616), Francis encourages readers to keep their eyes on Christ at all times so that they might always think and act as he did. As a practical way of following Christ, he suggests calling to mind the divine presence, making the right intention for our actions, and speaking often to God through short, heartfelt prayers. He also recommends attending Mass frequently, Communion, and devotion to Jesus's presence in the Most Holy Sacrament.[4]

Francis on the Eucharist

Although Francis often discusses the Eucharist, he expresses himself most clearly in Part Two of *Introduction to the Devout Life*, especially chapters fourteen, twenty, and

---

2. See Jozef Strus, "Salesian Spirituality," in *CSp*, 2:195–209; *NCDS*, s.v. "Salesian Spirituality," by Joseph F. Chorpenning;
3. See *DM*, s.v. "Francesco di Sales," by A. Pedrini; *CE*, s.v. "St. Francis de Sales," by Raphael Pernin, http://www.newadvent.org/cathen/06220a.htm (accessed May 12, 2009).
4. For general overviews of Francis' spirituality, see Jordan Aumann, *Christian Spirituality and the Catholic Tradition* (San Francisco/London: Ignatius/Sheed & Ward, 1985), 211–17; Strus, "Salesian Spirituality " in *CSp*, 2:195–209. *NCDS*, s.v. "Salesian Spirituality," by Joseph F. Chorpenning.

twenty-one, where he writes respectively on attending Holy Mass, and when and how to receive Holy Communion.

In chapter fourteen, Francis describes the sacrifice of the Mass as "the sun of all spiritual exercises."[5] Nothing can compare to it.

> the center of the Christian religion, the heart of devotion and soul of piety, the ineffable mystery that comprises within itself the deepest depths of divine charity, the mystery in which God really gives himself and gloriously communicates his graces and favors to us.[6]

He advises to make every effort to attend daily Mass so that with the priest we might offer Jesus's sacrifice to the Father for ourselves and for the good of the whole Church. In doing so, we unite ourselves with the worship of the angels and of all the faithful in heaven and on earth. If you cannot attend Mass on a particular day, he advises making a fervent prayer to enter the Church in spirit.[7]

Later in this chapter, Francis remarks that assisting devoutly at Mass includes six steps: (1) As the priest says his opening prayers at the foot of the altar, we should prepare ourselves with him by placing ourselves in the presence of God, recognizing our sins, and asking for pardon. (2) When the priest goes to the altar, we should ponder our Lord's coming and his life in the world. (3) From the Gospel to the Creed, we should reflect on the Lord's preaching and be resolved to live and die in accordance with his holy Word. (4) From the Gospel to the Our Father we should also apply our hearts to the mysteries of Jesus's passion and death. (5) From the Our Father to Holy Communion, we should stir up in our hearts a deep desire to be united with Jesus in the Most Holy Sacrament. (6) Finally, from Communion to the

---

5. Francis de Sales, *Introduction to the Devout Life* 2.14, trans. John K. Ryan, (Garden City, NY: Image Books, 1966), 103.
6. Ibid.
7. Ibid. (2.14), 104.

Francis de Sales: Health of the Soul 211

end of Mass, we should give thanks to Jesus Christ for his incarnation, life, passion, death, and love manifested for us in the Holy Sacrifice. All of these steps should stem from the intention to adore Christ in the Holy Sacrifice and to unite ourselves with him through our prayers and meditations.[8]

In chapter twenty, Francis notes that Jesus instituted the sacrament of his body and blood so that whoever eats of it would live forever. Receiving Communion frequently builds up the soul's health so that it can resist evil affections. A steady diet of such spiritual food will make us immune to death. Through the Eucharist, Francis says, God restores our souls to health and enables us to overcome the forces of evil. Although he does not specify how often one should receive Communion, he counsels:

> To receive Communion every week, it is required that one be free from mortal sin and from any affection for venial sin and have a great desire to communicate. To communicate every day it is necessary in addition that we overcome the great part of our evil inclinations and that we follow the advice of our spiritual director.[9]

Those who are serious about growing in the spiritual life, he maintains, should receive Communion at least once a month.[10]

In chapter twenty-one, Francis discusses preparation for Communion. The evening before receiving, we should make many acts of love to God. He suggests that we go to bed early and wake up a little bit earlier. If we should awaken during the night, we should immediately fill our hearts and lips with words of love and praise for Jesus. In the morning, we should fill ourselves with heightened expectation of the heavenly food we are about to receive. Having made our confession, we should approach the altar with humility,

---

8. Ibid. (2.14), 104–5.
9. Ibid. (2.20), 117.
10. Ibid. (2.20), 116.

aware of our own unworthiness. As we receive, we should open our mouths gently and lift our heads to let the priest place the host on our tongue and receive our Lord with sincere and heartfelt acts of faith, hope, and love. Having received, we should do homage to our Lord and Savior who has joined himself to us by becoming our very food and nourishment.[11]

When we cannot receive the actual host, Francis suggests receiving spiritually with a heartfelt desire to be united to Christ. We should receive Holy Communion "to advance, strengthen, and comfort ourselves in the love of God."[12] If asked why we receive Communion so often, we should respond: "...to learn to love God, be purified from imperfections, delivered from misery, comforted in affliction, and supported in weakness."[13]

Francis notes the two classes of people that should communicate frequently:

> ...the perfect, because being well disposed they would be very much to blame if they did not approach the source and fountain of perfection, and the imperfect, so that they rightly strive for perfection.[14]

He suggests going to Communion as often as possible, if so advised by a spiritual director. The connection between spiritual direction and participation in the Church's sacramental life highlights an important practice that many have found helpful (even essential) in their search for holiness.

Observations

The above presentation provides only the main contours of Francis' teaching on the Eucharist and in no way exhausts the quality of its depth and insights. The following remarks

---
11. Ibid. (2.21), 117–18.
12. Ibid. (2.21), 118.
13. Ibid.
14. Ibid.

seek to probe his teaching still further and highlight their relevance for today.

Francis' teaching on the Eucharist connects with the call of all the faithful to holiness. The Mass is not the sacrament of an elite few, but of all believers. It provides the spiritual nourishment necessary to brave the challenges of our earthly journey and prepare for life after death. Frequent reception returns our souls to health and empowers us to overcome our unruly passions. The Eucharist is the "center of the Christian religion" or, in the words of the Second Vatican Council, "the source and summit of the Christian life."[15] It offers every believer the strength to walk day by day in intimate friendship with God.

The Eucharist is connected to Francis' twofold emphasis on detachment (i.e. penance) and union (i.e., love) as the necessary means to holiness. Although everyone is called to holiness, only those who detach themselves at least interiorly from the things of this world will experience intimate union with God, the fruit of his love for us. God's love cannot flow into a soul already filled with a love for the things of this world. The Eucharist, a "sacrament of love," works in two ways. First, it loosens our ties to worldly desires; then it binds and strengthens our ties to Jesus Christ, the Lord of Life, the embodiment of God's love for humanity.

Francis teaches that a steady diet of the Eucharist will make our souls immune to death. He views the sacrament as food that strengthens the soul so that we can overcome the poisons of the flesh. At one point, he cites the example of an ancient king who used a special remedy called "mithridate" to make his body immune to poison.[16] The Eucharist functions in a similar way. When we receive it with reverence

---

15. *LG*, no. 11 (accessed April 23, 2012).
16. Francis de Sales, *Introduction to the Devout Life* (2.20), 114.

and devotion, it transforms our souls and gradually elevates us to a plane of existence that cannot be influenced by the destructive effects of unruly passions. The more we partake of the Eucharist, the more our souls will be free of the poisonous effects of concupiscence. Like Ignatius of Antioch, Francis views the Eucharist as a "medicine of immortality"[17] that overcomes sinful passions and so frees us from these toxic powers.

Even though Francis does not insist on daily communion, preferring to place such a judgment in the hands of a competent spiritual director, he does suggest assisting at Mass every day. He realizes the graces of the sacrament, especially when a person of faith participates attentively with a heart that yearns for God. Writing at a time before daily communion had become a widely accepted practice, he steers a middle path between laxist presumption and Jansenist rigorism. His reverence for the sacrament makes him recognize our responsibilities when receiving it, yet he also realizes the benefits of frequent communion. His emphasis on submission to one's spiritual director, spiritual communion, and frequent (at least monthly) sacramental communion is a prudent attempt to help believers approach the sacrament with devotion so as to receive the help they need.

Francis is a strong advocate of spiritual communion. He recognizes that sometimes it is impossible to receive communion. Our inability to receive, however, should not keep us from attending Mass. Francis recognizes the grace that those who participate in the sacrament with reverence and devotion receive. When we invite Jesus into our hearts, he comes personally and helps us to walk with him in friendship. Although spiritual communion cannot replace sacramental communion, it is the next best thing. The beauty of spiritual communion is that it bears much fruit and can be

---

17. Ignatius of Antioch, *Letter to the Ephesians*, 20.2.

received anytime, anyplace. Francis' endorsement of spiritual communion is a reminder that there is an alternative way to receive Jesus, even though it has fallen out of use in Catholic spirituality and perhaps needs to be retrieved and reaffirmed.

Francis explains carefully how to prepare to receive the Most Holy Sacrament. He encourages looking upon the greatness of sacramental communion and preparing for it with care and anticipation. When we receive important visitors, we clean our homes, wear our Sunday best, and prepare a refreshing repast for them. Similarly, we should ready our souls before receiving the sacrament by being awake and well rested, fill our hearts with prayers of love and praise, express sorrow for our sins, and approach the altar with a posture and gestures of reverence for what we are about to receive. Because in communion the natural and supernatural meet, Francis counsels awareness of the sacredness of the moment and proper preparation.

In addition to emphasizing how to prepare for Holy Communion, Francis describes what to do during celebration of the sacrament. Francis did write during a time when the Tridentine Mass was the ordinary form of the sacrament. Many would not understand the Latin prayers whispered by the priest throughout the celebration. The faithful therefore were to use prayers and meditations to raise their hearts and minds to God The Mass can provide an occasion to meditate and to thank God for the mysteries of Christ's incarnation, life, passion, death, and resurrection. Although the Tridentine Mass is now an extraordinary form of the sacrament, Francis' suggestions remind us of the connection between meditation and the sacraments; both are integral in the quest for holiness.

Conclusion

Francis de Sales inspired countless individuals through his deep apostolic zeal and numerous pastoral activities. He continues to do so through his writings and through the religious communities inspired by his spirituality—to name but a few, the Visitation Nuns, the Salesians of Don Bosco, and the Oblates of Francis de Sales. He was one of the great saints and spiritual writers of the early seventeenth century and is recognized as one of the giants of Catholic spirituality.

Francis was motivated by a deep love for God manifested in a selfless zeal for souls. He maintained that everyone is called to believe and that all believers are called to sanctity. His theological and spiritual outlook sprang from his desire to bring the treasures of Catholic spirituality to as many people as possible. All of his preaching, teaching, writing, and pastoral care was oriented to this end. The same can be said for his teaching on the Eucharist.

The Eucharist, for Francis, lies at the center of Catholic life. Because it lets us access the fruits of Christ's redemption, we must approach it with reverence and devotion. Francis emphasizes the sacrament's nutritional, sacrificial, and transformational aspects. He explains why we should attend Mass frequently and receive Holy Communion whenever we can. To those who cannot receive the sacrament, he recommends spiritual communion as an appropriate and efficacious alternative. Francis offers a balanced approach to holiness that can be embraced by people of all walks of life in their search for holiness. His spirituality, which is based on the Eucharist, still applies to believers today who seek to connect the devout life and sound sacramental practice.

Reflection Questions

- Francis believed that the Eucharist was the most important and sacred of all devotions, the "sun of all spiritual exercises." Why do you think he said that? How can you place the Eucharist at the center of your spiritual life? What can you do to make it even more so?

- Francis believes that receiving Communion frequently builds up the soul's health. When has the Eucharist helped you tame your passions and emotions? When has it helped you overcome temptation and walk more securely along the path of holiness?

- Francis saw a connection between the Eucharist and detachment from the things of this world. How might attachments to people or things hinder you in your journey to God? What people or things should you adhere to more closely?

Voice Eighteen

Alphonsus de Liguori: Friendship with God

My Jesus, I believe that you are in the Most Holy Sacrament. I love you above all things, and I desire to have you in my soul. Since I am not now able to receive you sacramentally, come to my heart at least spiritually. I embrace you. Never allow me to be separated from you.

Alphonsus de Liguori

Our next voice on the Eucharist, a giant of 18th century Catholic spirituality, had an impact on the devotional life of the faithful that continues even today. Noted for his prolific writing and zealous apostolic endeavors, he founded a religious congregation of men to preach conversion to the poor and abandoned. He served for nine years as bishop of a small town in the southern Italian countryside. A master of the popular mission, he found creative ways to evangelize those most in need by bringing them the spiritual treasures of the Church, especially prayer, the sacraments, and devotion to the Eucharist.

Apostle of Conversion

Alphonsus de Liguori (1696–1787) was born at Marianella, on the outskirts of Naples. A devout Catholic and a member of the lower nobility, he was educated at home until age 12, when he was enrolled in the University of Naples to study law. In four years, he completed a doctorate in Church and civil law (*in utroque jure*). He was on his way to a successful legal career when, in 1723, he lost an important civil case due to court corruption and intrigue. Disillusioned, he forsook the world of law and professed his desire to become a priest.

Alphonsus received his theological training at home under the direction of Don Julio Torni and in 1724 became a member The Congregation of the Apostolic Missions, a group of diocesan priests and clerics dedicated to preaching. Ordained on December 21, 1726, he devoted the next few years to preaching, catechetical instruction, and hearing confessions. In 1727 he organized the popular Evening Chapels, regular sessions in religious instruction, pious devotions, and charitable works for working class Neapolitans. In 1729 he took up residence in the Chinese College founded by Matteo Ripa (1682–1746) and devoted himself to local mission preaching.

A turning point came in 1730 when he journeyed south of Naples to Scala, a small town on the Amalfi coast. There, he met Thomas Falcoia (1663–1743), a member of the Pious Workers who had recently been consecrated bishop of nearby Castellamare di Stabia, and Sister Maria Celeste Crostarosa (1696–1755), a contemplative nun and mystic visionary living in a monastery at Scala. Each played an important part in establishing, in 1731, the Institute of the Most Holy Savior, a contemplative order of nuns later known as the Order of the Most Holy Redeemer (the Redemptoristines) and in 1732 the Congregation of the Most Holy Savior, an apostolic institute of priests and lay brothers, later known as the Congregation of the Most Holy Redeemer (the Redemptorists).

From 1732 on, Alphonsus devoted himself to living out this option for the poor. The major projects of his life—mission preaching, theological and spiritual writing, founding the Redemptorist Congregation, service as bishop of St. Agatha of the Goths, painting and musical compositions, a life of prayer—were motivated by his profound desire to spread the Good News of plentiful redemption in Christ, especially among those without easy access to the Church's spiritual treasures. During his 34 years of missionary experience he gave over 150 popular missions. He wrote 111 works, composed popular songs, many of which are still sung, and was an accomplished painter. He was beatified on September 15, 1816 by Pius VII, canonized in 1831 by Gregory XVI, declared a Doctor of the Church in 1871 by Pius IX, designated the "Doctor of Prayer" by Pius XI in 1934, and made the patron of confessors and moralists in 1950 by Pius XII.[1]

Alphonsus' Spirituality

Alphonsus' "Gospel Spirituality," rooted in the person of Jesus Christ, takes seriously the Lord's injunction that his apostles "make disciples of all nations" (Mt 28:19). His writings, although they differ in subject, length, or intended audience, all serve to draw people into a deeper and more intimate relationship with Christ.

Even a cursory survey of his voluminous literary output shows that Alphonsus was extremely well-read in the Scriptures, the Fathers of the Church, and the great spiritual masters of the Western Church.[2] Of all that he was exposed to, four streams of spirituality had a particular effect on his outlook. With St. Teresa of Avila (1515–82), one of the patrons of his religious institute, he shared the importance of practical realism, a deep sacramental sense, dogmatic orthodoxy, and a strong Catholic identity. Like St. Ignatius

---

1. All factual information and other historical data in this section comes from *NCE*, s.v. "Alphonsus Liguori, St.," by L. Vereecke; Jean Delumeau, "Preface," in Théodule Rey-Mermet, *St. Alphonsus Liguori: Tireless Worker for the Most Abandoned*, trans. Jehanne-Marie Marchesi (Brooklyn, N.Y.: New City Press, 1989), 7–10; Jones, *Alphonsus de Liguori*, 491–94.
2. For a list of his personal favorites, see Joseph W. Oppitz, *Alphonsian History and Spirituality: A Study of the Spirit of the Founder, Saint Alphonsus M. Liguori and of the Missionary Institute, The Congregation of the Most Holy Redeemer* (Rome, Suffield, Ct: Privately published [ad usum privatum], 2d printing, 1978), 28.

of Loyola (1491–1556), he emphasized a spirit of service based on effective, prudential love for the common good. He imitated St. Francis de Sales (1567–1622) in stressing the abundance and gratuity of salvation, the tenderness of God's love, and conformity to the divine will. Like him, Alphonsus also emphasized exclamatory prayer for personal recollection, the development of popular lay spirituality, and scholarship and the arts as aids to holiness. Finally, with the Oratorians of Naples, he emphasized such themes as participation in the Divine Image, the centrality of the Trinity, the Incarnation and Grace, and a devotional life based on the Incarnation and the Eucharist. He demonstrated an interest in the theology of states of life within the Church, and highlighted the simplicity, discipline, and training of an authentic spirituality of Christian childhood.[3]

In keeping with his highly focused and pragmatic spiritual ends, Alphonsus borrowed from these schools in a "creatively eclectic" way to develop a synthesis relevant to his mission in the Church of preaching the gospel to the poor and most abandoned.[4] His popular style enabled him to meet people where they were and bring them along in their walk with the Lord. His spirituality, best summarized in the phrase "crib, cross, and sacrament," is distinguished by close adherence to Jesus as "Redeemer" and proclaiming the need for fundamental conversion (*metanoia*). It is also marked by a deep devotion to Jesus's first and closest disciple, the Blessed Virgin Mary.

Alphonsus' vision of God's love for humanity focuses on the wonder of the Incarnation, the selfless giving manifested in Christ's passion and death, the Resurrected Lord's continuing presence in the Church through the Eucharist, and the compassionate love of Mary, the Mother of all believers.

---

3. This summary of the schools of Christian spirituality that influenced Alphonsus comes from Oppitz, *Alphonsian History and Spirituality*, 29–32.
4. The phrase "creatively eclectic" comes from Oppitz, *Alphonsian History and Spirituality*, 28.

Alphonsus on the Eucharist

In 1745, Alphonsus published *Visits to the Most Holy Sacrament and to Most Holy Mary*,[5] a small collection of 31 meditations designed to help believers pray daily before Jesus in the sacrament. Although he had written a few devotional pamphlets before this, *Visits* is the first of his works in which he is identified as the author. It therefore is often considered his first published work.[6]

In it, Alphonsus presents a Christ-centered "theology of the heart" coupled with a "spirituality of practice." "Paradise for God," he once wrote, "is the human heart."[7] He did not emphasize knowledge *about* Christ as much as *knowing* Christ himself. Although such a relationship is primarily the work of God, he knows it can be fostered by a life of heartfelt prayer sustained by a daily regimen of fervent yet moderate ascetical practices.[8]

Alphonsus considered it most appropriate to pray before the Blessed Sacrament. After all, where else could one conduct an intimate conversation with Jesus except by visiting him personally in the sacrament? Alphonsus wrote the *Visits* to show beginners how to do this. He provides words to be prayed vocally or mentally, individually or in a group, by which the faithful can conduct a heart-to-heart conversation with Jesus and his mother, Mary.

---

5. See Alphonsus de Liguori, *The Visits to the Blessed Sacrament and the Blessed Virgin Mary*, in The *Complete Works of St. Alphonsus de Liguori*, ed. Eugene Grimm, vol. 6 (Brooklyn, St. Louis, Toronto: Redemptorist Fathers, 1934), 109–212.
6. In part, this article depends on and is adapted from Dennis J. Billy, "Introduction," in Alphonsus de Liguori, *Visits to the Most Holy Sacrament and to Most Holy Mary*, trans. and commentator, Dennis Billy (Notre Dame, IN: Christian Classics, 2007), 9–21.
7. Alphonsus de Liguori, *The Way to Converse Always and Familiarly with God* in *The Way of Salvation and Perfection. The Complete Ascetical Works of St. Alphonsus de Liguori*, ed. Eugene Grimm, vol. 2 (New York, Cincinnati, Chicago: Benziger Brothers, 1886; reprinted., Brooklyn, St. Louis, Toronto: Redemptorist Fathers, 1926), 395.
8. This section depends upon and is adapted from Dennis J. Billy, *With Open Heart: Spiritual Direction in the Alphonsian Tradition* (Liguori, Mo.: Liguori Publications, 2003), 16–29.

The visits, therefore, are not an end in themselves but a series of carefully crafted meditations, the fruit of Alphonsus' own intimate conversations with Jesus and Mary, for deepening their relationship with God. These written examples of Alphonsus' approach to mental prayer follow a general structure of preparation, reflection, affection, petition, resolution, and conclusion. In the *Visits*, however, the structure is not presented as a formula, but woven into a seamless garment of devotional prayer with a simple and accessible literary style.

Recently, the changing contours of Catholic spirituality in the latter half of the twentieth century and decreased interest in Eucharistic adoration following the Second Vatican Council have lessened the popularity of the *Visits*. Nevertheless, it still has had lasting impact on the popular Catholic imagination. As one of Alphonsus' recent biographers claims: "Perhaps no other work, with the possible exception of *The Imitation of Christ*, has ever had such an effect on devotional practice throughout the whole Catholic world."[9]

Observations

When discussing the *Visits*, a number of other important factors should be kept in mind. The following list of observations, while in no way exhaustive, should help readers get a better grasp of the nature of what these meditations in the *Visits*, are and how they were meant to function in the life of believers. They should also suggest the theological and cultural lenses through which they should be viewed. The *Visits* reveal how Alphonsus immerses himself and his readers in "the voices of the past." He fills each visit with quotations and examples from the Scriptures and the lives of the saints. Nearly every page contains spiritual insights from the Old and New Testaments and passages by saintly

---

9. Frederick M. Jones, *Alphonsus de Liguori: The Saint of Bourbon Naples* (Dublin: Gill and Macmillan, 1992), 191.

giants such as Augustine, Bernard, Francis, Bonaventure, Albert the Great, Thomas Aquinas, Francis de Sales, and Teresa of Avila (to name just a few). This literary style steeps readers in the spiritual tradition of the Church. By allowing these saints to speak to his readers on their own terms, his audience experiences the richness of the Church's spiritual tradition that only a few could have accumulated on their own.

Alphonsus keeps his readers before him at all times. His presenting to them the wisdom of the Church's great spiritual masters is a pastoral service that will benefit many. He also connects devotion to the Blessed Sacrament and membership in the company of saints, thus giving those making the *Visits* the hope of one day being counted among them.

The Visits *reveal Alphonsus' image of Jesus and Mary.* His high Christology and Mariology may seem dated to contemporary readers, who tend to focus on Jesus's humanity rather than his divinity and Mary's solidarity with humanity rather than her strong intercessory powers. Alphonsus' writing, it must be remembered, reflects the cultural and spiritual climate of his day. Although he may not speak in ways relevant to present sensitivities, nothing he presents would have been considered irregular in his day and is in full accord with the teaching of the Church (both then and now). The difference between Alphonsus' day and now is a matter of emphasis. In his day, it was normal to begin with Jesus's divinity and eventually arrive at his humanity. It was also normal to emphasize Mary's great intercessory powers and her exalted role as Queen of Heaven rather than her solidarity with humanity and her role as the humble maiden from Nazareth and our sister in faith. Taking his cultural perspective into account, Alphonsus' *Visits* demonstrates how, within the bounds of legitimate Catholic orthodoxy, the relationship between the human and divine in Jesus and the variety of roles played by Mary in the Church can be construed. Those who disagree with Alphonsus' emphasis should consider his approach as an opportunity to examine their own faith more critically, to see whether they have been overlooking something very important.

The Visits *reflect Alphonsus' understanding of Redemption.* In Alphonsus' day the most common view of Redemption was the satisfaction theory of St. Anselm of Canterbury (1033–1109), which stated that the Word of God became man and died on the cross out of necessity in order to do what humanity itself could not accomplish. Through Jesus's passion and death, God's compassion satisfied the demands of God's justice over the infinite transgression of Adam's sin. Although Alphonsus recognized humanity's inability to satisfy the demands of God's justice, he did not believe that it was absolutely necessary for Christ to die. In his document on the dignity of the priesthood, the *Selva*, he says:

> It was not necessary for the Redeemer to die in order to save the world; a drop of his blood, a single tear, or prayer, was sufficient to procure salvation for all; for such a prayer, being of infinite value, should be sufficient to save not one but a thousand worlds.[10]

He believed that Christ chose to redeem humanity through his passion and death not out of necessity, but as an expression of God's unconditional love for humanity. Alphonsus understood God to be madly in love with humanity and willing to do anything out of love for them. Christ's passion and death is really God's attempt to show us how much he loves us. For Alphonsus, after receiving the sacraments, making a visit to the Blessed Sacrament was the best way to reciprocate that love.

---

10. Alphonsus de Liguori, *Dignity and Duties of the Priest*, or *Selva*, in *The Complete Works of Alphonsus de Liguori*, ed. Eugene Grimm, vol. 12 (New York, Cincinnati, Chicago: Benziger Brothers, 1889; reprint ed., Brooklyn, St. Louis, Toronto: Redemptorist Fathers, 1927), 26.

The Visits *are intimately related to sacramental worship.* Alphonsus demonstrates in the *Visits* how his readers can nurture their relationship with Jesus in ways other than sacramental worship. These suggestions are relevant for believers today. Jesus still remains present in the Blessed Sacrament, still yearns for our friendship, still desires that we visit with him. Mary still wishes to draw us closer to her Son, still plays an active role in our sanctification, she still looks upon us as her spiritual sons and daughters. We need only to step out in faith and talk to them. Although they do not exhaust the topic, the *Visits* do offer a comfortable point of departure. Readers who take them up and pray them as Alphonsus envisioned have much to gain. Because visiting Jesus in the Blessed Sacrament flows from the Eucharistic celebration, it necessarily leads back to it. Separating this devotion from its underlying orientation to the Mass reflects a fundamental misunderstanding of Jesus's presence in the sacrament. The Eucharistic action is the source and summit of the Church's life. Eucharistic devotion flows from that source and leads believers back to it for their primary source of spiritual nourishment.

The Visits *foster friendship with God.* In his opening dedication to Mary Alphonsus states his intention for writing the *Visits*: "Only so that souls may be more greatly inflamed with love for Jesus Christ."[11] He reinforces this unequivocal statement just a few sentences later, when he asserts that he writes not to be praised, but only so that his readers grow in devotion and affection for Jesus. Alphonsus notes that our love for God is founded upon "the tender and excessive love"[12] of Jesus's passion and the institution of the Most Holy Sacrament. He offers his readers a practical way to foster their personal relationships with Jesus and the Blessed Mother. This is best done as would be done with any other

---
11. See Alphonsus de Liguori, *Visits*, 111.
12. Ibid.

friends—simply by visiting them. Visits with Jesus and Mary differ from those with other friends, but in many ways are similar: preparation, dialogue, expressions of gratitude, frequency, order—to name but a few. The ritual of visiting a close friend has a well-developed, familiar pattern. Friends draw closer to each other by doing again and again the things they have done for years. Alphonsus recognizes the ritualistic dimension of human relationships and applies it to friendship with Jesus in the Blessed Sacrament and to Mary. In *The Visits,* he invites his readers to pray familiarly with Jesus and his mother Mary. Mary is not only Jesus's mother; she is our mother. Jesus is not only her Son; he is our Savior, our Lord—our Brother. Alphonsus does not want his readers to forget the close bond they share with Jesus by virtue of his becoming a human being, his suffering, death, and resurrection, and by virtue of the spiritual motherhood of Mary.

Alphonsus presents detailed directions for making a visit to the Blessed Sacrament. Each visit should begin with an act of love to Jesus which clearly states the three reasons for coming: thanksgiving, reparation, and adoration. The text of this opening prayer remains the same in each visit. It is followed by the visit itself (Alphonsus writes thirty-one in all—one for each day of the month), followed by an act of spiritual communion (he provides two versions), then the visit with Mary (again, thirty-one in all), and a concluding prayer to her (constant throughout). Alphonsus shapes the visits so that there is a balance between constancy and variety. He suggests a consistent pattern: (1) opening prayer to Jesus in the Most Blessed Sacrament, (2) visit to the Most Blessed Sacrament, (3) act of spiritual communion, (4) visit to the Blessed Virgin Mary, and (5) closing prayer to Mary. Within this structure, the first and last parts always remain the same; the second and fourth parts change each day in a cycle of thirty-one days; in the third part readers can choose between a formal prayer or a shorter version. In establishing a structure for the *Visits*, Alphonsus is careful to incorporate a rhythm of continuity and change. Something each day of every month will be the same; something will also be different. He includes enough structure to preserve the ritual of the devotion and enough innovation to allow for spontaneity. Although he realizes that spontaneity cannot be structured, he hopes that the visits themselves will turn into an outpouring of affection for Jesus and his Mother, Mary. The pious exclamatory prayers at the end of each *Visit* to the Blessed Sacrament and to Mary are intended to provide a bridge to such affectionate and spontaneous prayer.

Finally, the Visits *express Alphonsus' personal experience and missionary zeal.* Alphonsus writes with a single purpose: to lead as many as possible into an intimate relationship with Jesus Christ. He chooses the devotional genre of the *Visits* as the best way to accomplish this. He writes in a simple style that anyone can understand; he fills the *Visits* with stories from the lives of the saints and with scriptural quotations to provide models people can look up to and stories that will entertain and delight. His writing always reflects his missionary zeal. He writes his *Visits* as an apostle of Jesus Christ and as a servant of the Blessed Virgin Mary in order to draw others closer to them and raise up other disciples and servants for the vineyard of the Lord.

The *Visits* represent the fruit of Alphonsus' own deeply familiar and intimate conversations with Jesus and Mary. He wrote down what gushed forth from the depths of his heart, the product of his own deep awareness of God in his life. That is what he truly wishes to share with his readers, to let them find what he himself has tasted and seen. He also recognizes that the more his readers make fervent, devout visits to the Blessed Sacrament and to the Virgin Mother of God, the closer they will draw to each other. Through the

Visits, Alphonsus seeks to carry out his missionary task of spreading and building up the Body of Christ, the Church.[13]

Conclusion

Alphonsus' *Visits to the Most Holy Sacrament and to Most Holy Mary* is one of the great classics of popular Catholic devotion. Its popularity helped establish the practice of visiting Jesus in the Blessed Sacrament alongside other devotions such as the Rosary and The Stations of the Cross.

The fundamental metaphor of the entire work is "the visit." Here, Alphonsus provides a strong alternative to the rationalism of the Enlightenment that swept through Europe in the late-17th and 18th centuries, in which God was viewed as an impersonal force that designed the world and kept it in motion, but did not enter people's lives. Alphonsus, by way of contrast, glories in the traditional truths of the Catholic faith: God visited this world at the Incarnation through Mary in the person of Jesus; he also visits the world daily in the Holy Sacrifice of the Mass and remains hidden in the consecrated species of bread and wine. Since God visits the world in these mysterious ways, it makes perfect sense to reciprocate God's love for us by visiting Jesus in the Blessed Sacrament and by talking to Mary, who is never far from his side. The Church continues to proclaim these truths, even in a world that has moved past the of the confident progressivism of the Enlightenment and struggles in a sea of globalization and postmodern uncertainty.

In the *Visits*, Alphonsus highlights God's personal nature and the invitation extended to each person to know God better. The act of spiritual communion, moreover, is a reminder that God visits not only in the concrete dimensions of time and space (i.e., in the Incarnation and in the Eucharist), but also in the deepest recesses of the human heart. We visit the

---

13. This section depends upon and is adapted from Dennis J. Billy, *Plentiful Redemption: An Introduction to Alphonsian Spirituality* (Liguori, MO: Liguori Publications, 2001), 41–52.

Blessed Sacrament precisely because we want God to visit us and to dwell within our hearts. This mutual indwelling of God in us and of us in God is one characteristic of the divine-human friendship that Jesus made possible by his passion, death, and resurrection. It is the deepest longing of the human heart and the greatest desire of a God madly in love with his people.[14]

Reflection Questions

- Alphonsus says that paradise for God is the human heart. What evidence do you see for this? How does it make you feel to realize that God's deepest yearning is to dwell in your heart? What must you do for God to dwell there? How can you prepare your heart for him? What role does the Eucharist play?

- Alphonsus believed that the most appropriate place for prayer was in the presence of the Blessed Sacrament. Where do you like to go for prayer? What is the difference between praying in your own private space, or in nature, or in the presence of the Blessed Sacrament?

- Alphonsus's *Visits* are a collection of meditations before the Blessed Sacrament. How do you meditate? What makes it easy to meditate? What makes it difficult? What method do you use to pray? How do you talk to God? Why is it important to share your innermost thoughts and feelings with him?

---

14. This conclusion depends upon and is adapted from Billy, *Plentiful Redemption*, 47–48.

Voice Nineteen

St. John Vianney: Loving Presence

> Our Lord is hidden in the Blessed Sacrament, waiting for us to come and visit Him.... See how good He is!... If He had appeared before us now in all His glory, we should not have dared to approach Him; but He hides Himself like one in prison, saying: "You do not see Me, but that does not matter; ask Me for all you want."
>
> *John Vianney*

Our next voice on the Eucharist came from obscure French peasant stock but came to be renowned worldwide for his holiness and nobility of life. During his lifetime, he was known as a simple parish priest with great gifts for directing souls and working miracles. The curate of the country parish in the small southern French town or Ars, he labored for more than forty years to revitalize an area that the depredations of the French revolution had left spiritually depressed. His intense ascetical life and reputation for holiness are surpassed only by his deep, endearing love for the Eucharist.

Patron of Priests

Jean Mary Baptist Vianney (1786–1859), universally known as the Curé of Ars, was born of devout Catholic parents in the French town of Dardilly, not far from Lyons.

At the age of twenty, he entered a preparatory school for seminarians at Ecully under the tutelage of M. Charles Balley. Because he had little prior education he struggled academically, especially in Latin. His studies were cut short when he was conscripted into the French army, an event complicated by an unintentional desertion that forced him to live in hiding under an assumed name for a period of time. Years later, when he re-contacted his family, his brother arranged to take John's place in the army so that he could resume his studies for the priesthood.

John entered the minor seminary at Verrieres in 1812, but failed the required entrance examinations for the major seminary; he was admitted only after retaking the exams three months later. He struggled with his studies throughout his time in the seminary, but was finally ordained on August 13, 1815 by the bishop of Grenoble. He was made the assistant to M. Balley at Ecully and, after his mentor's death in 1818, was assigned the parish of Ars, a small village on the outskirts of Lyons.

John threw his whole heart and soul into the spiritual care of his parishioners. He became known as a man of prayer with a deep love for the people. Shortly after his arrival at Ars he established "The Providence," an orphanage for destitute girls. His catechetical instructions for the children became so popular that other parishioners also requested them. In time, he gained a reputation in Ars and beyond as a preacher and teacher of God's Word and director of souls. His exemplary life of prayer and asceticism drew countless individuals back to the faith. At one point, his bishop did not allow him to attend the annual diocesan clergy retreats so that he could attend to the crowds coming to see him. By 1847, more than twenty thousand pilgrims from throughout France had come to Ars.

In 1859, after more than forty years of serving the people of Ars as their pastor and friend, he died. Known throughout the world as a holy confessor and director of souls, he was said to possess the gift of reading people's hearts when they came to him for direction. He was known for healing the sick and for obtaining food and money for charitable causes. He was canonized in 1925 by Pope Pius XI; recently Pope Benedict XVI declared him the patron saint of priests.[1]

The Curé's Spirituality

During his life and ever since his death, John has been acclaimed as a model of priestly life and holiness. He is noted for a rich, deep spiritual outlook that touches many areas of a priest's daily life. He was especially noted for a spirited embrace of the evangelical counsels of poverty, chastity, and obedience, qualities normally associated with the religious life. As a diocesan priest, John recognized that these counsels were meant not for a select few, but for every state of life in the Church. He lived the counsels in a way typically suited for a diocesan priest serving in a remote country parish, and encouraged others to live them in ways suitable for their own life situations.[2]

John's spiritual outlook centered on prayer, especially daily meditation, visits to the Blessed Sacrament, recitation of the rosary, and the examination of conscience.[3] He promoted these practices not for their own sake, but as well-tried means of sustaining an intimate relationship with God. He thought them to be especially important for priests:

> The thing that keeps us priests from gaining sanctity is thoughtlessness. It annoys us to turn our minds away from external affairs; we don't know what we really ought to do.

---

1. The historical details in this section come from *The Catholic Encyclopedia*, vol. 8 (New York: Robert Appleton, Company, 1910), s.v. "St. Jean-Baptiste-Marie Vianney," http://www.newadvent.org/ cathen/08326c.htm (accessed September 26, 2009). See also Abbé Francis Trochu, *The Curé of Ars: St. Jean-Marie-Baptiste Vianney* (trans. Ernest Graf (Rockford, IL: Tan Books, 1977); Idem, *The Curé of Ars: A Biography of St. Jean-Marie Vianney*, trans. Ronald Matthews (Manila: Sinag-Tala Publishers, 1986).
2. See *SNP* nos. 11–35.
3. Ibid., no. 42.

What we need is deep reflection, together with prayer and an intimate union with God.[4]

His life demonstrates how he never allowed external affairs, even pastoral service to his people, from interfering with his life of prayer and intimate conversation with God.[5] He has left numerous sayings about the centrality of prayer for a Christian's life:

We are beggars who must ask God for everything.[6]

How many people we can call back to God by our prayers![7]

Ardent prayer addressed to God: this is man's greatest happiness on earth![8]

To be loved by God, to be joined to God, to walk before God, to live for God: O blessed life, O blessed death![9]

These sayings of the blessed Curé of Ars remind us of the necessity of prayer for our lives. Through prayer and by God's grace, we can foster an intimate of relationship with the Lord of life. Without it, we forget the final goal of our lives and go through life without purpose or direction. For John, the spiritual life centered on prayer. It also sustained him his pastoral endeavors.

John was also a true shepherd of souls. When he first came to Ars, the community was immersed in the faithless, immoral aftermath of the French revolution. He met resistance at first, but gradually began to win people over through the authentic witness of his life. To stir up the love of God in his parish he first stirred it up within his own heart: "Good shepherd! O Shepherd who lives up to the commands and desires of Jesus Christ completely! This is

---

4. See *Secret Vatican Archives*, v. 227, p. 131. Cited in *SNP*, no. 37.
5. See *SNP*, no. 37.
6. See *Secret Vatican Archives*, v. 227, p. 1100. Cited in *SNP*, no. 38.
7. See *Secret Vatican Archives*, v. 227, p. 54. Cited in *SNP*, no. 38.
8. See *Secret Vatican Archives*, v. 227, p. 45. Cited in *SNP*, no. 38.
9. See *Secret Vatican Archives*, v. 227, p. 29. Cited in *SNP*, no. 39.

the greatest blessing that a kind and gracious God can send to a parish."[10]

John lived a life of deep prayer and holiness—and the people followed. He won them over not through sophisticated arguments or by demands and obligations, but by being a good and holy priest who was present to his people and who helped them as best he could in their spiritual and material struggles. As he himself realized, doing so often meant suffering for them and with them: "If I had known when I came to the parish of Ars what I would have to suffer, the fear of it would certainly have killed me."[11]

One thing sustained him throughout his many trials during his long tenure at Ars—his deep love for and devotion to the Eucharist. Prayer was central to his life, and the Eucharist the very heart of his prayer: "Without the Eucharist," he believed, "there would be no happiness in this world; life would be insupportable."[12]

John on the Eucharist

John's teaching on the Eucharist had many dimensions. First, he believed in the real presence with all his heart: "Jesus Christ is present in the Eucharist with his Body, his Blood, his Soul, and his Divinity."[13] The love that Jesus expresses through the sacrament, moreover, deserves our reciprocal response: "He is the one Who has loved us so much; why shouldn't we love Him in return?"[14] John therefore saw that being a confessor and spiritual director chiefly consisted in reconciling others to God so that they might worthily receive the Eucharist. He encouraged people to attend Mass

---

10. See *Sermons*, 1.c., v. 2, p. 86. Cited in *SNP*, no. 64
11. See *Secret Vatican Archives*, v. 227, p. 991. Cited in *SNP*, no. 70.
12. St. John Vianney, "Eucharistic Quotes," http://www.acfp2000.com/Saints/St_John_Vianney/st_john_vianney.html (accessed September 26, 2009).
13. Abbé H. Convert, ed., *St. John Vianney, The Curé of Ars: Eucharistic Meditations*, trans. Sr. Mary Benventura (Trabuco Canyon, CA/Wheathampstead Herts, Great Britain: Source Books/Anthony Clarke, 1993), 23.
14. See *Secret Vatican Archives*, v. 227, p. 1103. Cited in *SNP*, no. 46.

daily, to receive Jesus in spiritual communion when they could not receive him sacramentally, and to visit him often in the Blessed Sacrament. He also taught them to pray before the sacrament in a simple, heartfelt way:

> You do not need many words when you pray. We believe in faith that the good and gracious God is there in the tabernacle; we open our souls to Him; and feel happy that He allows us to come before Him; this is the best way to pray.[15]

When the Curé asked a simple peasant about his prayer before the tabernacle, he is said to have responded, "I look at him and he looks at me."[16] John encouraged such contemplative gazing before the Blessed Sacrament and was heartened to see it practiced so faithfully by one of his parishioners.

John also believed in the innumerable benefits that come from quiet adoration before the Blessed Sacrament. Priests who did so were inflamed with a burning love for Christ and those charged to their pastoral care. Their souls nourished with the grace of the Spirit, they were empowered to place the interest of others before their own. Such heartfelt devotion rarely went unnoticed. He believed that priests' Eucharistic devotion influenced the lives of their parishioners. When they see their priests sitting or kneeling in silent prayer before the Blessed Sacrament, they themselves are often inspired to take time to make a visit. John therefore believed that a priest could demonstrate deep pastoral care for the faithful by fostering in his own a life a deep devotional love for Jesus, present in the Blessed Sacrament.[17]

For John, however, adoration of the Blessed Sacrament could not compare with the Holy Sacrifice of the Mass. He always celebrated Mass with reverence and devotion,

---

15. See *Secret Vatican Archives*, v. 227, p. 45. Cited in *SNP*, no. 47.
16. Cited in *Catechism of the Catholic Church*, no. 2715, http://www.vatican.va/archive/ENG0015/ P9M.HTM (accessed September 26, 2009).
17. See *SNP*, nos. 48–49.

allowing ample time to prepare for the great mystery he was about to celebrate and to give thanks afterwards for the great gift of the Eucharist. John oriented his entire ministry toward celebration of the Eucharist. It inflamed his pastoral zeal for souls and sustained him in his long hours of teaching the truths of the Catholic faith, in the confessional, and in preparing sermons that would touch peoples' hearts. His pastoral life was an extension of his interior life, which in every respect was thoroughly Eucharistic. John's pastoral zeal for souls was intimately related to his thirst for holiness which, in turn, was oriented entirely toward his deep love for the Eucharist. John was a man for others first and foremost because he was a man for God. By placing God before all things, he understood how to take up his cross daily and follow the way of the Lord Jesus.[18]

The Curé's teaching on the Eucharist can be summarized thus: The Blessed Sacrament contains Jesus' real presence. The Mass itself is both a sacrifice that atones for our sins and a banquet that supplies food for our souls. The Eucharist unites us to Jesus Christ by increasing sanctifying grace in us, so giving us a pledge of eternal life and planting in us the seed of a glorious resurrection. It is a source of great joy that should be received with the proper dispositions. We should therefore be grateful for this sacrament and visit Jesus often in the tabernacle. We should also try to attend Mass as often as possible, even daily, and allow ample time before to prepare ourselves properly for worthy reception of the sacrament and after to give God proper thanks for the graces received. Priests should be especially grateful for the great dignity God has bestowed on them in ordination. They bring Christ, the Lord of Life to others. In doing so they are both nursing mothers and spiritual fathers for the faithful. "The priesthood," John said, "is the love of the

---

18. See *SNP*, nos. 50–55.

heart of Jesus."[19] He could just as easily have said, "The priesthood is the love of the Eucharist of Christ."

Observations

The main contours of John's teaching on the Eucharist are expanded in the following remarks, which probe his teaching further and highlight its relevance for today.

John's spirituality is thoroughly Eucharistic. His interior life is intimately related to his ministry of pastoral care for souls—and vice versa. There is an intrinsic continuity between his inner and outer life, established by the Eucharist. He is devoted to the Eucharist not only because it is the primary means of his own walk to sanctity, but also because it is essential for the holiness of the souls under his care. His entire ministry consists in bringing Christ to others, the Eucharist being the most concrete and visible way for accomplishing this. His ministry as a teacher, preacher, and spiritual director derive from this underlying Eucharistic orientation of his life. The Eucharist is the reason for his ascetic lifestyle and deep yearning throughout his life to be a good and holy priest.

As did many other saints, John saw an intimate connection between visiting Jesus in the Blessed Sacrament and celebrating the Holy Sacrifice of the Mass. He recognized attendance at Mass as the primary way by which Christians (and priests especially) express the Eucharistic dimension of their prayers, but also time and again asserted the importance of adoring Jesus in the tabernacle. He did not see adoration before the Blessed Sacrament as opposed to celebration of the Eucharist, but as an impetus to desiring more deeply to participate in the Mass and to receive Jesus in Holy Communion. The Mass emphasizes the sacrament's dimensions of sacrifice and banquet; adoration emphasizes

---

19. Convert, ed., *St John Vianney, The Curé of Ars: Eucharistic Meditations*, 133.

in a special way Jesus's presence. John understood that a proper understanding of the Catholic teaching requires that all three dimensions. As recent years have demonstrated, a lack of devotion to Jesus's presence in the Blessed Sacrament leads to a neglect of this essential of the Catholic faith.

John also saw a special relationship between the Eucharist and his ministry as a confessor and spiritual director. As a physician of souls, he understood that healing a soul requires not only forgiveness, but also restoration to health through proper care and spiritual nourishment. As a confessor and spiritual director, he sought to lead people to the Eucharist. He believed that Eucharistic devotion—either at Mass or in adoration before the Blessed Sacrament—was the fullest expression of prayer. The Eucharist, the prayer of Christ's body, the Church, was essential for restoring individuals to health and by grace transforming them into the person as God has envisioned from all eternity. John saw that Eucharist has the power to cure and to transform. His teaching reminds us that the sacrament can satisfy all our needs and elevate us to a supernatural plane of existence.

John recognized that prayer before the Eucharist can take many forms. We can speak to God aloud through the responses at Mass, or in a hushed voice before the tabernacle (*vocal prayer*). We can raise our minds to God and speak to him in the quiet of our hearts (*meditation*). We can also sit before the tabernacle and rest in his presence in a quiet, wordless prayer (*contemplation*). John also was aware that because prayer engages our whole being, it is important to follow the proper gestures at Mass and to sit or kneel respectfully before the tabernacle. Above all, John considered prayer to be our response to the movement of grace in our lives. He understood that because prayer requires faith, it requires the help of the Holy Spirit. He taught his parishioners to pray to God in the way that suited them best and encouraged them to be mindful of how the Spirit might be prompting them to lift up their hearts and minds to God

Finally, John's great love and devotion for the Eucharist reflects his deep sense of the dignity of the priesthood. The priest alone has been entrusted with the power to consecrate bread and wine as they become the body and blood of Christ. As a pillar of the Christian faith and a true spiritual father, a priest should be a living image of Jesus who leads his parishioners to Christ. Without a priest, a believing community's light of faith will grow dim or die. Rooted in the love of the heart of Jesus, priests extend the mystery of redemption through time. Their vocation asks of priests a love so overwhelming that they can fully understand their calling only in heaven, when they see God face to face.[20] Only then will they understand their crucial role in God's plan of salvation. Only then will they understand what a great privilege it is to celebrate Mass.

Conclusion

John Vianney was a saintly priest who identified completely with his pastoral ministry. That title by which he is universally known, the "Curé of Ars"—a name that emphasizes his responsibility for the care and cure of souls in a particular place—personifies the self-effacing man of God who loved the people of his small country parish and for whom he would go to any length to insure their spiritual health and well-being.

Although unsophisticated and sickly, he did not let these shortcomings limit his desire to do great things for God. The heart of his spiritual outlook, communion with God through constant prayer, permeated his life, internally as well as externally. Prayer sustained him and gave him the energy to place others' needs before his own, enabling

---

20. See Ibid., 131.

him to endure rigorous fasts, spend hours in silence before the Blessed Sacrament, and receive long lines of penitents as a loving, merciful father. His quest for holiness was intimately related to his priestly vocation and ministry. At the heart of this identity was Mass and devotion to the Blessed Sacrament.

John considered Eucharist to be humankind's greatest gift. It represents God's desire to love us intimately by pouring himself into the simple elements of bread and wine to become our food and drink. It also embodies the essence of prayer. John believed that Jesus could be thanked for his hidden presence in our midst only by worthy reception of the Eucharist during Mass or by making a visit to the Blessed Sacrament. Through this great "sacrament of love," Christ continues his ministry of love through time. The essence of church, of the tabernacle, of the community of faith is the Eucharist John Vianney dedicated his life to serving this community by bringing Jesus to others through the Eucharist so that they might be transformed by grace and one day become partakers of the Father's glory.

Reflection Questions

- The Curé believed in the real presence with all his heart. How deep is your conviction? What would you be willing to give up for it? How do you demonstrate this conviction through your actions?

- The Curé believed that the love Jesus expresses through the sacrament, moreover, deserves a reciprocal response. How do you reciprocate the love Jesus has shown you in the sacrament? How do you demonstrate the love he bears for you in the love you bear for others?

- The Curé believed in the innumerable benefits that come from spending time in quiet adoration before the Blessed Sacrament. When have you received such benefits? What were they? How has the practice increased your love, deepened your faith or increased your hope?

Voice Twenty

John Henry Newman: Devotion to the Real Presence

O most Sacred, most loving heart of Jesus, you are concealed in the Holy Eucharist, and you beat for us still. Now as then you say, *Desiderio desideravi*," "With desire I have desired." I worship you then with all my best love and awe, with my fervent affection, with my most subdued, most resolved will. O my God, when you condescend to suffer me to receive you, to eat and drink you, and you for a while take up your abode within me, O make my heart beat with your heart. Purify it of all that is earthly, all that is proud and sensual, all that is hard and cruel, of all perversity, of all disorder, of all deadness. So fill it with yourself, that neither the events of the day nor the circumstances of the time may have power to ruffle it but that in your love and your fear it may have peace.

John Henry Newman

Our next voice on the Eucharist was an Anglican priest, theologian, and Oxford fellow. His conversion to Catholicism in 1845 alienated him from friends and colleagues in the Church of England and sparked debate among Catholics as well as Protestants. Having substantially changed his understanding of religious assent and the development of doctrine, he overcame his own prejudices and embraced the faith of the Church of Rome. This ripening of thought and devotion influenced every area of his faith, especially his approach to the Eucharist. All through his life his appreciation of the sacrament grew and the doctrine of the Real Presence became central to his devotional life and practice of the faith.

Path to Conversion

Although John Henry Newman (1801-90) was raised an Anglican and took delight in reading the Scriptures, in *Apologia pro Vita Sua* he states that he had no firm religious convictions until his embrace of low church Evangelicalism (a modified form of Calvinism) at the age of fifteen.[1] During his studies at Trinity College, Oxford, his probing mind eventually led him to begin delving more deeply into the origins of his religious faith, a process that years later would lead him to Rome.

Shortly after his election as fellow of Oxford's Oriel College in 1822, he began considering the Anglican priesthood. He was ordained in 1824 and for two years was the curate of St. Clement's, Oxford. In 1828 he became Vicar of St. Mary's, the university church where he delivered his famous *Parochial Sermons*. Around this time he began to explore the teachings of the Church Fathers and developed his *Via Media*, in which he describes the Church of England as being situated in the middle ground between Catholicism and Calvinism. During this time he associated with the high church reform known as the Oxford Movement, a relationship that led him to break from his low church affiliations. These developments, together with his belief in the religious nature of a college tutorship, led to a disagreement with the authorities of Oriel College and his eventual resignation.

Newman's study of the Fathers led him to embrace the high church reform party of Anglicanism and eventually

---

1. John Henry Newman, *Apologia pro Vita Sua* (London and New York: Longmans, Green, 1903), Chap. 1. See also *EN*, 15-19.

to break ties with the Church of England itself. A visit to Rome during a Mediterranean tour in 1832–33 also shaped him in his journey to Roman Catholicism, for it gave him an unforgettable, deep sense of Anglicanism's roots in the faith and rituals of this ancient patriarchal see. Although he would not take the final step until a decade later, the foundations of his conversion had been laid.

Upon returning to England, Newman dedicated himself to the intellectual tenets of the Oxford Movement. In 1833 he began his career as a High Anglican polemicist with *Tracts for the Times*, a series of pamphlets dedicated to rooting the Church of England in sound doctrine and discipline. A turning point came in 1841 with Tract 90, which examines the doctrinal tenets of the Church of England and tests their compatibility with Catholic doctrine. In it, he argues that the differences lie not in substantive issues, but in errors and misunderstanding.

The indignation of high-ranking officials in the Church of England about this *Tract* sealed Newman's movement toward Rome. He broke ties with the Oxford Movement in 1842 and retired to a life of study and practical piety with a small group of followers at Littlemore. There, on October 9, 1845, the Italian Passionist Dominic Barberi formally received him into the Roman Catholic Church.[2]

Newman's Spirituality

Shortly after his conversion, Newman published *An Essay on the Development of Doctrine* (1845). This treatise examines the nature of theological change and, in some respects, foreshadows elements of Darwin's theory of

---

2. The historical information in this section comes from Jean Honoré, *The Spiritual Journey of Newman*, trans. Sr. Mary Christopher Ludden (New York: Alba House, 1992), 249–50. For more on Newman's conversion to Catholicism, see Brian Martin, *John Henry Newman: His Life and* Work (New York/London: Paulist Press/Geoffrey Chapman Mowbray, 1990), 56–74. For important Newman biographies, see Ian Ker, *John Henry Newman: A Biography* (Oxford: Clarendon Press, 1988).

evolution. It also mirrors many of the changes in his own theological outlook that eventually led him to the Church of Rome.

Once he embraced the Catholic faith, Newman threw himself headlong into its theological and ecclesiastical affairs. He went to Rome, was ordained a Catholic priest in 1846, and was awarded the Doctor of Divinity degree by Pope Pius IX. He returned to England in 1847 and as a member of the Oratorians worked diligently to establish the order on British soil. He eventually established an Oratory in Birmingham, where he spent most of the rest of his life immersed in the religious discipline of his order and in scholarly pursuits that gained him international fame. During this time, he composed some of his most important works, such as *Idea of a University* (1852, 1858), *Apologia Pro Vita Sua* (1865–66), *The Dream of Gerontius* (1865), and *An Essay in Aid of a Grammar of Assent* (1870). Newman, an extraordinarily prolific author wrote in a number of literary genres: novels, poetry, letters, essays, tracts, treatises—to name just a few. He is considered a master of Victorian prose and one of the great theologians of the nineteenth century.[3]

Newman's spiritual outlook, historical and personal in tone, anticipated the twentieth-century existential search for Truth. He opposed the "enlightened" rationalism of Descartes that narrowed the scope of human knowledge. Instead, he fostered awareness of the underlying mystery of God and creation. He believed that reality was a mixture of both light and darkness, and that knowledge was not a matter of "clear and distinct" ideas, but a growth in wisdom that developed over time.[4] He realized that human language can never express the mysteries encountered by the human

---

3. Honoré, *The Spiritual Journey of Newman*, 249–50. For an assessment of Newman's theological and literary legacy, see Martin, *John Henry Newman*, 142–56.
4. *EN*, vi. For an assessment of Newman's theological and spiritual outlook, see Honoré, *The Spiritual Journey of Newman*, 225–31.

mind. Newman therefore understood the limitations of his own thinking and acknowledged that his ideas were subject to change, as *An Essay on the Development of Christian Doctrine* states: "To live is to change, and to be perfect is to have changed often."[5] His willingness to hold positions loosely so that they might mature over time, however, did not contradict his fundamental conviction that the mystery of truth, rooted in the mystery of God, was essentially unchanging. For Newman, change occurs not in the nature of truth itself, but in a person's growing awareness of it over time. He believed that time itself would confirm his ideas or prove them wrong.[6]

Newman's ideas on development and the personal grasp of truth led to his distinction between notional and real assent. True knowledge is not an abstract, intellectual pursuit but something that involves the whole person in his or her actual historical existence. Concerning the mysteries of the Christian faith, doctrines need intellectual assent, but even more a full embrace in heart and mind manifested in piety and devotional practice. For Newman, the sacraments provide Catholics with an opportunity for genuine religious assent, the Eucharist being the means by which such assent can be constantly affirmed in the daily life of the believer.[7]

Newman on the Eucharist

Although Newman did not contribute anything particularly original to the theology of the Eucharist, the sacrament held a central place in his life and devotion. According to the late Church historian John Tracy Ellis:

---

5. John Henry Newman, *An Essay on the Development of Christian Doctrine* (London and New York: Longmans, Green, 1885), Chap. 1, Sec. 1. See also *EN*, 118–123.
6. *EN*, vi-vii. For a treatment of Newman's ideas on the development of doctrine, see Ker, *John Henry Newman*, 257–315.
7. *EN*, 284–85, 288–95. For a treatment of Newman's ideas on the justification of religious belief, see Ker, *John Henry Newman*, 618–50.

> Where he [Newman] contributed most...was in the painstaking explanations he gave concerning his understanding of the Eucharist, but even more, perhaps, by the example of his personal devotion to the Blessed Sacrament and his virtually lifelong adherence to the doctrine of the Real Presence.[8]

Newman's belief in the Real Presence developed over time. When he was a low church Evangelical it was not significant in his theology and life of faith. His belief deepened as his affiliation with high church Anglicanism deepened, especially through the influence of Richard Hurrell Froude, a friend who introduced him to the doctrine of the Real Presence and to devotion to the Blessed Virgin.[9] In 1828, when at the age of twenty-seven Newman preached his first sermon on the Eucharist, he asserted that Jesus's Eucharistic Presence was a presence to faith rather than a presence to sight. In his early Anglican years, he emphasized that God conveys his gifts through the sacraments and that they need to be exercised in faith.[10]

By 1838, seven years before his conversion to Catholicism, Newman already had a highly nuanced belief in the Real Presence. It differed from Catholic doctrine only in terms of the doctrine of transubstantiation, which held that the substance of bread and wine were changed into the very substance of Christ's Body and Blood and that only the accidents of bread and wine remained.[11]

When he became a Catholic in 1845, he added transubstantiation to his belief in the Real Presence, even though he did not fully understand it. At this point, Newman's humility led him to submit his ideas to the truth and the authority

---

8. John Tracy Ellis, "The Eucharist in the Life of Cardinal Newman," *Communio* 4 (Winter, 1977): 339.
9. See Ellis, "The Eucharist in the Life of Cardinal Newman," 323.
10. See Alf Härdelin, *The Tractarian Understanding of the Eucharist* (Uppsala, 1965), 132. Cited in Ellis, "The Eucharist in the Life of Cardinal Newman," 323.
11. Ellis, "The Eucharist in the Life of Cardinal Newman," 324.

of the Church's teaching. In speaking of this doctrine in relation to Newman's conversion, Stephen Dessain notes:

> He [Newman] had long believed and taught most earnestly the doctrine of the real presence; he now added to it that of transubstantiation, thinking it to be included in the Church's teaching. But he knew that the reality of Christ's presence in the Holy Eucharist could not be adequately explained in words, and exclaimed: 'What do I know of substance or matter? Just as much as the greatest philosophers, and that is nothing at all.'[12]

Newman recognized that the mystery of the Eucharist could not be captured in human language and was satisfied that the Church has the authority to teach on issues that lie beyond human comprehension. As a Catholic, he recognized the incomprehensible mystery of the Eucharist, which he placed at the center of his spirituality. Jean Honoré points out,

> What is new and significant is not so much the fact that Newman understood the dogma of the Eucharist more clearly, but that he found in it a universal prayer and a bond of unity for all the faithful. This contemplation never left him feeling alone. This invisible world peopled with presences, angels, and saints, was never absent from his prayer life.[13]

Newman's diaries and letters clearly convey the centrality of devotion to Christ's Real Presence in the Eucharist in his life.[14] In 1846, for example, he wrote to his friend Henry William Wilberforce,

---

12. Cited in Charles Stephen Dessain, *John Henry Newman* (London: Thomas Nelson and Sons Ltd, 1966), 89. See also Ellis, "The Eucharist in the Life of Cardinal Newman," 324.
13. Honoré, *The Spiritual Journey of Newman*, 159.
14. See Placid Murry, *Newman the Ortorian. His Unpublished Oratory Papers* (Dublin: Gill and Macmillan Ltd., 1969), 43–58, 124. See also Ellis, "The Eucharist in the Life of Cardinal Newman," 325.

> I am writing next room to the Chapel — It is such an incomprehensible blessing to have Christ in bodily presence in one's house, within one's walls as swallows up all other privileges and destroys, or should destroy every pain. To know that He is close by — to be able again and again through the day to go in to Him.[15]

Such daily prayer before the Blessed Sacrament sustained Newman during the darkest periods of his life. It helped him to weather the controversy surrounding his leaving the Anglican fold for Catholicism. It kept him firm during the difficulties involved with establishing an Oratorian presence in England. It gave him courage and strength when his theological writings were held suspect and he had fallen out of favor with the authorities in Rome. In the Blessed Sacrament Newman found "the strongest moral support of his personal life."[16] The deep sense of security and help that he received from the sacrament fueled his desire to explain it to others.

Observations

After this glimpse into Newman's teaching and love for the Eucharist, the following remarks should deepen our appreciation of his devotion to the Real Presence and help us apply it to our own lives.

Newman's appreciation of the centrality of the Eucharist in the life of the faithful developed considerably throughout his life, his beliefs changing in his conversion from Evangelicalism to High Anglicanism and then to Roman Catholicism. His theory of the development of doctrine is important for understanding how Church teaching has matured over time. Believers can apply it analogously in their

---

15. Newman to Wilberforce, Maryvale, February 26, 1846 in Stephen Dessain, ed., *Letters and Diaries*, vol. 11 (London: Thomas Nelson and Sons Ltd, 1961), 129. See also Ellis, "The Eucharist in the Life of Cardinal Newman," 326.
16. Ellis, "The Eucharist in the Life of Cardinal Newman," 337.

own lives to understand how their own understanding of the faith matures. Such an understanding challenges us to examine our stand concerning the truths of the faith and to assess honestly, as Newman did, what we actually believe. For Newman, the doctrine of the Real Presence was not an abstract teaching to which he gave intellectual assent, but a vital reality that he embraced fully with mind and heart.

Friendship played an important role in Newman's developing appreciation of the Eucharist. Newman's faith did not develop in a vacuum. His friend, Richard Hurrell Froude, helped him recognize the importance of the doctrine of the Real Presence, an insight that eventually led him to move from the low Evangelical church to High Anglicanism. Conversely, friendship did not prevent Newman from following the strength of his own convictions. His friends in the Oxford Movement opposed him when his ideas about the nature of the faith (including those on the Eucharist) moved beyond the *Via Media* position he had developed years earlier. Nevertheless, he did not give in to their pressure and set a straight course for Rome.

The doctrine of the Real Presence was important to Newman because it provided a concrete sign of God's abiding love and friendship for the believer. Newman reciprocated that love by visiting the Blessed Sacrament often, praying before it, and resting in its presence. Moreover, his belief in the doctrine of the Real Presence did not displace his conviction that Jesus is present in the human heart. He did not consider them in opposition to one another, but as complementary. True devotion to the Blessed Sacrament could only deepen one's friendship with Christ—and vice versa. True friendship with Christ enables believers to see with the eyes of faith his hidden presence in the consecrated elements of bread and wine, in one another.

Because Newman realized that human language cannot fully express the mysteries of the faith, he was not troubled when he could not grasp the Catholic doctrine of transubstantiation. Instead, he embraced it wholeheartedly as an integral part of the Catholic faith for which he had come to feel reverence and great love. He understood that a prerequisite for the real assent of faith is not understanding, but trust. Like the Apostle Paul, in the present life we can only "see darkly as in a mirror."[17] His awareness of the limitations of human language, however, did weaken his belief that one day Truth would penetrate the human mind and reveal itself in all its fullness. That came about in Jesus Christ some 2,000 years ago and is achieved today in the Eucharist, which is foremost a sacramental mystery and secondarily a doctrine of the faith.

Finally, Newman's faithful embrace of what he did not fully understand indicates his deep humility before the Truth and his willingness to subject himself to those in the Church entrusted with elucidating its doctrine. Although recognized as one of the great theologians of his day, Newman's humility enabled him to acknowledge the limits of his mind before the mysteries of the faith. His humility was coupled with the courage to face the obstacles he encountered as he pursued the Truth—personal prejudices, friends, religious upbringing, cultural mores, and so forth. His humility before the Truth and courage to pursue it at all costs helped Newman navigate turbulent religious waters. He did so with such skill because his daily prayerful rest before the Blessed Sacrament nurtured these traits, giving him the strength to persevere.

Conclusion

John Henry Newman, a great nineteenth-century theologian, is recognized as a significant figure in Church history.

---

17. See 1Cor 13:12.

His long, arduous journey of faith led him from low church Evangelicalism to high church Anglicanism, and eventually to the Church of Rome. Even after his conversion to Catholicism, he suffered for his convictions of conscience and desire for Truth. Certain members of the Roman hierarchy were deeply suspicious of the forward-looking articles on the role of the laity in the Church that he published in *The Rambler* in 1859. Afterwards, he confined himself to a self-imposed exile of meditation and study at the Birmingham Oratory, feeling more and more resigned to his seeming lack of influence in Church affairs. Amid these and other failures, he developed a sense of abandonment and surrender to God's will, nourished by a life of prayer and solitude.[18]

Newman's multidimensional theological outlook was based on his examination of the origins of Christian doctrine, especially in the Scriptures and the Church Fathers. His writings on the development of Christian doctrine are a hallmark in the Church's self-understanding. Although at first his work met resistance and even outright hostility, it eventually gained acceptance and is now generally seen as a useful explanation of how the Church's theology matured over time.

In 1879, Pope Leo XIII made Newman a cardinal in recognition of his contribution to Catholic theology. Through the course of a long life, his growing maturity of mind and heart could have come only from the gentle movement of God's providential hand. Newman remained steadfast in his devotion of mind and heart to a search for Truth and maintained the strength to withstand the obstacles he had to face because of his deep love for the Eucharist and his unfailing devotion to Christ's Real Presence in the Blessed Sacrament.

---

18. Honoré, *The Spiritual Journey of Newman*, 182–86, 215–224, 229.

Reflection Questions

- Newman's belief in the Real Presence developed over time. When did you come to believe in the sacrificial nature of the Mass? In the Real Presence? How have your views toward the sacrament changed over time?

- Friendship played an important role in Newman's appreciation of the Eucharist. Which of your friends has helped you in this way? When have you played such a role in the lives of others? In what sense is the Eucharist a concrete sign of Christ's lasting and abiding friendship?

- Daily prayer before the Blessed Sacrament sustained Newman during his darkest periods. How does prayer before the Blessed Sacrament sustain you in your daily life? When has it helped you in the dark periods of your life?

Voice Twenty-One

Thérèse of Lisieux: Kiss of Love

How sweet it was, the first kiss of Jesus to my soul! Yes, it was a kiss of Love. I felt I was loved, and I too said: "I love Thee, I give myself to Thee forever!" Jesus asked nothing of me, demanded no sacrifice. Already for a long time past, He and the little Thérèse had watched and understood one another... That day our meeting was no longer a simple look but a fusion. No longer were we two: Thérèse had disappeared as the drop of water which loses itself in the depths of the ocean, Jesus alone remained; the Master, the King! Had not Thérèse begged Him to take away from her, her liberty? That liberty made her afraid; so weak, so fragile did she feel herself that she longed to be united forever to Divine Strength.

Thérèse of Lisieux

Our next voice on the Eucharist, one of the most beloved saints of modern times is revered for her childlike simplicity and trust in God's loving care She emphasizes the importance of seeking the Lord in all things and in placing every anxiety and care within his benevolent embrace. Her teaching on the Eucharist, which reflects this childlike trust in the Father's love, lies at the heart of her spiritual doctrine.

A Little Flower

St. Thérèse of Lisieux (1873–1897), "The Little Flower," is known for her "Little Way," or doctrine of spiritual childhood. She was the youngest of the nine children in a devout Catholic family in Alençon, Normandy. At fifteen, she entered the Carmelite monastery in Lisieux and died there of tuberculosis at twenty-four. In those nine years at Carmel, she lived a hidden life rooted in faith yet steeped in anguish and inner turmoil. Uniting herself to the sufferings of Christ, she offered herself entirely to God. Just before her death she stated that she would like to spend her life in heaven doing good on earth.

After her death Thérèse's reputation for sanctity blossomed; she was soon looked upon as a close friend of God with great powers of intercession. Pope Pius XI canonized her on May 17, 1925 and on October 19, 1997 Pope John Paul II declared her a Doctor of the Church. Widespread devotion to her has never waned. Today, her tomb in Lisieux is the second most popular pilgrimage site in France, after Lourdes. She outlines her spirituality in her autobiography, *The Story of a Soul* (1895–97), and in many letters written both before and after she entered Carmel. Her teaching on the Eucharist, based on her doctrine of spiritual childhood, affirms her position as a great spiritual master for the third millennium.[1]

Thérèse's Spirituality

Thérèse's "Little Way" contains three basic principles:

> (1) We must fully recognize our spiritual poverty, our incapacity, and accept this condition. (2) We must have recourse to God with blind and filial confidence, in order that He may accomplish in us what we cannot do by our own powers; for

---

1. For a historical account of Thérèse's life and spiritual journey, see Guy Gaucher, *The Spiritual Journey of St. Thérèse of Lisieux*, trans. Sr. Anne Marie Brennan (London: Darton, Longman and Todd, 1987). For testimonies and a genealogy of Thérèse's family, see idem, 219–27.

God is our Father; He is Love infinitely merciful. And (3) We must believe in Love and apply ourselves to the practice of love.[2]

These insights are rooted in Jesus's gospel message of becoming like a little child in order to enter the kingdom of God.[3] Thérèse herself says that she embraces "a little way to Heaven, very straight and direct, an entirely new way."[4] For her, holiness is not difficult to attain, but a gift of God's free and abundant grace. We need only a childlike acceptance that we cannot achieve holiness by ourselves and the humility to open our hearts to God's help.

Thérèse uses the image of an elevator to convey the newness of her spiritual message:

> We live in an age of inventions now, and the wealthy no longer have to take the trouble to climb the stairs; they take a lift. That is what I must find, a lift to take me straight up to Jesus, because I am too little to climb the steep stairway of perfection. So I searched the Scriptures for some hint of my desired life until I came upon these words from the lips of Eternal Wisdom: 'Whosoever is a little one, let him come to Me.'...Your arms, My Jesus, are the lift which will take me up to Heaven.[5]

These demonstrate the thoroughly Christocentric nature of Thérèse's spirituality. He alone is "the way, the truth, and the life."[6] He alone can bring us into the presence of our Father in heaven by lifting us up into his glorified humanity. He came into the world and became one of us for one purpose: to commune with us in a personal, intimate way.

---

2. François Jamart, *Complete Spiritual Doctrine of St.Thérèse of Lisieux*, trans. Walter van de Putte (Staten Island, NY: Alba House, 1961), 274.
3. See Mk 10:15; Mt 18:3; Lk 18:17.
4. Thérèse of Lisieux, *The Story of a Soul: The Autobiography of St. Thérèse of Lisieux*, trans. Michael Day; Foreword, Vernon Johnson (Westminster, MD: The Newman Press, 1952), 135.
5. Ibid. For the Scripture reference, see Prv 9:4.
6. Jn 14:6.

She responded to Jesus's love by trying at all times to live in, with, and through Jesus. Holiness, for her, meant living a life of intimate union with Jesus:

> [I]f you want to be a saint...occupy yourself with 'the one thing necessary,' that is to say: while you give yourself up devotedly to exterior works, your purpose is *simple*: to please Jesus, to unite yourself more intimately to Him.[7]

When once to write what she remembered most about her childhood, Thérèse said she would be glad to write the story of "the little flower gathered by Jesus... to make known all the gifts that Jesus has given her."[8] In her mind, Jesus was responsible for the many graces she had received in life, and to him she felt most indebted. It was Jesus who revealed to her over time the tenets of her "Little Way." This spiritual doctrine is linked to her special love for the Child Jesus, a devotion that later in her religious life gave way to a deep love for the Holy Face of Jesus. Walking the way of holiness meant gazing upon Jesus and having our eyes fixed on him at all times. By contemplating the face of Christ in this way, gradually we become conformed to his way of thinking and habituated to his way of acting. Shortly before her death she wrote to her sister Céline:

> Jesus is on fire with love for us...look at His adorable Face!... Look at His eyes lifeless and lowered! Look at His wounds.... Look at Jesus in His Face.... There you will see how he loves us.[9]

For Thérèse, contemplating the face of Christ puts us in touch with Jesus's humility. The disfigured face of her

---

7. Letter to Sister Léonie, July 16, 1897. See *Letters of St. Thérèse of Lisieux*, vol. 2, 1890–1897, trans. John Clarke (Washington, D.C.: Institute of Carmelite Studies, 1988), 1149.
8. Thérèse of Lisieux, *The Story of a Soul*, 7–8.
9. Letter to Céline, April 4,1889. See *Letters of St. Thérèse of Lisieux*, vol. 1, 1877–1890, trans. John Clarke (Washington, D.C.: Institute of Carmelite Studies, 1982), 553.

Savior is hidden, forgotten by the rich and powerful. By contemplating His face, Thérèse developed a desire to share in her Lord's sufferings and to be hidden in his: "If only my face, like the Face of Jesus, 'could be hidden from everyone,' that none on earth might take notice of me! I longed to suffer and to be despised."[10]

Thérèse on the Eucharist

Thérèse also manifested her love for Jesus in her love for the Holy Eucharist. She remembers how this love seemed when she received her first Holy Communion:

> How lovely it was, that first kiss of Jesus in my heart—it was truly a kiss of love. I knew that I was loved, and I said 'I love You, and I give myself to You for ever.' Jesus asked for nothing, He claimed no sacrifice. Long before that He and little Thérèse had seen and understood one another well, but on that day it was more than meeting; it was a complete fusion. We were no longer two, for Thérèse had disappeared like a drop of water lost in a mighty ocean.[11]

This fusion of hearts stands at the center of "The Little Way." Like the image of the elevator, she likens Jesus in the Eucharist to an eagle that carries her into God's presence:

> You are the Eagle whom I love…You who flew down to this land of exile, to suffer and die, that You might bear all souls away and plunge them deep into the bosom of the Blessed Trinity, the eternal home of Love. It is You who, though ascending to inaccessible light, yet stay in our valley of tears, hidden under the appearance of a small white host, to nourish me with Your own substance…. I hope that one day You will swoop upon me and carry me off to the furnace of love, and plunge me into its glowing abyss, that I may become forever its happy holocaust.[12]

---

10. Thérèse of Lisieux, *The Story of a Soul*, 106.
11. Ibid., 52.
12. Ibid., 195.

Thérèse attributed the many graces she received from Jesus to her close contact with him in the Eucharist. In this intimate communion of hearts, she received deep consolations and also a deep desire to share in the sufferings of Christ. She cites her Christmas communion of 1886 in particular as a time when she received a special grace of "conversion."[13]

Because receiving his body and blood nourished her close contact with Jesus, Thérèse yearned to receive him as often as possible. At a time when frequent communion was uncommon in Catholic practice and devotion, her confessor gave her permission to take Holy Communion several times a week.[14] Although Thérèse could not receive communion daily, she deeply desired to do so. On those days when she could not, she opened her heart to Jesus by making a spiritual communion. She desired to receive the sacrament as often as possible and enthusiastically encouraged the other sisters in the convent to do the same.[15]

That is not to say that Thérèse always felt consolation when receiving Holy Communion. Sometimes she received the sacrament in the midst of a deep lethargy, aridity, and dryness of soul. Such times did not discourage her, however, because she believed that she was receiving Jesus not for her own sake, but to give him pleasure.[16] She considered holiness to be Jesus's work, not hers. She believed that there was no more effective way of being completely transformed in Christ than by worthily receiving his body and blood.[17]

By receiving the Eucharist Thérèse also felt a communion with all the living members of Christ's Mystical Body. This strong sense of communion with Jesus and the community of the faithful made her treasure the interces-

---

13. See Jamart, *Complete Spiritual Doctrine of St.Thérèse of Lisieux*, 246.
14. Thérèse of Lisieux, *The Story of a Soul*, 70. See also Madeline Grace, "Thérèse of Lisieux and Frequent Communion," *Emmanuel* 105 (no. 3, 1999): 166–71.
15. See Jamart, *Complete Spiritual Doctrine of St.Thérèse of Lisieux*, 246–47.
16. Thérèse of Lisieux, *The Story of a Soul*, 124.
17. See Jamart, *Complete Spiritual Doctrine of St.Thérèse of Lisieux*, 247.

sory power of prayer and deepened her desire to help others through her own prayers. It also strengthened her desire to dwell in Jesus's heart and to be an instrument of love for others in life as well as death.[18]

Observations

Thérèse's spirituality demonstrates her love for Christ and the centrality of the Eucharist in her daily walk of faith. The following observations will present further insights concerning her teaching on the Eucharist and connect it to everyday life.

The Eucharist connects closely with Thérèse's way of spiritual childhood. The analogy is clear. Just as little children must rely on their parents for every necessity of life, so must we must rely on God for every necessity for our spiritual journey. Thérèse considered the Eucharist to be food from heaven that strengthened those on a spiritual journey, but also brought them into intimate communion with God's Son, Jesus Christ. This communion with Jesus places us in a new relationship to God the Father. We relate to Father through Jesus the Son, so much so that we can now be called God's sons and daughters. Thérèse realized that Jesus's presence in the Eucharist made this intimate relationship with the Father possible. When receiving the Eucharist, she felt that the Father was feeding her. In childlike simplicity she even referred to God as "Papa, the good Lord."[19]

Thérèse's love for the Eucharist put her in close contact with the person of Christ and with his paschal mystery. Receiving the sacrament intertwined her journey more and more with Jesus's passion and death. As her intimacy with Jesus grew, Thérèse came to embrace her own suffering as he embraced his cross. By her relationship with Christ,

---

18. Ibid., 247–49.
19. Ibid., 242

moreover, she embraced her excruciating anguish of body and soul and found meaning in it. By uniting her suffering to Christ's, she passed through her turmoil to the profound joy that comes from total resignation to the will of God. The Eucharist helped Thérèse unite herself to Jesus and with him offer her entire self to the Father. Through it, she found consolation in her suffering and even a foretaste of heaven's joy.

The Eucharist helped Thérèse appreciate the hidden nature of Jesus's mission. Through her devotion to the Holy Face she came to understand Jesus's humility in becoming man and undergoing an ignoble death. Jesus reveals that same humility in becoming present in the bread and wine, which gives us spiritual nourishment for our journey to God. The Eucharist indeed is the "sacrament of love," but is also the "sacrament of humility." Jesus's presence there is hidden. He remains in the tabernacle day and night, concealed in the bread and wine, yearning to be visited and to be consumed in Holy Communion. Jesus's hiddenness in the sacrament inspired Thérèse to live in a similar manner. She longed to be forgotten by the world, far from the center of attention. Jesus was enough for her, and following Jesus meant walking the way of humility.

Thérèse connected her appreciation of Jesus's hiddenness in the Eucharist with the Eucharist's centrality to her life of prayer. Just as she yearned to contemplate the Jesus's Holy Face, she understood that Holy Communion brought her into intimate union with Jesus himself. Jesus's presence within enabled her to contemplate him in the most profound way possible. Prayer, for Thérèse, was the soul's intimate conversation with God. She recognized how much pleasure her receiving Holy Communion brought to Jesus and that her contemplation of Jesus was reciprocated by Jesus's contemplation of her. She believed that there was no better time to enter into intimate conversation than after receiving the sacred host. Worthy reception of the Eucharist brings a person closest to Jesus. From this intimate union unfolds the transformation of our lives.

Communion with Christ in the Eucharist also allowed Thérèse to appreciate her connection with other believers and to see the meaning and purpose of intercessory prayer. If Jesus intercedes for us with the Father, then those united to him as members of his body can share in his intercession. Thérèse connected the doctrine of the Communion of Saints with her understanding of the Church as Christ's Mystical Body. When we receive Holy Communion, we celebrate our intimate union not only with Christ, but also with other believers. As a result, our prayers for others are joined to Jesus's prayer to the Father on our behalf. When we receive Jesus in Holy Communion, therefore, our prayers mingle with his and are carried into the Father's presence, where they are received, pondered, and judiciously acted upon. Because of their intimate union with Jesus, the prayers of the saints, the true "friends of God," are given special attention and blessed with a special efficacy. More than anything else, Thérèse desired to be Christ's close, intimate friend.

Thérèse desired to receive Holy Communion as often as possible, even though the Catholic world generally adhered to more rigid practices due to the lingering effects of persistent Jansenist influences, even after they had been condemned. Not until 1905, during the pontificate of Pius X, was daily communion encouraged as a devotional practice among the Catholic faithful. Her views on receiving Holy Communion, which were ahead of her time, demonstrate her single-hearted devotion to a loving and merciful God. These views flowed from her overall spiritual outlook, which focused on God's kindness and generosity instead of devotional rigorism. Thérèse's attitude toward frequent

Communion reflects a spirituality that celebrates God's generous and constant longing to dwell within the human heart. If "everything is grace," as she often said, then the Eucharist, the source of his constant stream of transforming grace, expresses God's love for us.

Finally, it is important to understand how the various strains of Thérèse's spirituality converge in her teaching on the Eucharist. Her "Little Way" of spiritual childhood, her Christocentrism, her devotion to Jesus's Holy Face, her desire to do God's will, her embrace of suffering, her desire to lead a hidden, forgotten life, her belief in the communion of saints and the power of intercessory prayer, her desire for daily communion, her joy and gratitude for the many graces she received, all of these aspects of her spiritual outlook come together in the Eucharist and find their home there. For Thérèse, Jesus's arms were like an elevator that lifted her into the Father's presence, or an eagle whose wings carried her to the threshold of the divine; and the Eucharist was the visible, divinely-chosen instrument by which Jesus carried out his plans. The Eucharist, for her, went beyond imagery and symbolism, and represented God's visible, transforming action in the world and in the lives of all who believe in him and receive him worthily.

Conclusion

As a doctor of the Church, Thérèse of Lisieux has been recognized for the value of her spirituality for believers of all ages and in all times. As the Church's youngest and most recently declared doctor, she has particular significance for today's believers, many of whom struggle, as she did, with anxieties of heart that sometimes even border on despair. Amid such dark and ominous interior forces, she witnesses to the power of simple, childlike faith. This is why she has been heralded as a doctor for the new millennium.

Thérèse's spiritual outlook is keenly suited to contemporary sensitivities. Although she died at the end of the nineteenth century, her spirituality anticipates the intense spiritual struggles that believers would face in the twentieth century and beyond. And as a new millennium dawns, her message of complete dependence on God continues to strike a resonant chord in all who seek God with a sincere heart. This is true especially concerning her teaching on the Eucharist.

Thérèse felt that she was truly resting in the heart of Christ just after having received Holy Communion. In that moment, the Lord physically made his abode in her, shedding many graces upon her. She, in turn, opened her heart to him in the deepest and most intimate of unions, one that spanned all of human experience, from abandonment and desolation to heights of joy. Throughout her life, the Eucharist was at the center of Thérèse's spirituality; the means by which she was transformed interiorly into a real disciple of Christ, into someone who took delight in taking up her cross daily and following wherever he might lead. In this way, her "Little Way" demonstrates how to follow the "Way of Christ." And her spirituality can also be described as the "Way of the Eucharist."

Reflection Questions

- When receiving Jesus in the Eucharist, Thérèse felt that she had disappeared like a drop of water in a mighty ocean. How does that image describe the relationship between God and his creatures? How does that image reflect Thérèse's experience of spiritual intimacy?
- Through the Eucharist, Thérèse also felt a communion with the living members of Christ's Mystical Body. When you receive, how might the sacrament allow you to feel a communion with the other members of his Body, the Church?
- In the Eucharist, Thérèse felt she was being fed by the Father. In her childlike simplicity she even would refer to God as "Papa, the good Lord." What is the relationship between Thérèse's devotion to the Eucharist and her doctrine of spiritual childhood? How did the Eucharist lead her to this spiritual outlook?

Voice Twenty-Two

Charles de Foucauld: Nearness to Jesus

> What is it we are asking here, O God? We are asking, both for today itself, and the whole of life (a life that in reality is no longer than a day) for that bread which is more precious than anything else: that is, our supernatural bread, the only bread we really need, the only bread absolutely necessary to us if we are to reach our goal — the necessary bread of grace.
>
> *Charles de Foucauld*

Our next voice on the Eucharist, one of the most enigmatic Catholic figures of the early twentieth century, attracted few, if any, followers during his lifetime. Nevertheless, he has inspired many to model their own lives on Jesus' hidden life at Nazareth. His emphasis on being present to the poor and abandoned, and offering them hospitality conveys with stark simplicity its gospel focus on bringing Christ to others through the witness of one's own life. The Eucharist holds a striking place in his understanding of spiritual life and permeates his understanding of vocation.

Desert Dweller

In his fifty-eight years, Charles de Foucauld (1858–1916) had a wide range of life experiences. Born to an aristocratic family of Strasbourg, he was orphaned at an early age, by the age of twenty inherited a huge fortune, entered the

French military as an officer, lost his faith in God, and soon gained a reputation for an extravagant bohemian lifestyle. During military service in Algeria, he consumed fine food and drink and openly kept a young woman as his mistress. He abruptly left his post when his commanders asked him to change his immoral ways, but out of loyalty returned when his unit came under attack.

After his military service he returned to France for a short time before returning to explore the African desert, first along Morocco's Algerian border and later in southern Algeria and Tunisia. During his travels in North Africa he developed a fascination with the Arabic language and Islam. He returned to Paris to lecture and to publish his findings. At that time, he had a remarkable conversion experience through the influence of his cousin, Marie Moitessier, and an encounter with l'Abbé Huvelin, a French priest assigned to the Church of St. Augustine in Paris. He made a sincere confession and received Holy Communion.

Charles's life was transformed. Within a few short years, he entered the Trappist monastery of Our Lady of the Snows in France. Six months later, he asked to be sent to a much poorer monastery in Syria, eventually moving to the Holy Land to serve the Poor Clares in Nazareth. During his time in the Middle East, the idea came to him to establish a religious order based on the hidden life of Jesus. He returned to France in 1900 for ordination, then moved to Morocco in 1901 to live in the Sahara as a hermit.

For the next fifteen years Charles lived a life of adoration, presence, and hospitality in a Touareg village. Throughout these years, the Eucharist was central to his life and spirit. During an insurrection against French colonial power, he was betrayed by a trusted guide and was murdered by a Senoussi *rezzou* on December 1, 1916. He was beatified by Pope Benedict XVI on November 13, 2005.[1]

---

1. For the important dates and events of de Foucauld's life, see Jean-Jacques Antier,

Foucauld's Spirituality

Charles's was a new kind of apostolate, one of evangelizing, not by word, but by presence of the Most Blessed Sacrament, by offering the divine Sacrifice, praying, doing penance, practicing the evangelical virtues, sharing even one's last mouthful of bread with any of the poor, guest, any stranger, and being host to any human being as to a beloved brother.[2]

He modeled his own style of missionary presence on Jesus's hidden life at Nazareth. He considered Jesus's early life in a small Galilean village as important to his public ministry. During this time Jesus sanctified the ordinary activities of daily life, by growing up as a young child in the household of Joseph and Mary and in his young adult life by learning the carpenter's trade, earning his daily bread by the work of his hands and the sweat of his brow.

Charles saw that Jesus's hidden life at Nazareth proclaimed God's presence amid his people. To be Emmanuel, "God with us," Jesus did not need to preach, or teach, or cast out demons; he merely dwelt among his people, lived with them and shared in their daily struggles. Such presence, a powerful witness in its own right, prepared him for his public ministry and his suffering, death, and resurrection. For Charles, Nazareth represented the hidden life that during his public ministry Jesus carried with him throughout Galilee and Judea, even to the summit of Calvary.

Charles also realized that the main element of Jesus's hidden life was self-denial—forgetting himself in order to live for others. In his writings he often emphasized this virtue:

Charles de Foucauld (*Charles of Jesus*) (San Francisco: Ignatius Press, 1997), 335–39. See also Kate White, "The Hidden Life of Charles de Foucauld: An Explorer, Monk, Priest Who Did Nothing by Half-Measures,"*National Catholic Reporter* (Novermber 11, 2005): 13–15.

2. Cited in Leon Cristiani, *Charles de Foucauld: Life and Spirit* (Derby, NY: St. Paul Publications, 1965), 95.

We must no longer live for ourselves but for our neighbor, who is Jesus. We must forget about ourselves, which is the first thing that Jesus wants of his disciples. Not only must we do good to others at certain times, but we must never let a chance to do good to a neighbor pass by without acting upon it.[3]

He viewed self-denial as integral to discipleship. Picking up one's cross and following Christ meant, first and foremost, placing the concerns of others before one's own.

Charles's spirituality can be summed up in three words: contemplation, communion, and presence. Every day he spent hours in adoration before the Blessed Sacrament, pouring out his heart to Jesus and sharing his most intimate thoughts. Taking to heart St. Paul's injunction to "pray without ceasing" (1Thes 5:17), he prayed before the Blessed Sacrament with his whole being, even experiencing profound moments when he would simply rest in wordless prayer in intimate communion with his Lord and Savior. He took this deep communion with him to the Touareg village in the Southern Sahara. He did not preach to the Berber villagers or try to convert them with sophisticated arguments. He believed, simply by entering into communion with them, that Christ himself would also become present to them.

Charles's mission was to bring the contemplative presence of Christ's hidden life at Nazareth to areas untouched by the proclamation of the gospel. It also included recognizing Christ in the stranger and unbeliever, preparing them to recognize Christ in themselves and others. During his years of desert solitude, he wrote a rule of life that embodied this spiritual outlook and sought to establish a religious order dedicated entirely to witnessing the silent, hidden presence of Christ in the poor, forsaken outposts of the world. He was martyred, however, without a single follower. Years passed

---

3. Charles de Foucauld, *Scriptural Meditations on Faith* (New York: New City Press, 1988), 66.

before his spiritual legacy inspired others to continue his work and mission. And at the heart of the family that grew up after him was the Eucharist, just as it was at the heart of Charles's spirituality.

Foucauld on the Eucharist

We can understand Charles's teaching on the Eucharist by looking at the way he prayed before the sacrament. We are fortunate to have some of his prayers to the Holy Eucharist, written presumably during quiet adoration or after having received Holy Communion.

One meditation begins:

> Lord Jesus, you are in the Holy Eucharist. You are there a yard away in the tabernacle. Your body, your soul, your human nature, your divinity, your whole being is there, in its twofold nature. How close you are, my God, my Savior, my Jesus, my Brother, my Spouse, my Beloved![4]

With these words, Charles sums up Catholic Eucharistic belief and conveys his deep sense of Jesus's closeness to us in the Blessed Sacrament. He also lets us glimpse the many ways in which he related to Jesus, as if no single human relationship was enough to describe the intimate bond they shared.

At one point, Charles offers a beautiful description of Jesus's nearness in the sacrament:

> "You were not nearer to the Blessed Virgin during the nine months she carried you in her womb than you are to me when you rest on my tongue at Holy Communion. You were no closer to the Blessed Virgin and St. Joseph in the caves at Bethlehem or the house at Nazareth or during the flight into Egypt, or at any moment of that divine family life than you are to me at this moment—in the tabernacle. St. Mary

---

4. Charles de Foucauld, *Spiritual Autobiography of Charles de Foucauld,*. ed. Jean-Franois Six, trans. J. Holland Smith (New York: P.J. Kennedy & Sons, 1964), 98.

Magdalene was no closer to you when she sat at your feet at Bethany than I am here at the foot of this altar. You were no nearer to your apostles when you were sitting in the midst of them than you are to me now, my God. How blessed I am![5]

Charles considered receiving Jesus in Holy Communion the greatest privilege a person could ever hope for. Overwhelmed by Jesus's nearness in the sacrament, he longed to bring that quiet presence to others, especially those who lived in desolate, distant places where Christianity had not yet taken root.

While Charles respected those who went on pilgrimage to the Holy Land, to the places where Jesus had once walked, he believed that such journeys paled in comparison with simply visiting Jesus in the Blessed Sacrament:

O God, to go and kiss the places you made holy during your life on earth—the stones of Gethsemane and Calvary, the ground along the Way of Sorrows, the waves of the sea of Galilee—but to prefer it to your tabernacle would be to desert the Jesus living beside me, to leave him alone, going away alone to venerate the dead stones in places where he is no longer.[6]

It would be foolish to value such locations over the Real Presence:

It would be to leave the room he is in—and with it his divine companionship—to go to kiss the floor of a room he was in, but is in no longer. To leave the tabernacle to go and venerate statues would be to leave the Jesus living at my side to go into another room to greet his portrait.[7]

Charles saw an infinite difference between making a pilgrimage and making a simple visit to Jesus in the Blessed Sacrament.

---

5. Ibid.
6. Ibid.
7. Ibid., 98–99.

Receiving Holy Communion is the most important act any of us could do; the next best, Charles believed, would be to visit and spend time with the Blessed Sacrament:

> Is it not true that someone in love feels that he has made perfect use of all the time he spends in the presence of his beloved? Apart from this, is not that time used best which is employed in doing the will or furthering the welfare of his beloved in some other place?[8]

At one point in his meditation, Charles has Jesus himself affirming the essential teaching of the Eucharist:

> Wherever the sacred Host is to be found, there is the living God, there is your Savior, as really as when he was living and talking to Galilee and Judea, as really as he now is in heaven."[9]

Jesus's nearness in the sacrament reveals his infinite love for humanity and longing that we receive him in the sacrament:

> Never deliberately miss Holy Communion. Communion is more than life, more than all the good things of this world, more than the whole universe: it is God himself, it is I, Jesus. Could you prefer anything to me? Could you, if you love me at all, however little, voluntarily lose the grace I give you in this way? Love me in all the breath and simplicity of your heart.[10]

Charles's intimate friendship with Jesus allowed him to converse with him in the depths of his heart and inspired him to share what he felt in writing. So intimate was this relationship that he even wrote in the voice of Jesus, his Lord, his Master, and his Savior.

---

8. Ibid., 99.
9. Ibid.
10. Ibid.

Observations

Because of his ardent love for Christ, Charles found Eucharist to be essential in his daily walk of faith. The following remarks explore his teaching on the Eucharist and suggest how to apply it in our own lives.

Charles demonstrated his missionary character by being present to others through hospitality. He considered the Eucharist to be the strongest testimony of God's love for humanity. God loves us so much that he desires to be present everywhere. God wishes not only to dwell among us, but also to become our spiritual nourishment. Charles considered "presence" and "hospitality," the two vital and intimately related dimensions of the sacramental mystery, to represent the concrete outpouring of Christ's redemptive mission. Christ saved us through his sacrificial death on the cross; the passing from death to new life is mediated to humanity through Christ's constant, hospitable presence in the Holy Eucharist. Our faith asks us to be present and hospitable to others as Christ is present to us in the Eucharist.

Charles took this last insight to heart: the missionary character of Christ's hospitable presence in the Blessed Sacrament shaped his apostolate of hospitable presence to the people of the Southern Sahara. Like Jesus in the Eucharist, his hidden presence made itself known in quiet, unobtrusive ways. He saw the connection between Jesus's hidden life in Nazareth and his presence in the Eucharist hidden beneath the appearances of bread and wine, and lived out that connection. His decision to live a hidden life in one of the most remote corners of the world reflects Jesus's redemptive journey from the heart of the Father to live amid an impoverished and sinful humanity. Charles's simple life of presence and hospitality demonstrates how all believers can also carry Jesus's presence to others.

During his hidden life at Nazareth, Jesus realized his intimate relationship with the Father. He carried this intimate relationship wherever he went, professing his desire to do the Father's will, whatever it might entail. Jesus's hidden life at Nazareth is connected to his intimate relationship with the Father, his desire to do the Father's will, and his ultimate embrace of the cross at Calvary. Through his intimate bond with Jesus in the Eucharist, Charles also connected his own hidden life among the Touareg of the Sahara and his desire to carry out God's will. He loved the people with whom he lived and chose to remain with them even when his life was in danger. His violent death at the hands of marauding thieves was an extension of his mission of loving presence that emerged from his love for the sacrament, the Father's will, and the people he served. Such courage in the face of adversity reminds us that a true disciple of Christ will go to any length to do God's will.

Charles's ministry of presence and hospitality in non-Christian environs prefigured the emphasis on pre-evangelization that became so important for the Church's missionary efforts around the world. This ministry is founded on the recognition that the hearts of unbelievers must be prepared for the preaching of the Word by saintly figures who mediate the presence of Christ to them by their very lives. Bringing Christ to others means much more than merely preaching the truth about Christ. Just as Christ entered our world, gave himself completely to become our nourishment and source of hope, so are we called to do the same for others. Charles recognized that inculturation of the gospel is an extension of Christ's incarnation, which prepared peoples' hearts for receiving the Word. In this light, his ministry of presence and hospitality can be seen as evangelization in the truest sense of the word. He brought Christ to others simply by dwelling among them and loving them with all his heart.

Finally, Charles's spirituality of contemplation, communion, and presence demonstrates the interrelated nature of the contemplative and missionary nature of the Church. Contemplation leads to communion with Christ. This intimate relationship then propels us to missionary activity which, in turn, leads us back to contemplation. A circular relationship between *contemplatio, communio,* and *missio* generates a dynamic, persevering missionary presence even in hostile environments. This dynamic presence reflects the immanent and economic relationships within the Trinity, is embodied in the person of Jesus Christ, and continues through time in the celebration of the Holy Sacrifice of the Mass and in Jesus' presence in the Blessed Sacrament. Such authentic discipleship, which inspires people to give their lives to Christ—even to the point of dying for him—sustains all the Church's missionary activity.

Conclusion

Charles de Foucauld was a missionary hermit in one of the most desolate places on earth. He lived this life out of his conviction that God had called him to make Christ present in places where the people had never before experienced him. He chose a foreign land and culture not because he felt superiority or needed to escape his own cultural surroundings, but out of his love for the local people, who he befriended over time and who eventually befriended and accepted him.

|Charles's spirituality may be described as a "contemplative missionary presence." It was mystical, meaning that he sought to live out the gospel and share it with others by living among them and partaking in their daily lives. His mysticism did not retreat into a world of isolated personal bliss, but manifested itself in "a charitable life of helping

the poor."[11] He learned how to love and nourished it through his unfailing devotion to Jesus in the Most Holy Sacrament.

Charles's life, spirituality, and missionary presence to the Berber tribes of the southern Sahara centered on the Eucharist. It alone caused him to embark on so perilous a life. It provided for him a spiritual oasis for his thirsting soul in a desert wasteland amid people from a vastly different culture and religion. He never tried to convert his Muslim neighbors, but never concealed his convictions about Christ's saving presence in the Eucharist. Like Christ, he extended a loving, hospitable presence to others by offering himself on their behalf, even to the point of dying for them.

Reflection Questions

- Foucauld had a strong sense of being present to others through hospitality. How did the Eucharist foster this attitude of hospitality? How does the sacrament represent the hospitality of God? How might such hospitality be called "missionary"?

- Foucauld connected Jesus's hidden life in Nazareth and his hidden presence in the Eucharist beneath the appearances of bread and wine. How does Jesus's hidden life at Nazareth connect to your own? What draws you it? What do you find appealing about it? How does it challenge you?

- Foucauld's spirituality demonstrates the relationship between the contemplative and missionary nature of the Church. How would you describe this relationship? What is the importance of each dimension? How do they depend on each other?

---

11. Antier, *Charles de Foucauld*, 256.

Voice Twenty-Three

Thomas Merton: Living Bread

> Jesus wants us to "come to him" not only in faith, but also in sacramental union: for union with Christ in all the sacraments and particularly in the Blessed Eucharist not only signifies and symbolizes our complete mystical integration in him, but also produces that which it signifies. "He who eats my flesh and drinks my blood abides in me and I in him. As the living Father has sent me and as I live because of the Father, so he who eats me, he also shall live because of me" (Jn 6:57–58).
>
> *Thomas Merton*

Our next voice on the Eucharist was a Trappist monk of Our Lady of Gethsemani Abbey in Kentucky, whose renowned autobiography, *The Seven Storey Mountain*, captured the religious imagination of an entire generation; he is considered one of the great masters of the spiritual life. Since his unfortunate death more than four decades ago, his many writings on prayer and contemplation continue to shape the hearts and minds of those searching for a deeper experience of the Christian faith. His writings have inspired people worldwide to integrate contemplative prayer with their daily lives. While some have followed his own path into a monastic setting, many more have sought to carry his spirit of prayer and solitude into their busy and active lives. His teaching on the Eucharist offers a wonderful starting point from which believers can foster a spirit of contemplation while living in a world of frenzied action.

Monastic Solitude

In his early life, Thomas Merton (1915–1968) reveals a restless spirit desperately searching for an identity and place to call home. Born at Prades, France on January 31, 1915, he lost his mother when he was six and his father at sixteen. When his father was still alive, he studied for a time in France and then in England, where he attended Oakham and Cambridge. A few years after his father's death, he went to Douglaston, L.I., to live with his maternal grandparents. While there, he attended Columbia University in New York, earning his B.A. in English in 1938 and his M.A. in the same subject the following year.

During these early years, Merton experienced bouts of intense loneliness, which he tried to numb with smoking, alcohol, partying, and other assorted Bohemian escapes. While at Cambridge he had even fathered a child. He also found himself questioning the meaning of his life and seeking to understand the philosophical grounds for the structure of reality. While at Columbia he began to consider seriously the Catholic faith. He began attending Mass regularly and eventually decided to take instruction.

Although pulled in various directions and trying to focus his energies on his literary career, he felt an urge (almost a compulsion) to enter the Church. As he listened to the quiet stirrings of his heart, he even began entertaining thoughts about entering a religious order, possibly even becoming a priest. While teaching at St. Bonaventure University in Olean, NY from 1939 to 1941, he briefly considered joining the Franciscans. Although that path led him nowhere, another opened up during a retreat at the Trappist monastery at Gethsemani. Struck by a deep sense of belonging and an even deeper intuition that he could find peace in a life of monastic solitude, he sought permission to enter and was accepted. On December 10, 1941 he walked through the gates of the Abbey of Gethsemani,. His monastic vocation shaped not only his own life, but also those of many others. He died on the twenty-seventh anniversary of his entrance into monastic life half a world away, in Thailand.

Merton's Spirituality

Merton's life before his entrance into the monastery reveals a man in search of his deepest self. His contemplative outlook reflects such restlessness, for it is rooted in the distinction between a person's true self and false self. Throughout his writings Merton asserts that, for much of our lives, we follow the desires and urges of a false identity that masks our true identity. Over time, we find ourselves possessed by attitudes and debilitating habits that divide us from our deepest needs and truest selves. Merton's spiritual life involved a journey from surface appearances and attachments to the depths of his heart, where he encountered God in solitude and was able to live from his center. "We experience God," he once wrote,

> in proportion as we are stripped and emptied of attachment to His creatures. And when we have been delivered from every desire we shall taste the perfection of an incorruptible joy.[1]

In contemplation, Merton discovered a state of being in communion with God that spilled over into his daily activities. Oriented toward both God and others, it manifests itself in action flowing from the depth of solitude. Being and doing are intimately related. The transformation of the world begins by seeking to nurture a contemplative outlook and permitting God to change us from the inside out. Love

---

1. Thomas Merton, *Seeds of Contemplation* (London: The Catholic Book Club, 1950), 182.

of God and neighbor are intimately related. Merton puts it this way:

> The truth I must love in my brother is God Himself, living in him. I must seek the life of the Spirit of God breathing in him. And I can only discern and follow that mysterious life by the action of the same Holy Spirit living and acting in the depths of my own heart.[2]

Throughout his writings Merton declares that, by plumbing the depths of our hearts, we discover our common ground with others, eventually encountering the Spirit of God. Illumined by God's grace, this experience leads us to discover our true selves. Merton says that the contemplative journey rests upon this discovery and lies at the heart of reality. It is what unites us to ourselves, others, and God. He expressed this through John Donne's notion that "No man is an island," even using it as a book title.[3] He took these words of the poet to heart and pondered them often. We are all connected by our common humanity, created in the image and likeness of God. Contemplation, for Merton, brings about an awareness of true identity and prepares us for our journey home. The Eucharist, in turn, provides the food we need on our journey of self-discovery.

Merton on the Eucharist

In his book *The Living Bread*, Merton's discusses his views on the Eucharist. In the Prologue, he calls the Eucharist: "...the greatest of all the sacraments, the crown of the whole Christian life on earth... the sacrament of charity... in which Christ not only gives us grace but actually gives us Himself."[4]

---

2. Thomas Merton, *No Man Is an Island* (Garden city, NY: Image, 1955), 22.
3. Ibid., 9.
4. Thomas Merton, *The Living Bread* (New York: Farrar, Strauss and Cudahy, 1956), ix.

Affirming Catholic teaching, he also states that in this sacrament of love "Jesus Christ Himself is truly and substantially present, and remains present as long as the consecrated species of bread and wine continue in existence."[5] He goes on to identify the Eucharist with "the very heart of Christianity" since it contains Christ Himself and is the primary means by which Christ unites the faithful to himself in one mystical body.[6]

Merton explains that the Eucharist extends the Incarnation of God's Word through time, reaching into human hearts and souls to fulfill God's plan that all things be reconciled in Christ.[7] He also notes the connection between the Eucharist and Christ's sacrificial death on Calvary:

> ...the Eucharistic sacrifice makes present on the altar the sacrifice of Calvary, by which man is redeemed; the Eucharist re-enacts the most important event in the history of mankind. It communicates to all men the fruits of Redemption.[8]

For Merton, the Eucharist also signals the future consummation of human history. For this reason, it "is a prophetic sign of the Last Judgment and of the general resurrection and of our entrance into glory."[9]

Merton considers the Eucharist, which lies at the heart of Catholic faith and ultimately constitutes the Church, to be "the central mystery of Christianity."[10] Concerning this, he quotes St Bonaventure:

> It is by this Sacrament that the Church continues in existence, by this sacrament that faith is made strong, that the Christian religion and divine worship flourish. It is by reason

---

5. Ibid.
6. Ibid., ix-x.
7. Ibid., ix.
8. Ibid., x.
9. Ibid.
10. Ibid.

of this Sacrament that Christ says: 'Behold I am with you all days even to the end of time' (Mt 28:20).[11]

The Eucharist keeps the memory of the Christ event fresh in the mind of the Church; it makes Christ's person and sacrificial action present to the members of his mystical body; it offers food and sustenance for their pilgrim journey through life and to the consummation of time.

Those who receive the Eucharist worthily "[come] into contact with the Logos, the Word of Life, and [are] by that very fact filled with spiritual life."[12] Merton maintains that Christ instituted the Eucharist so that he could enter into us and commune with us intimately. Having partaken of the Lord's Body and Blood, we are filled with the Holy Spirit and united with the Logos "as if He were the soul of our own soul and the being of our own being."[13] Holy Communion centers our lives totally on Christ, enabling us to communicate with our deepest and truest selves. Such unique and intimate contact with Christ allows deeper insights into the dimensions of the contemplative journey. In the context of the Eucharist, contemplation means allowing the Incarnation to take root in our hearts so that the narrative of Christ's paschal mystery can manifest itself in our lives, enabling us to be a loving and healing presence to others. It also means sharing in the solitude of Christ and making it our own so that the hidden attitudes and attachments of our false selves will dissipate so that we can be moved and led by the promptings of the Spirit.

Observations

Thomas Merton's teaching on the Eucharist has even greater quality and depth of insight than these notes have conveyed. The following remarks probe his teaching further and highlight its relevance for today.

---

11. Ibid., x-xi. See also St. Bonaventure, *De preparatione ad Missam*, i,3.
12. Merton, *The Living Bread*, 109.
13. Ibid., 110.

Merton sees an intrinsic link between Eucharist and prayer, especially the particular form of wordless prayer known as "contemplation." Because the Eucharist is the worship of the Church par excellence, those who receive it should experience a gradual increase in the quality and depth of their relationship with God. The prayer of the Church, in other words, strengthens the prayer of its individual members and improves its quality and depth. It highlights the relationship between the individual and the community and encourages each individual to find his or her proper place in the body of Christ.

Merton acknowledges each person's unique and irreplaceable relationship with God. Although the Christian tradition contains many insights into the nature of prayer and an extensive body of rules and guidelines, he recognizes that because no two people pray in exactly the same way each individual should choose his or her particular method of prayer. In Christ's mystical body each person makes a unique contribution to the good of the whole. People are called to worship God through different types of prayer (e.g., *oratio, meditatio, contemplatio*); some may even be called to different levels or degrees of contemplation.

In the Eucharist, the Incarnation of God's Word extends itself through time, reaching into and transforming the human heart. The Eucharist therefore is central to Christian spirituality. Merton appreciates how the Eucharist helps individuals share with Christ on ever deeper levels of consciousness. By enabling us to commune with Christ, the Eucharist lets us contact our truest, deepest selves. In turn, it makes self, others, and the divine into one. Thus, through the Eucharist, Christ continues his redemptive mission through time.

By participating in the sacrifice of the Eucharist, we come in contact with Christ's paschal mystery. Communing with

Christ in the sacrament allows us to enter into the narrative of this mystery. There comes about a unique experience of the Christ event that helps us to embrace the mysteries of life and death with the attitude of Christ. The Eucharist, in other words, enables us to become so closely united with Christ that we begin to see the world through his eyes. Contemplation, in this sense, means pondering our world as Christ pondered it and striving to act in it as he did—always in accordance with the will of the Father.

As a prophetic sign of the Last Judgment, the general resurrection, and our entrance into glory, the Eucharist focuses on the eschatological dimension of our lives, encouraging us to live in anticipation of the coming of the kingdom while keeping before us the last things and our ultimate end. The Eucharist helps us recollect the marvels of God's past saving actions and celebrate our present life, aware that God's kingdom is somehow already in our midst. It also invites us to anticipate the consummation of time when all things will be recapitulated in Christ. For contemplatives, it means living in expectation of the fulfillment of God's promises not only for individuals, but for the Church and for all humanity.

The Eucharist is bread for our journey through life, nourishing and strengthening us to confront and overcome the dangers of the road. It purges the attractions and enticements of our old lives and helps us take up the attitudes and values of our new lives rooted in Christ. The Eucharist helps us detach ourselves from the things of the world and make ourselves one with those of Christ's kingdom. As bread for our journey, the Eucharist reminds us that, as followers of the way of the Lord Jesus, we are passing through to the world that is to come.

The Eucharist is a sacred banquet, a celebration of Christ's marriage to the Church. Through his passion, death, and resurrection we are united in one mystical body. There is no life without banquet, a celebration that underscores the communion between believers and Christ, by which they are incorporated into and made members of his body. The sacred meal that is the Eucharist is the deepest, most mystical prayer of Christ and his Church. All authentic Christian prayer flows from it and is directed back toward it. Our contemplation, our meditations, our vocal prayers, even our private devotions are part of the *sacrum convivium* of the Most Holy Eucharist.

Finally, Merton points out that the mystical contemplation of Christ in the Eucharist is not a flight from the world but an embrace of the responsibilities of our particular state in life by virtue of our membership in Christ's mystical body. He explains that Christ is present in the sacrament in four ways: in his body and blood, in his passion, in the sanctifying grace he bestows, and in his anticipated glory.[14] In a similar way, we who receive Christ in the sacrament are called to offer our entire lives—body, soul, and spirit—for building up the kingdom, to be conformed to his passion and death, to be transformed by the grace of the sacrament, and to live in anticipation of the glorified existence to come. This fourfold presence of Christ inspires us to carry on his redemptive mission in the circumstances of our daily lives.

Conclusion

Thomas Merton fostered a love for solitude and prayer. In keeping with his monastic vocation, his insights into the spiritual life were rooted not in abstract speculation but in personal experience. His autobiography, in which he narrates his own conversion experience, catapulted him into renown as a writer. It has even been described as a modern-day *Confessions*, the spiritual classic of St. Augustine, whose writings have helped to shape monastic theology and

---

14. Ibid., 87.

spirituality. Like Augustine, Merton reflected on many topics: his life, his conversion, his relationships, his faith, his writings. He also reflected on his experience of the liturgy, especially his experience of the Eucharist.

Merton's views on the sacrament reflect of the essentials of Catholic teaching: the sacrificial nature of the Mass, the transformation of the bread and wine into the real presence, the eschatological orientation of the Eucharistic table toward the messianic banquet. He emphasizes both the communal and individual fruits of the sacrament and highlights what he calls the "sacramental contemplation" of Christ during its celebration. He also considers the Eucharist as an extension of the mystery of the Incarnation through time by Christ being born through it in the human heart.

The Eucharist, for Merton, is a divine and human action that makes present the redemptive mystery of Calvary and points to the consummation of all things in Christ. It is the "sacrament of love" that celebrates and puts into action Christ's commandment that we love one another as he has loved us. It provides food for our spiritual journey and is a visible reminder of Christ, our constant companion, our fellow sojourner on our journey home. It is a memorial of a past event, a celebration of a saving action, and a prophetic sign of the kingdom to come. It is a *sacrum convivium*, a sacred banquet, which celebrates the union of Christ with his mystical body, the Church, and his intimate friendship with each individual believer. It is a sacrament to be celebrated with deep reverence, a loving presence to be received with great joy, and a hidden mystery to be contemplated in the solitude of one's heart and in the heart of Christ's mystical body, the Church.

Reflection Questions

- Merton says that contemplation of Christ in the Eucharist should not involve a flight from the world but a bold embrace of the responsibilities of our particular state in life. What is your present state in life? Through the Eucharist, how might you embrace it boldly, and with courage?
- Merton believes that the narrative of Christ's paschal mystery is manifested in our lives through the Eucharist. How has the sacrament made Christ's passion, death, and resurrection present in your life? In which of your life experiences has the Eucharist been manifested?
- For Merton, we center our lives totally on Christ through Holy Communion, enabling us to get in touch with our deepest and truest selves. How can you center your life totally on Christ? What changes do you need to make for this to happen? What have you realized about your own deepest and truest self through Holy Communion?

Voice Twenty-Four

Teresa of Calcutta: Face of the Poor

> If I can give you any advice, I beg you to get closer to the Eucharist and to Jesus...[W]e must pray to Jesus to give us that tenderness of the Eucharist. Parish priest, ask your people to have adoration in your churches wherever you can. Make it even once a week, so that the tenderness of love may grow in your heart to share it with others...The cross is the proof that he loved us and the Tabernacle is the proof that he loves us now with tender compassion.
>
> *Teresa of Calcutta*

Our next voice on the Eucharist, founder of the Missionaries of Charity and winner of the 1979 Nobel Peace Prize, had a deep love for Christ and the poor. She believed that Christ came to reveal the depths of the Father's love for us and to unite himself to us so that we might express this same love to others, especially the poor and destitute. The Eucharist, which was central to her spirituality, it gave her the strength to carry out her mission to the abandoned of India's slums and enabled her to see the presence of Christ in those she served. The Eucharist gave her and her followers, disciples of Christ in service of the poor, the grace to accomplish beautiful things for God.

Belonging to the World

Blessed Mother Teresa of Calcutta (1910–1997) once said this about herself: "By blood, I am Albanian. By citizenship, an Indian. By faith, I am a Catholic nun. As to my calling, I belong to the world. As to my heart, I belong entirely to the Heart of Jesus."[1] This statement conveys this saintly woman's larger-than-life character.

Born on August 26, 1910 in Ottoman-ruled Skopje, in present-day Macedonia, she was baptized Gonxha Agnes, the youngest child of Nikola and Drane Bojaxhiu. When she was eight her father died, leaving her family impoverished. This did not prevent her being raised in a loving and faith-filled environment and becoming active in the local Jesuit parish.

When she was eighteen, Gonxha expressed her desire to become a missionary. She left Skopje for Ireland to join the Sisters of Loreto. Having received the religious name Sr. Mary Teresa, she left for India in 1929, made her first vows in May of 1931, and her final profession in May of 1931. All during this time, she taught at St. Mary's School for girls in Calcutta, becoming the school's principal in 1944. Her life with the Loreto Sisters was marked by prayerfulness, peace, and abiding joy. Little did she know that the Lord would soon call her to a very different kind of missionary work.

On September 10, 1946, during a journey by train from Calcutta to Darjeeling for her annual retreat, Teresa first perceived the Lord's call to serve him in the poor and destitute. This "call within a call" became the motivating force of her life. In her heart, she heard Jesus asking her to found a new missionary order dedicated to serving the poorest of the poor.

---

1. Cited in Vatican: The Holy See, "Mother Teresa of Calcutta (1910–1997)," http://www.vatican.va/news_services/liturgy/saints/ns_lit_doc_20031019_madre-teresa_en.html (accessed May 28, 2010).

After a period of discernment, she received permission to begin this new work. She left her Loreto convent on August 17, 1948, taking as her habit the traditional dress of Indian women, a sari, colored white with a blue border. After a course with the Medical Mission Sisters in Patna, she went back to Calcutta, stayed for a time with the Little Sisters of the Poor, and began visiting the slums on December 21.

The Missionaries of Charity were officially established in the Archdiocese of Calcutta on October 10, 1950. Within a decade, Teresa was sending her sisters to other regions of India and eventually to other parts of the world. As her order grew in size and significance, she founded other congregations to assist in their work for the poor: Missionaries of Charity Brothers (1963), a contemplative branch of the Sisters (1976), a contemplative branch of the brothers (1979), the Corpus Christi Movement for Priests (1981), and the Missionaries of Charity Fathers (1984). In addition to communities in religious life and the priesthood, she also established lay movements for those drawn to her charism and missionary spirit. By the time of her death in 1997, Mother Teresa's Sisters numbered nearly 4,000, with 610 foundations in over 120 countries.[2]

The religious family Teresa founded continues to grow. It has made an impact on the world's spiritual landscape, traversing boundaries of creed and denomination to inspire countless believers to see the presence of Christ in those living in extreme poverty and on the verge of death.

---

2. All historical information in this section comes from "Mother Teresa of Calcutta (1910–1997)." For biographical notes on Teresa, see Renzo Allegri, *Teresa of the Poor: The Life of Mother Teresa of Calcutta* (Ann Arbor, MI: Servant Publications, 1998), 167–75. For helpful biographies, see Navin Chawla, *Mother Teresa: The Authorized Biography* (Boston/Shaftesbury/Melbourne: Element, 1992); Eileen Egan, *Such a Vision of the Street: Mother Teresa—The Spirit and the Work* (Garden City: Doubleday, 1985).

Teresa's Spirituality

At heart Teresa was a contemplative, but in action a missionary. Her spirituality takes its inspiration from Jesus's words in Matthew's Gospel:

> For I was hungry and you gave me food, I was thirsty and you gave me something to drink, I was a stranger and you welcomed me, I was naked and you gave me clothing, I was sick and you took care of me, I was in prison and you visited me....Truly I tell you, just as you did it to one of the least of these who are members of my family, you did it to me.[3]

She carried these words in her heart wherever she went — and acted upon them.

Because she saw Jesus in the people she served, especially the sick and destitute, Teresa contemplated his face in everyone she met. By becoming ever more conscious of Christ's presence in those around her, she served him by placing their needs before her own. Hers is a spirituality and ministry of presence. The corporal works of mercy — feeding the hungry, giving drink to the thirsty, clothing the naked, sheltering the homeless, visiting the sick, visiting those in prison, and burying the dead — filled her daily life. Jesus, she believed, was especially close to the poor and downtrodden. By comforting them, she believed she was bringing comfort to the suffering Christ, who gave himself up to death on our behalf.[4]

Key to Teresa's understanding of Christ's presence in the poor and underprivileged was her belief in Christ's mystical body. In the paschal mystery, Jesus has passed through death to a level of existence in which he has overcome time and space to be present to our broken humanity. She embraced Christ in the leper, the beggar, the blind, the dumb,

---

3. See Mt 25: 35–37, 40. For Teresa's interpretation of these verses, see Egan, *Such a Vision of the Street*, 420.
4. For examples of Teresa's work with the poorest of the poor, see Allegri, *Teresa of the Poor*, 99–122; Egan, *Such a Vision of the Street*, 63–89.

the crippled, the addicted, the prostitute, the prisoner, the old, the dying. By comforting the suffering, she believed that she was comforting the crucified Christ.[5]

Teresa's connecting the suffering Christ with his presence in suffering humanity stems from her conviction that by becoming man Christ irrevocably tied human experience, even the most banal, to his. As a result, he still lives and moves among us, but in a mystical way. Because of his passion, death, and resurrection, every person in some way is living out his story. In their suffering and dying, every man, woman, and child is walking the same path that Jesus once walked. Teresa considered it a privilege to minister to Christ in the forgotten masses of India's slums and sought to be present to them in a spirit of humble service. In the Eucharist, she realized, Christ's suffering presence on the cross became a compassionate presence to human suffering in the world.[6]

Teresa on the Eucharist

Teresa's life and the spirituality of the missionary institutes and associations that she founded center on the Eucharist. She spoke of this often during her long life, both publicly to the world and privately to her missionary sisters and associates.

Of particular note is Teresa's address to the International Eucharistic Congress at Nairobi, Kenya, in 1985.[7] In it, she outlines the features of her teaching on the Eucharist. Jesus has come to us for one purpose: "...to tell us that God loves us, that we are precious to him, that we have been created to

---

5. For a moving description of how Teresa saw Jesus in the poor, see Egan, *Such a Vision of the Street*, 396–97.
6. For an eloquent description of Teresa's embrace of the poorest of the poor as a spiritual countersign to the unrestrained use of violence, see Egan, *Such a Vision of the Street*, 406–16. For Teresa's understanding of prayer, contemplation, and the centrality of the Eucharist to her life, see Idem, 426–27.
7. Cited in *RPA*, 204–5.

love and to be loved, and that we must love one another as he loves us, as the Father has loved him."[8]

She also points to the cross and the tabernacle as concrete symbols of God's love for humanity: "When we look at the cross we know how he loved us. And when we look at the Tabernacle we know how he loves us still."[9]

She believes that this intimate connection between the suffering Christ and his presence in the tabernacle spills over into the world's suffering:

> He made himself this Bread of Life to satisfy our hunger for this love. And as if that were not enough for him, he made himself the hungry one, the naked one, the humblest one so that you and I can satisfy his hunger for our human love. This is something so wonderful—the sick, the poor, the unwanted, the unloved, the lepers, the drug addicts, the alcoholics, the prostitutes—Christ in the distressing disguises.[10]

She believed that *they* are the privileged ones, for they are blessed to embody him twenty-four hours a day.

In this same speech, Teresa highlights the importance of personal sacrifice in making God's tender and compassionate love present in the world today:

> Sacrifice is his love in action. God sent Jesus to teach us this love. And you will find out in your own life. Have you ever experienced the joy of loving? Have you ever shared something with the sick, with the lonely, together making something beautiful for God? This is something that has to come from within us. That is why Jesus made himself the Bread of Life—to create that in our life.[11]

For Teresa, in the Eucharist God's sacrificial love is given to us to be eaten and digested so that it can divinize us and

---

8. Ibid., 204.
9. Ibid.
10. Ibid.
11. Ibid.

become a part of our very selves. When we receive it, God empowers us to love others with the same love that Christ has shown us. In this way, the sacrament helps us to bring Christ's love to the poor and to perceive him in them.

Teresa believes that to see Jesus in others we need purity of heart:

> 'Blessed are the clean of heart, for they shall see God.' Now unless we see God in each other we cannot love each other. And so it is important for us to have a clean heart. With a clean heart we will be able to be only all for Jesus and to give Jesus to others. That is why Jesus made himself the Bread of Life. That is why he is there twenty-four hours. That is why he is longing for you and for me to share the joy of loving.[12]

She then offers one clear piece of advice: "I beg you to get closer to the Eucharist and to Jesus....Parish priest, ask your people to have adoration in your churches wherever you can. Make it even once a week, so that the tenderness of love may grow in your heart to share it with others."[13]

She understood that devotion to Jesus in the Blessed Sacrament will deepen our devotion to his presence in the poorest of the poor. This twofold presence lies at the heart of her Eucharistic spirituality and the charism of the religious institutes she founded.[14]

Observations

This is only a partial sketch of Teresa's teaching on the Eucharist. The following remarks will explore her teaching further and underscore its relevance for today.

The Eucharist is central for Teresa's mission to serve the poor and destitute. The Eucharist is indispensable, she be-

---

12. Ibid., 205.
13. Ibid.
14. For more on Jesus' twofold presence, see James A. Mohler, "Thérèse and Teresa on the Eucharist," *Emmanuel* 100 (no. 8, 1994): 494–95.

lieved, in reaching out to the forgotten and underprivileged masses as she and her missionary sisters have done. Their daily sustenance with Jesus' body and blood gave them the physical and emotional strength to reach out to those in direst need. The Eucharist enabled them to see and to serve Christ in others.

Teresa saw a close connection between contemplation and mission, both of which at their core are Eucharistic. Prayer before the Blessed Sacrament empowered her to reach out to the Jesus who confronted her at every turn: in the poor, the lonely, the hungry, the sick, and the dying. Contemplation and mission are two poles of the one missionary spirit that she sought to live with all her heart and to instill in her sisters. Contemplation sent her out to mission; in turn, mission drew her back to contemplation. This reciprocity lies at the heart of her missionary spirituality.

Jesus's real presence in the Eucharist parallels his mystical presence in the poor and destitute. Teresa believed that both could be seen only with a clean heart and through the eyes of faith. She therefore emphasized the importance of a simple life, detached from worldly desires and possessions. Although in themselves good, worldly allurements can distract from what really matters in life: seeing and serving Christ in others. Teresa and her sisters live a simple life of penance and self-denial in order to cleanse their hearts so that Jesus might dwell in them and through them reach out to others. Their ascetic life is not an end in itself, but a way of emptying their hearts in order to fill them with divine love.

Teresa loved to refer to the Eucharist as the Living Bread, a term that resonates deeply in Scripture and has significance for the Christian community in its journey through time.[15] This Living Bread is the "manna from heaven," the divine food that sustains God's people on their pilgrim way and enables them to remain faithful to the New Covenant established by Christ's paschal mystery. This food is the body and blood of Christ himself. Like all faithful Catholics, Teresa and her sisters believed that by eating his flesh and drinking his blood they become more deeply united to Christ and his Mystical Body, the Church. In doing so, they also see themselves more deeply united in a "holy communion" to the poor and the destitute.

Finally, in the Eucharist Teresa found a profound source of peace that penetrated the darkness she experienced in the world and in the depths of her soul.[16] As the source and summit of the Church's life and worship, the Eucharist enabled her to put things in perspective and to keep in mind that, in the end, the missionary work she was doing was not her own, but the Lord's. Teresa felt most herself at Mass or in adoration before the Blessed Sacrament. Because her heart belonged entirely to Jesus, in his presence she could rest and be herself. The peace and strength she received from such moments enabled her to go out to others and to rest and be herself when she was with them. In the presence of the poor and destitute Teresa was in the presence of Christ. By seeing Christ beneath a disguise of bread and wine, she could see him as well in the "distressing disguises" of the poor.

Conclusion

Teresa of Calcutta arose from humble origins to worldwide acclaim as a "living saint" and messenger of God's peace to the poor and broken-hearted. Starting with next to nothing, through the generosity of those who believed in her work and message she was able to work miracles.

---

15. See Jn 6:52–58.
16. For Teresa's struggle with darkness and inner turmoil, see Brian Kolodiejchuk, ed., *Mother Teresa: Come Be My Light* (New York: Doubleday, 2007), 208–34.

As a child and adolescent up in Macedonia, as a teacher with the Sisters of Loreto, and as a servant of the poor with the Missionaries of Charity, she lived for Jesus. Because of her intimate relationship with the Lord, she could see his presence everywhere, especially in the poor and destitute of India's slums.

The outlook of Teresa's spirituality is both contemplative and missionary. She centered her life in prayer, which nourished her relationship with the Lord and let her see the world around her through the eyes of faith. She took Jesus's words to heart that what we do to the least of our brothers and sisters, we also do to him. Her closeness to Christ in prayer helped her to hear his call to serve the poor and respond with all her heart, mind, and soul. What she started alone on a hot August day in 1948 eventually became a great spiritual family of women and men who desire only to see the face of Christ in the poor and serve them with tender compassion.

Her life and mission are based in her devotion to Jesus offering himself in the Holy Sacrifice of the Mass and his personal presence in the Blessed Sacrament. Contemplating the presence of Christ in this sacrament led Teresa to experience his presence in the suffering of those around her.

The sacrament purified her heart and deepened her love. In living out her "call within a call," Teresa imparted a Eucharistic spirituality to her followers, emphasizing the intimate connection between Christ's sacramental presence and his presence in those they served. Above all else, she wanted her followers to understand that they must be rooted in God's love in order to share it with others. Only the Living Bread of the Eucharist can bind our wounds, strengthen our resolve, and sustain us on our journey.

Reflection Questions

- Teresa notes that the cross and the tabernacle are concrete symbols of God's love for humanity. What do they symbolize for you? How do they relate to each other? How do they relate to Christian life? How does each of them embody God's love for humanity?

- Teresa believes that the suffering of Christ and Jesus's presence in the tabernacle relate to the world's suffering. How is Jesus present for you in the sick, the unwanted, and the unloved? How does Jesus's hidden presence in the Blessed Sacrament help you recognize his hidden presence in the poor and afflicted?

- Teresa believes that we can see Jesus in others if we have purity of heart. What does it mean to be pure of heart? How do purity and single-heartedness help us to focus on what really matters in life? How does having our hearts focused on Jesus help us to perceive his presence in others, especially the abandoned and the underprivileged?

Voice Twenty-Five

Chiara Lubich: Forging Unity

> The Eucharist does not only bear good and beautiful fruits of love and sanctity; nor is its primary purpose to increase our unity with God and with one another (as unity is commonly understood) and thus serving to nourish the presence of Jesus in our midst. Yes, this too. But the task of the Eucharist is something else. This is the purpose of the Eucharist: to make us God (by participation). By mixing our flesh with Christ's life-giving flesh, which is given life by the Holy Spirit, the Eucharist divinizes us in soul and body. Therefore it makes us God.
>
> *Chiara Lubich*

Our next voice on the Eucharist, the founder of the Focolare Movement, is a great voice for renewal in the Church. The spirituality of communion that emerged from her experience and that of her first companions has inspired countless people from all walks of life to dedicate themselves to living a life of gospel fellowship with themselves, others, and God. This spirituality, which touches upon the need for Christian fellowship or koinonia, expresses one of the key values of the Church's self-understanding. As someone who could see what is invisible (see Heb 11:37), Chiara committed her entire life to express and transform into life the certainty that Jesus is alive, that he is among us. All the other presences of Jesus in the Church (in the Word, in the Eucharist, in the ordained ministry, in the neighbor, and so on) tend toward and draw their origin from this presence of Jesus in the midst. She believed that living in communion with one another lie at the heart of the gospel message. She also saw it as central to the meaning of the Eucharist and what is accomplished in each of us when we receive the sacrament.

Work of Mary

Chiara Lubich (1920–2008) was born on January 22 in Trent, Italy. At eighteen she began a career as an elementary school teacher, first in the small villages of Castello and Livio, and later at Trent. She began her studies in philosophy at the University of Venice, but could not continue when World War II broke out. In 1939, while visiting the Marian shrine at Loreto during a convention of young people associated with Catholic Action, she intuited that there could be another "House of Loreto" like the one in which the Holy Family had lived, where consecrated virgins and married couples live with Jesus in their midst. A few years later, as a member of the Franciscan Third Order, inspired by Clare of Assisi's desire to live the gospel in a radical way, she took the name "Chiara." On December 7, 1943 she dedicated herself to God through vows of chastity, poverty, and obedience. Although she did this as a private act, that turning point in her life is considered the date when the Focolare Movement began.

During the aerial bombardment of Trent, Chiara discovered the only thing that bombs could not destroy: love. She and her first companions, all young women, took up residence together on the Piazza Cappucini, in an apartment that came to be known as the "focolare," which means "hearth." The community around them called it that because they sensed a special presence there of warmth and family. In 1947 the Movement was approved by Carlo de Ferrari, the Archbishop of Trent. A focolare for men was opened the following year.

Each summer between 1949 and 1959, she and her companions would retreat to the mountains near Trent, an experience that gave rise to the *Mariapolis*, a regular gathering of a small community of believers—people from every walk of life, age, vocation, single and married—dedicated to living a gospel spirituality. During this time she included married men and women in the focolare households (1953), and founded branches for diocesan priests and members of religious orders (1954).

Lubich's activities eventually extended to the fields of publishing, ecumenism, societal transformation, and even economics. In 1956 the first edition of a magazine, *Città Nouva* ("New City"), was published. In that same year, when the Soviet Union invaded Hungary, she founded the *Volunteers of God*, a group of men and women dedicated to bringing God, the source of all unity, to every corner of society throughout the world. In 1960, she began working to spread the Movement to countries under communist rule. In 1961 she initiated the movement's ecumenical activities when she met with a group of Lutheran pastors who wanted to learn about her spirituality. In 1962 the movement received papal approval and was officially recognized as *The Work of Mary*, a name that suggests its purpose—like Mary, to make Jesus present in the world.

In 1964, she opened a house of formation for the movement's members at Rocca di Papa near Rome, and the first of the movement's little towns at Loppiano, near Florence. A branch for young adults, known as the *Gen* (*Gen* standing for New Generation), came to life in 1966, followed by the *New Families* Movement (1967) and a *Gens 2* branch for seminarians (1968). In 1970, a *Gen 3* movement for children and younger teenagers emerged, and in 1971 a Focolare branch for women religious. In 1976, she organized a group for bishops who are friends of the movement and in 1984 the *Gen 4* for even younger children. During a visit to Brazil in 1991, she called for a project to help those living in poverty, now known as "Economy of Communion." This has established a new economic praxis and theory that has spread throughout the world, involving hundreds of businesses.

As founder and president of the Focolare Movement, Lubich has been invited to many leadership positions and has received many honors. She was awarded the Templeton Prize for Progress in Religion (1977), was named consultant to the Pontifical Council for the Laity (1985), received the Augsburg Peace Prize (1988), and was named one of the honorary presidents of the World Conference on Religion and Peace (1994). In 1996, UNESCO recognized her work with its Peace Education Prize and she was named honorary citizen of Rome and Florence in 2000. She spoke as a representative of the Roman Catholic Church at the 2002 Day of Prayer for Peace in the World, in Assisi. She also has been granted honorary degrees in various disciplines from Catholic and secular universities in Argentina, Brazil, Mexico, the Philippines, Poland, Taiwan, the United Kingdom, and the United States.

On March 14, 2008, sixty-five years after her "yes" to God that marked the beginning of what would become the Focolare Movement, Lubich died in her home at Rocca di Papa, Italy. In the years prior to her death, the movement had spread to 182 countries, eighty-nine of which had established centers. Its membership numbered 140,300 with millions more sharing in its spirituality in a less organized manner. Besides Catholics, those associated with the movement include approximately 47,000 other Christians from some 350 Churches and ecclesial communities, about 30,000 from other religions (including Jews, Muslims, Buddhists, Hindus, and Sikhs) and some 10,000 who profess no religious orientation. This extended family continues, held together by a spiritual outlook committed to working for unity on all levels of the human community. It is an outlook rooted in Lubich's experience of God and forged in the deep interior spaces of her soul.[1]

Lubich's Spirituality

Lubich's "spirituality of unity" lies at the heart of the Focolare Movement. This spirituality is a response to the deep call she and her first companions felt as they read the gospels in the bomb shelters, especially Jesus's prayer, "... that they may all be one. As you, Father, are in me and I am in you, may they also be in us, so that the world may believe that you have sent me" (Jn 17:21). This spirituality of unity is "the soil from which its [the movement's] many activities and projects draw sustenance."[2] Through it, the members seek "to contribute to building universal brotherhood and to recompose the human family in the unity for which Jesus prayed.[3] They do so through five important dialogues: (1) "within the Roman Catholic Church, or for other Christians within their own churches"; (2) "with other Christian Churches and ecclesial communities"; (3) "with those who follow other religions"; (4) "with those who do not subscribe to any particular religious conviction"; and (5) "in various areas of culture as a whole."[4]

In her 1996 address to UNESCO, Lubich describes the communitarian dimension of this spirituality of unity, which is rooted in a profound awareness that God is love and therefore by nature both personal and social. God relates to us as a loving Father and asks us only to open our hearts to him in faith. That same love is the inner dynamic of authentic human relationships. Mutual love, a reflection

---

1. All significant dates and other historical information from this chapter come from *CLEW*, 383–99.
2. Ibid., 395.
3. Ibid.
4. Ibid.

of God's love in our lives, makes Christ present. By striving for unity, she says, we bring Christ's peace to the world, witnessing to that peace even when the world rejects it. For Lubich, Christians are called to witness God's great love for humanity to the world, and by living in communion with each other to radiate that love to others. The community of believers, the Church, stands at the forefront of this mission to herald in the kingdom of God.[5]

In a 1995 address Lubich explains that in its essence gospel spirituality is a way of going to God not as individuals, but together.[6] She says that the Holy Spirit "is inspiring people to walk together, in fact, to be of one heart and soul with all who share their convictions."[7] Referencing saints such as Basil the Great and Augustine of Hippo, she points out the importance for Christian living of mutual love and unity.[8] She also cites the Carmelite Jesus Castellano, an expert in Christian spirituality, concerning the importance of a communitarian "ecclesial spirituality," and the Jesuit Karl Rahner, one of the great theologians of the twentieth century, on the importance of "a communally lived spirituality" for the future.[9] Unity, Lubich maintains, comes about by union in Christ through charity:

> Just as two poles of electricity, even when there is a current, do not produce light until they are joined together, likewise two persons cannot experience the light of this charism [of unity] until they are united in Christ through charity.[10]

Although the spirituality of unity is the specific charism of the Focolare Movement, she points out that it "is for the whole people of God whose vocation is to become ever more

---

5. Ibid., 12–15
6. Ibid., 27–28.
7. Ibid., 28.
8. Ibid.
9. Ibid., 28–29.
10. Ibid., 31.

united and ever more holy."[11] For her, the Eucharist plays a central role in this quest for unity and holiness.

Chiara Lubich on the Eucharist

For Lubich, Jesus in the midst and true unity, sharing in and through our relationships in God together, is both the fruit and the end of the Eucharist. We are made one with one another through our sharing together in God; and we live this out when we live with Jesus in our midst. Jesus in the midst makes us fully Jesus, and so fully sharers in God. The Eucharist, therefore, gives us the condition for having these fruits, which are aspects of the living out and the completion of our divinization. The Eucharist deepens our unity with each other and fosters Jesus' presence in our midst; it does nothing less than to divinize us, "to make us God (by participation)."[12] When we receive the sacrament worthily, our flesh is mixed with Christ's life-giving flesh by the power of the Holy Spirit.[13] We are elevated to a higher plane of existence and made to share deeply and intimately in the divine life. Although the distinction between us as creatures and God as our creator is maintained, we enter into the heart of the Father, to the center of the life of the Trinity. Also, the Eucharist does this not only for us as individuals, but as a community, as the Church.[14] The Eucharist creates and sustains this community, and brings us into a divinized existence through Christ in the bosom of the Father.

Echoing figures like Irenaeus and Tertullian, Lubich notes that the Church "is made up of divinized people, made God, united to Christ who is God and to each other."[15] In more scriptural terms, it "is a body, whose head is the

---

11. Ibid., 32.
12. Ibid., 129.
13. Ibid.
14. Ibid.
15. Ibid.

glorious Christ."[16] Since Christ exists in the bosom of the Trinity, so must the Church. The Eucharist accomplishes this for believers here on earth and will ultimately bring it about for all humanity, which will bring the rest of creation with it. For Lubich, everything that comes from God ultimately will return to God. Seen in this light, the Eucharist is the beginning of the New Creation. Through it, all of humanity and all of creation will return through Christ and enter into the bosom of the Most Holy Trinity.[17]

Since the Church is intimately related to Christ, its head, Lubich asserts that the Eucharistic celebration is an extension of the love between brothers and sisters of the believing community: "If a community is not 'realized' in Christ, in full communion, it is evangelically unsuited to offer to God befitting worship."[18]

She also maintains that this important insight must not be lost amid the concerns of individual religiosity which can numb our senses to the importance of mutual charity in community, "Christianity's true strength."[19] When people are truly united, their experience at Eucharist deepens: "The face of the Church would turn out to be beautiful in its full splendor and would attract the world as once Jesus attracted the crowds."[20]

The celebration of the Eucharist thus belongs both to Jesus and to the community of believers: It is "His Mass, our Mass."[21] His presence in the tabernacle, moreover, awakens within our souls profound stillness and silence. We must therefore give thanks for all that Jesus has done for us. He took humankind as his bride and has remained faithful to her.[22] His passion, death, and resurrection give us hope. By

---

16. Ibid.
17. Ibid.
18. Ibid., 130.
19. Ibid.
20. Ibid.
21. Ibid., 131.
22. Ibid., 133.

his presence in all the tabernacles of the world heaven pours itself onto the earth: "The earth is big, because it is dotted everywhere with the Eucharist: God with us, God among us, God for us."[23]

Observations

We have outlined only the main contours of Lubich's deep and extensive teaching on the Eucharist. The following remarks seek to probe her teaching further to bring out its deeper significance for believers.

For Lubich, the Eucharist is essentially relational. The presence of Christ in us makes each of Jesus, so we can become one with the Jesus in our neighbor. And when the Jesus in us makes himself one with the Jesus in the others, we become still more Jesus. When we receive the Eucharist united with one another—each of us Jesus and so all of us Jesus together—we become one in Jesus; we become more Jesus. In this way, we are "made God." Unity is a work of God, the Word-made-flesh who has entered our world to bring humanity into the life of the Father, Son, and Spirit. This work comes from God, is implemented by God, and is ultimately completed by God. By its divinizing powers, the Eucharist is one of the primary means by which God accomplishes the redemptive work of Christ in us and draws us to Himself, into the heart of the Trinity.

Lubich makes it clear that the Eucharist divinizes us both individually and communally. The unique relationship between the individual and community is most important in the Christian message. Although Christians do not lose their identity by being submerged into a larger social body, the believing community of which they have become a part has its own unique and irreplaceable life. For Lubich, individual believers maintain peace and unity among them

---
23. Ibid., 134.

because they and the community together look to Christ as their head. A lack of unity within the community reveals the reality of sin within the life of the individual and the community. While God works to form ever stronger bonds of communion among believers and all people of good will, Chiara acknowledges that human beings can decide not to cooperate with this work and even to work actively against it.

For Lubich, the Eucharist lies at the heart of the Church. Through the Eucharist the community of believers is being gradually transformed into the humanity established by Christ through his paschal mystery and drawn into the heart of God. Her understanding of divinization by participation and her insistence that the Church itself must live through Christ and by the power of the Holy Spirit in the bosom of the Father provides the Church with a clear understanding of its origin, purpose, and destination. Through the Eucharist and the community of believers it brings about, God gathers humankind and all of creation into Himself. In this sense, the work of unity, a work of God, is also a human work.

By building the community through Jesus in the midst, Lubich dedicated her life to corresponding with God's work for unity. She recognized that humanity's sharing in the life of divinity requires active participation in building the life of the kingdom. The spirituality of unity to which she dedicated her life is a charism, a gift of the Holy Spirit that inspired all that she did. The Eucharist, a sharing in God together, is central to her charism because it brings about that unity. Receiving the Eucharist is an individual and communal commitment to building the kingdom by lives dedicated to mutual charity. With the Eucharist God draws humanity to intimate community with the Trinity. Dialogue, both within and beyond the Church, prepares people to receive God's love and ultimately to participate in its fullness. Eucharist and dialogue go hand in hand. When one is lacking, the other cannot be what God fully intends it to be.

Finally, Lubich revels in Jesus's presence in the Blessed Sacrament and sees in it a divine outpouring upon the earth that confirms God's desire to attract humanity and eventually all of creation back to its origins. Through the Eucharist, as he does with all the sacraments, Jesus makes himself concretely present in thousands upon thousands of places on earth. Through his paschal mystery, he multiplies himself and is present to us in a personal, intimate way. By receiving the Eucharist, we embrace Jesus' glorious vision for humanity as our own and dedicate ourselves to making it a reality. We too must give ourselves to others and "die in order to multiply."[24] We understand that because God is with us and among us and for us, we too must be with, among, and for our brothers and sisters, especially those in need.

Conclusion

Throughout her life, Chiara Lubich called for unity—within the Catholic Church, among all Christian churches and ecclesial communities, other religions, and all men and women of good will. The movement she inspired has spread throughout the world, building community through a commitment to authentic dialogue and doing whatever is necessary to alleviate the sufferings of those in need, especially the poor and underprivileged.

What she brought to the world can be summed up by the simple words, "spirituality of unity." She firmly believed that we have been brought into existence to live in intimate union with ourselves, others, and God. Her contribution to the history of spirituality lies in the way she let God transmit this spirituality of unity through her and put it into practice

---

24. Ibid.

through a life of dialogue and mutual charity. In her lifetime, her extended family came to embrace all age groups, all states of life within virtually all Christian churches, the world's major religions, and even those who do not believe. That family continues to grow and develop.

At the core of Lubich's spirituality is the belief that God is drawing humanity and all of creation to the bosom of the Trinity. The Incarnation, Christ's paschal mystery, and the Eucharist were ordained by God through the power of the Holy Spirit to achieve this end. Lubich understood the Eucharist's divinizing power and saw in this sacrificial meal the presence of the glorious Christ, the head of his community of believers. Because it makes us one Christ together, she saw the essential value of this sacrament in bringing about an intimate union of minds and hearts. It did so and continues to do so by enabling us to share in the life of the Trinity itself and by drawing us into ever deeper bonds of intimate, communal love.

Reflection Questions

- For Lubich, the Eucharist divinizes humanity. How does the Eucharist make us more like God? What is the relationship between this sacrament and the spirituality of communion? In what way is being in communion with others a reflection of the divine life?
- Lubich believes the Eucharist creates and sustains community. How does the Eucharist create community? What creative forces does it unleash? How does it bring people together? How does it enable them to put aside their differences and establish communion with each other? How does it fulfill Jesus' prayer, "That they may all be one"?
- Lubich believes the celebration of the Eucharist belongs both to Jesus and to the community of believers. Do you feel the Mass belongs to you? Do you actively participate in it or are you merely a passive observer? Do you contribute to building the body of Christ in your family, local parish, and larger community?

Voice Twenty-Six

Pope John Paul II: School for Peace

The Christian who takes part in the Eucharist learns to become a *promoter of communion, peace and solidarity* in every situation. More than ever, our troubled world, which began the new Millennium with the specter of terrorism and the tragedy of war, demands that Christians learn to experience the Eucharist as *a great school of peace,* forming men and women who, at various levels of responsibility in social, cultural and political life, can become promoters of dialogue and communion.

John Paul II

Our next voice on the Eucharist, one of the towering figures of the twentieth century, led the Catholic Church through a sea of changes. His literary output would fill many shelves and his accomplishments are too many to list in a short article. He headed the Catholic Church at a critical moment in its history and guided it in addressing the challenges of the new millennium. His love for the Eucharist lay at the heart of his courageous missionary spirit.

The Polish Pope

Karol Józef Wojtyła (1920–2005) was born in Wadowice, a village about 30 miles outside of Krakow, Poland. Ordained in 1946, he taught moral theology and social ethics in the major seminary of Krakow and in the Faculty of Theology of Lublin from 1953–1958, before being consecrated an auxiliary bishop of Krakow in 1958. He became archbishop of Krakow in 1964, was made a cardinal in 1967, was elected Pope on October 16, 1978, died on April 2, 2005, was declared venerable in 2009, and was beatified in 2011.

One of the longest reigning popes in the history of the Church, John Paul II affirmed Catholic orthodoxy, contributed to the fall of Communism and the collapse of the Soviet Union, and made innumerable papal visits throughout the world. During his pontificate, he made a lasting impression on the Church, especially in his teaching on the "spirituality of communion" and its relationship to the Church's missionary efforts in the new evangelization.

In his personal life, John Paul had a profound attachment to the Eucharist as a sacrament and as a private devotion, and saw a deep connection between the two. His Eucharistic teaching appears in many of his writings, especially in his last encyclical, *Ecclesia de Eucharistia* ("Church of the Eucharist"), promulgated on April 17, 2003 and in *Mane Nobiscum Domine* ("Stay with Us, Lord"), his Apostolic Letter for the Year of the Eucharist (October 2004–October 2005), promulgated on October 7, 2004.[1]

John Paul's Spirituality

John Paul II affirms his spirituality in these passages from *Ecclesia de Eucharistia*: "The Church draws her life from the Eucharist"; it "recapitulates the heart of the mystery of the Church" (no. 1). He quotes the Second Vatican Council that the Eucharist is "the source and summit of the Christian life" (no. 1) and that it "contains the Church's entire

---

1. All biographical information in this paragraph comes from: The Holy See, http://www.vatican.va/ news_services/press/ documentazione/documents/santopadre_biografie/giovanni_paolo_ii_biografia _breve_en.html (accessed February 10, 2013).

spiritual wealth" (no. 1).[2] This "mystery of faith" anticipates Jesus's passion, death, and resurrection, and carries on his redemptive mission wherever it is celebrated (no. 4).

It also reveals the mystery of the Church, which took shape in the Upper Room when Jesus celebrated his Last Supper with his disciples and was born by the gift of the Holy Spirit on the feast of Pentecost (no. 5). The pope affirms the centrality of the Eucharist for the Church's life and mission and reaffirms the teaching of the Councils and his predecessors on the sacrament (no. 9).

The encyclical has six major sections. The first, "The Mystery of Faith," states that the Eucharist is "the gift par excellence" for it represents not only God's saving work, but also his true gift of self (no. 11). The Eucharist "shows us a love...which knows no measure" (no. 11). Therefore, it is a sacrificial gift to God the Father of Jesus and his body, the Church, which "makes present not only the mystery of the Savior's passion and death, but also his resurrection" (no. 14). This sacrifice is "intrinsically directed to the inward union of the faithful with Christ through communion" (no. 16) and brings about the forgiveness of sin and union with Christ's Spirit (nos. 16–17). It also "expresses and reinforces our communion with the Church in heaven" and "increases, rather than lessens, our sense of responsibility for the world today" (nos. 19–20).

The second section, "The Eucharist Builds the Church," points out the "causal influence of the Eucharist" in the very origins of the Church (no. 21). The Apostles present with Jesus when he instituted the sacrament "were both the seeds of the new Israel and the beginning of the sacred hierarchy" (no. 21). When they entered into sacred communion with Jesus for the first time, they were drawn into his redemptive mission and commissioned to carry this saving action to every corner of the earth (nos. 21–22). In this sense, the

---

2. *LG*, no. 11 (accessed April 23, 2012); *PO*, no. 5 (accessed April 23, 2012).

Eucharist is also "the source and summit of all evangelization" (no. 22).

The third section, "The Apostolicity of the Eucharist and of the Church," explains how "the Eucharist builds the Church and the Church makes the Eucharist" (no. 26). This intimate relationship constitutes the Church as "one, holy, catholic, and apostolic" (no. 26). Recalling the Church's teaching as expressed in the *Catechism of the Catholic Church*, the pope points out three senses of the Church's apostolic nature. First, she is built on the foundation of the Apostles. Second, she preserves and passes on Christ's teaching through the guidance of the Holy Spirit. Third, she "continues to be taught, sanctified, and guided" by the successors of the apostles, the bishops, in union with the pope, the successor of St. Peter (nos. 27–28).[3] The Eucharist expresses all three senses of apostolicity, but the pope underscores apostolic succession. The priestly ministry, he writes, "is a gift which radically transcends the power of the assembly and is in any event essential for validly linking the Eucharistic consecration to the sacrifice of the Cross and to the last supper" (no. 29). He reaffirms the teaching of the Second Vatican Council that the Eucharist is "the center and root of the whole priestly life" (no. 31).[4]

The fourth section, "The Eucharist and Ecclesial Communion," places the sacrament in the context of an "ecclesiology of communion." Through the Eucharist, the Church "constantly lives and grows" (no. 3). The Eucharist is often called "Communion" because it embodies the primary purpose of the Church—maintaining and promoting "communion with the Triune God and communion among the faithful" (no. 34). Therefore, the pope says "it is good to cultivate in our hearts a constant desire for the sacrament of the Eucharist" (no. 34). He also notes, however, that "it

---

3. See *CCC*, no. 857 (accessed April 23, 2012).
4. *PO*, no. 1(accessed April 23, 2012).

presupposes that communion already exists, a communion which it seeks to consolidate and bring to perfection" (no. 34). "It is an intrinsic requirement of the Eucharist," therefore, " that it should be celebrated in communion" (no. 35). It would be "a great contradiction if the sacrament *par excellence* of the Church's unity were celebrated without true communion with the Bishop" (no. 39). There is close connection between the Eucharist and the sacrament of Penance (no. 37), and there are some rare conditions under which non-Catholics may receive the Eucharist (nos. 43-46).

The fifth section, "The Dignity of the Eucharistic Celebration," describes the Eucharist as a sacrificial banquet to be conducted with dignity and honor (no. 48). The sacrament, "while shaping the Church and her spirituality, has also powerfully affected 'culture,' and the arts in particular" (no. 49). Liturgical artists must balance the needs of inculturation with the timeless values expressed in the sacrament. For this reason, "[i]t is necessary...that this important work of adaptation be carried out with a constant awareness of the ineffable mystery against which every generation is called to measure itself" (no. 51). Indeed, "[n]o one is permitted to undervalue the mystery entrusted to our hands: "it is too great for anyone to feel free to treat it lightly and with disregard for its sacredness and its universality" (no. 52).

The sixth and final section, "At the School of Mary, 'Woman of the Eucharist,'" describes how Mary lived her Eucharistic faith even before the Lord instituted the sacrament "by the very fact that she offered her virginal womb for the Incarnation of God's Word" (no. 55). Her *Fiat* in response to the angel corresponds to the "Amen" that every believer says when receiving the body of the Lord (no. 55). Mary's entire life, not only her standing at the foot of the cross on Good Friday, was a sharing in "the sacrificial dimension of the Eucharist" (no. 56). In a similar way, "[i]n the Eucharist the Church is completely united to Christ and his sacrifice, and makes her own the spirit of Mary (no.

58). The encyclical concludes with a call for all the faithful "to undertake with renewed enthusiasm the journey of Christian living" (no. 60). It ends with the following exhortation: "The mystery of the Eucharist—sacrifice, presence, banquet—does not allow for reduction or exploitation; it must be experienced and lived in its integrity, both in its celebration and in the intimate converse with Jesus which takes place after receiving communion or in a prayerful moment of Eucharistic apart from Mass" (no. 61). The pope calls us to take our place "at the school of the saints, who are the great interpreters of true Eucharistic piety" (no. 62).

John Paul on the Eucharist

John Paul II's apostolic letter, *Mane Nobiscum, Domine* proposes that an entire year be dedicated to studying the themes of *Ecclesia de Eucharistia* more deeply (no. 3). It uses the image of the two disciples on the way to Emmaus (Lk 24: 13–35) as "a fitting guide" for this year (no. 2). John Paul II states: "Amid our questions and difficulties, and even in our bitter disappointments, the divine Wayfarer continues to walk at our side, opening the Scriptures and leading us to a deeper understanding of the mysteries of God" (no. 2). Coming soon after a year dedicated to contemplating the mysteries of the Rosary, the pope wishes to emphasize "the Eucharistic dimension of the whole Christian life" (no. 5).

In the wake of the Second Vatican Council and the Great Jubilee Year 2000, the pope says, "Jesus Christ stands at the center not just of the history of the Church, but also the history of humanity" (no. 6). During the Year of the Rosary, the pope proposed "contemplating the face of Christ from a Marian perspective, by encouraging once more the recitation of the Rosary" (no. 8). For the Year of the Eucharist, he suggests that the faithful contemplate the Eucharistic face of Christ in the sacrament (no. 10).

The Eucharist, the pope maintains, is "a mystery of light" (no. 11). It is a mystery because Jesus, who described himself as "the light of the world" remains hidden (no. 11). It is light "because at every Mass the liturgy of the Word of God precedes the liturgy of the Eucharist in the unity of the two 'tables,' the table of the Word and the table of the Bread" (no. 12). This mystery of light has three dimensions: a meal, a sacrifice, and a "real" presence (nos. 1–16). It is a great mystery "which above all must be well celebrated" (no. 17). He therefore suggests that during the year each parish community spend some time studying the General Instruction of the Roman Missal (no. 17). He also describes the presence of Jesus in the tabernacle as "a kind of magnetic pole attracting an even greater number of souls enamored of him" (no. 18). He suggests that Eucharistic adoration outside Mass become a particular focus of parish and religious communities during the year (no. 18).

The pope goes on to describe the Eucharist "as the source of ecclesial union and its greatest manifestation" (no. 21). This communion, both hierarchical and fraternal, places certain demands on us through a "'spirituality of communion' which fosters reciprocal openness, affection, understanding, and forgiveness" (no. 21). At Mass, "we are called to measure ourselves against the ideal of communion which the Acts of the Apostles paints as a model for the Church in every age" (no. 22). "In a certain sense," he continues, "the People of God of all times were present in that small nucleus of disciples, the first-fruits of the Church" (no. 23). Like the disciples, we must relive at Sunday Mass the experience of the apostles when the Risen Lord appeared to them when they were gathered together (no. 23).

The Eucharist gives the Church the principle and plan of her mission. The pope says, "the Eucharist is a mode of being, which passes from Jesus into each Christian, through whose testimony it is meant to spread throughout society and culture" (no. 25). "For this to happen," however, "each member of the faithful must assimilate, through personal and communal meditation, the values which the Eucharist expresses, the attitudes it inspires, the resolutions to which it gives rise" (no. 25). In this sense, "[t]he Eucharist is not merely an expression of communion in the Church's life; it is also a project of solidarity for all of humanity" (no. 27). Moreover, "[t]he Christian who takes part in the Eucharist learns to become a promoter of communion, peace and solidarity in every situation" (no. 27).

The Eucharist, "a great school for peace," urges the community toward "a practical commitment to building a more just and fraternal society" (no. 28). The letter concludes with the hope that all the Christian faithful might rediscover the gift of the Eucharist as a source of light and strength for their daily lives (no 30). The pope asks the Blessed Virgin Mary, "whose whole life incarnated the meaning of the Eucharist," to help the Church acknowledge with new enthusiasm "that the Eucharist is the source and summit of her entire life" (no. 31)

Observations

Taken together, *Ecclesia de Eucharistia* and *Mane Nobiscum, Domine* provide a comprehensive synthesis of the Church's teaching on the Eucharist and underscore its significance for today's believers. What follows are further insights into John Paul II's teaching that should help us appreciate this great "mystery of faith" even more.

The documents complement one another. Although each is independent, read together their complementarity becomes evident. The encyclical presents a comprehensive account of John Paul II's teaching on the Eucharist; the apostolic letter emphasizes the importance of meditating upon this teaching and making it one's own. An entire year is to be dedicated to the Eucharist in order to invite the faithful to ponder this great mystery of their faith and make it even more vital and necessary to their daily lives.

Read together the two documents promote Novo Millennio Ineunte *(2001), John Paul II's apostolic letter on the new millennium, which asks the faithful to "contemplate the face of Christ."*[5] They should ponder the face of their Lord so that they may witness to the reality of God's love in their lives. The encyclical and apostolic letter suggest that such contemplation begin with the mystery of the Eucharist. The faithful can see the face of Christ in their midst every time they celebrate Mass, and whenever they pray before Christ's hidden presence in the Blessed Sacrament.

In addition to contemplation of the face of Christ, the encyclical and apostolic letter also promote a "spirituality of communion," which John Paul II highlights in Novo Millennio Ineunte. *It has become an interpretive key for understanding his pontificate.*[6] As the Church embarks on the new millennium, he urges the faithful to live out in their own lives this spirituality of communion, modeled upon the communion of the Holy Trinity, especially the intimate bond of union between the Jesus and his Father. Contemplating the face of Christ in the Eucharist leads to a more profound awareness of how the "sacrament of unity" constitutes the Church and how the Church herself constitutes a sacrament of unity.

The encyclical and the apostolic letter both underscore the ecclesial dimension of the Eucharist by placing the sacrament at the heart of the mystery of the Church. The Eucharist is a sacrificial banquet that brings into our midst the person of Christ himself and the reality of his paschal mystery, revealing the mystery of Christ's redemptive love

---

5. *NMI*, nos. 16–26 (accessed April 23, 2012).
6. Ibid., nos. 43–45.

and the Church's participation in it. Through this "sacrament of love" the Church understands its true purpose and mission. The Church draws her life from this sacrament, receiving the strength and courage to proclaim the redeeming Christ to the whole world.

Finally, in both documents the pope highlights Mary as a model of Eucharistic love and devotion that all the faithful should emulate. Linking her *Fiat* to the angel with the "Amen" we say when receiving the Eucharist, he underscores the Marian dimension of the sacrament and explains why, as "Mother of Christ," she is also "Mother of the Eucharist." As the closing lines of the apostolic letter state: "The Eucharistic bread which we receive is the spotless flesh of her Son" (no. 31). In the Incarnation, in his public ministry, in his passion and death, and in his glorious resurrection and ascension into heaven, Mary knew what it meant to contemplate the face of her Son. She also knows what it means to contemplate the face of her son in the Eucharist, the great sacrament and mystery of our faith.

Much more can be said about John Paul II's teaching on the Eucharist. These insights, however, suggest the general content and direction of his thought, and highlight the significance he saw in the sacrament for the Church's life, unity, and mission. They also demonstrate the centrality of this great "mystery of faith" to his thought and its importance as the Church embarks on the new millennium.

Conclusion

The Eucharist permeates John Paul II's writings, especially two documents composed near the end of his long pontificate: the encyclical, *Ecclesia de Eucharistia*, and the apostolic letter *Mane Nobiscum Domine*. These are intimately related. The first presents a comprehensive teaching on the sacrament, and the second, an introduction to the

Year of the Eucharist, invites the faithful to spend time reflecting on this teaching and making it their own.

The two documents also advance two themes presented in John Paul II's apostolic letter on the new millennium, *Novo Millennio Ineunte*: contemplating the face of Christ and promoting a "spirituality of communion." They give a Eucharistic interpretation to these themes and look to the Blessed Virgin Mary as the model par excellence of someone who embraced a Eucharistic spirituality from the first moment of her divinely inspired *Fiat* to her glorious Assumption and coronation as Queen of Heaven.

In union with the Magisterium of the Church as manifested in the teaching of the Church Fathers, the Ecumenical Councils, his predecessors in the papacy, the doctors of the Church, and the lives of the saints, John Paul II sees in the Eucharist "the heart of the mystery of the Church." This ecclesial dimension of the Eucharist is rooted in the love of the Trinity, the self-emptying sacrificial offering of the Son, and the outpouring of the Spirit upon the disciples at Pentecost. It also has its roots in Jesus's institution of the Eucharist in the Upper Room, when he linked his paschal Mystery to the sacrificial meal in which he was both priest and victim.

During the Year of the Eucharist in 2004 as the new millennium was just getting under way, the pope invited bishops, priests, religious, and all the faithful to place at the center of their lives this great "mystery of faith," this "sacrament of unity," and "sacrament of love" from which all else flows .

Reflection Questions

- John Paul II says that the Eucharist is often called "Communion" for good reason. How has the sacrament inspired you to promote communion in your life? With whom do you share this communion—yourself? Others? God? How is the Eucharist the "sacrament of unity?"

- John Paul II describes the Eucharist as "a great school for peace." How is peace more than a simple lack of violence? More than imposing law and order on the unruly elements of society? What positive feelings and actions constitute peace? What is the relationship between peace and justice?

- John Paul II says that Mary lived her Eucharistic faith "by the very fact that she offered her virginal womb for the Incarnation of God's Word." How does the Eucharist continue and extend the mystery of the Incarnation? In what sense is receiving the Eucharist an extension of this mystery in your own life?

Conclusion

That which is beautiful elicits wonder. Whatever it may be—a work of art, music, a novel—it draws us out of ourselves and lets us see the world in a different light. Beauty is both objective and subjective. It does reside in the eye of the beholder, but it also emanates from the thing itself. We are attracted to beauty because we were made for it. It awakens in us a desire not merely to behold its mystery, but to become one with it. In doing so, it brings us to the threshold of the sacred and the world beyond.

This book has explored the mystery of the Eucharist. The twenty-six saints and mystics presented within its pages had a deep love for the sacrament and wrote of how receiving it or simply being in its presence deepened their desire for holiness and communion with God. Although they may have lived in different historical epochs and in varying cultural circumstances, their voices resonate still in a litany of heartfelt praise and thanksgiving for the divine gift of the Eucharist. The sacrament filled them with wonder at God's passionate love for humankind and led them to a deep awareness of living the gospel. They did so because the mystery of the Eucharist filled their hearts and transformed their souls.

The Eucharist is also beautiful because it makes us beautiful. God gives us this gift to divinize us and make us holy. It elicits wonder because it comes from Beauty itself, the God who created us in his image and likeness and who yearns to dwell within our hearts. Through this great sacrament, these twenty-six saints and mystics experienced the transforming power of God. Each of these unique voices in the history of the Church cooperated with God's grace—sometimes startlingly so. Each sang in the rhythms and melodies of his or her time in ways that touch the deepest yearnings of the heart. Each provides special insight into the beauty of the sacrament and of the soul. Believing that we too, like them, might one day be saints, we feel inspired to raise our voices to God,. They remind us of our call to holiness and make us realize our longing to experience God in the depths of our souls. Their voices, expressions of heartfelt gratitude, proclaim the beauty of God's love and marvel at his accomplishments in the human heart and in the world.

The Eucharist comes from the heart of God to touch the heart of the Church and every human being. These voices constitute a great symphony, joined by Christians throughout history and the world over, to render praise and thanksgiving to God for the gift of this sacrament. It is a particularly beautiful symphony, moreover, in which the Spirit is simultaneously composing, performing, and conducting its various movements within our hearts. The piece remains unfinished, however, an encounter with the divine still taking shape within our hearts, not to be completed until the end of time when all things find their final consummation in Christ. These saints and mystics invite us, by joining our voices with theirs, to let the beauty of the sacrament penetrate every aspect of our lives. In doing so, we offer praise and thanksgiving to God that will resonate in our hearts and in the hearts of those we serve.

The beauty of the Eucharist is all about the new creation God has ushered in through Christ's paschal mystery. This beauty allows us to share in the timeless and transcendent mystery by opening our hearts to the transforming love of the Spirit. The voices of these saints and mystics remind us that the Spirit is still working in the human heart, from there being poured out on all creation. May the voices of our hearts join those of these holy men and women so that the Spirit's divinizing work may be accomplished in us as it was in them. May every aspect of our lives be placed under the all-encompassing prospect of God's redeeming and sanctifying grace.

Acknowledgments

Parts of this book were previously published as:

"Pseudo-Dionysius on the Eucharist," *Emmanuel* 133 (no. 5, 2007): 407–17 [Voice One].

"John Damascene on the Eucharist," *Emmanuel* 113 (no. 4, 2007): 313–22 [Voice Two].

"Anselm of Canterbury on the Eucharist," *Emmanuel* 115 (no. 3, 2009): 220–31 [Voice Three].

"Bernard of Clairvaux on the Eucharist," *Emmanuel* 114 (no. 1, 2008): 4–14. [Voice Four].

"Hildegard of Bingen on the Eucharist," *Emmanuel* 113 (no. 6, 2007): 486–96 [Voice Five].

"Aelred of Rievaulx on the Eucharist," *Emmanuel* 115 (no. 1, 2009): 24–33 [Voice Six].

"Albert the Great on the Eucharist," *Emmanuel* 114(no. 4, 2008): 320–28 [Voice Seven]. "Bonaventure on the Eucharist," *Emmanuel* 114 (no. 2, 2008): 106–114 [Voice Eight].

"Thomas Aquinas on the Eucharist," *Emmanuel* 114 (no. 3, 2008): 225–34 [Voice Nine].

"Meister Eckhart on the Eucharist," *Emmanuel* 115 (no. 4, 2009): 292–302 [Voice Ten].

"Catherine of Siena on the Eucharist," *Emmanuel* 115 (no. 5, 2009): 417- 25 [Voice Eleven].

"Julian of Norwich on the Eucharist," *Emmanuel* 116 (no. 1, 2010): 4–13 [Voice Twelve].

"Thomas à Kempis on the Eucharist," *Emmanuel* 115 (no. 6, 2009): 509–16 [Voice Thirteen].

"Ignatius of Loyola on the Eucharist," *Emmanuel* 116 (no. 2, 2010): 135–43 [Voice Fourteen].

"Teresa of Avila on the Eucharist," *Emmanuel* 116 (no. 3, 2010): 210–20 [Voice Fifteen].

"John of the Cross on the Eucharist," *Emmanuel* 116 (no. 4, 2010): 292–301. [Voice Sixteen].

"Francis de Sales on the Eucharist," *Emmanuel* 116 (no. 5, 2010): 410–19. [Voice Seventeen].

"St. Alphonsus de Liguori on the Eucharist," *Emmanuel* 117 (no. 1, 2011): 4–14 [Voice Eighteen].

"St. John Vianney on the Eucharist," *Emmanuel* 117 (no. 4, 2011): 292- 302. [Voice Nineteen].

"John Henry Newman on the Eucharist," *Emmanuel* 116 (no. 6, 2010): 486–96 [Voice Twenty].

"Thérèse of Lisieux on the Eucharist," *Emmanuel* 117 (no. 3, 2011): 196–206 [Voice Twenty-One].

"Charles de Foucauld on the Eucharist," *Emmanuel* 117 (no. 5, 2011): 404–13 [Voice Twenty-Two].

"Thomas Merton on the Eucharist," *Emmanuel* 118 (no. 1, 2012): 4–13 [Voice Twenty-Three].

"Teresa of Calcutta on the Eucharist," *Emmanuel* 118 (no. 2, 2012): 132–41 [Voice Twenty-Four].

"Chiara Lubich on the Eucharist," *Emmanuel* 118 (no. 3, 2012): 235–39, 245–49 [Voice Twenty-Five].

"John Paul II on the Eucharist," *Emmanuel* 119 (no. 1, 2013): 4–14 [Voice Twenty-Six].

Except for those within direct quotations from the authors studied, all Scriptural citations come from *Holy Bible: New Revised Standard Version with Apocrypha* (New York/Oxford: Oxford University Press, 1989).

In keeping with the book's popular tone, footnotes have been kept to a minimum. The strictly historical material in the book is not original to the author. Those interested in pursuing particular points of interest can begin by looking to such works as Hubert Jedin et al., ed. *History of the*

Church, 10 vols. (New York: Crossroad, 1965–81); Karl Bihlmeyer and Hermann Tüchle, *Church History*, 3 vols. trans. Victor E. Mills (Westminster: The Newman Press, 1968); Louis Bouyer, François Vandenbroucke, and Jean Leclercq, *A History of Christian Spirituality* (New York: The Seabury Press, 1982); and *Christian Spirituality*, 3 vols. (New York: Crossroad, 1985–89).

A special word of thanks goes to Gary Brandl, Tom Masters, Jim Webber, and Julie James of New City Press for their invaluable help at every stage in the evaluation, preparation, marketing, and distribution of this book.

NEW CITY PRESS
of the Focolare
Hyde Park, New York

New City Press is one of more than 20 publishing houses sponsored by the Focolare, a movement founded by Chiara Lubich to help bring about the realization of Jesus' prayer: "That all may be one" (John 17:21). In view of that goal, New City Press publishes books and resources that enrich the lives of people and help all to strive toward the unity of the entire human family. We are a member of the Association of Catholic Publishers.

Further Reading—Books by New City Press

Books by Fr. Dennis J. Billy
Beauty of the Eucharist	978-1-56548-328-6	$17.95
Living in the Gap	978-1-56548-392-7	$12.95
Tending the Mustard Seed	978-1-56548-475-7	$11.95
Gospel Joy: Pope Francis and the New Evangelization	978-1-56548-566-2	$11.95

Books by Maire O'Byrne:
Now - This Moment Matters	978-1-56548-500-6	$7.95

Periodicals
Living City Magazine,
www.livingcitymagazine.com

Scan to join our mailing list for discounts and promotions or go to www.newcitypress.com and click on "join our email list."